Pieter Bruegel the Elder
at the Kunsthistorisches Museum in Vienna

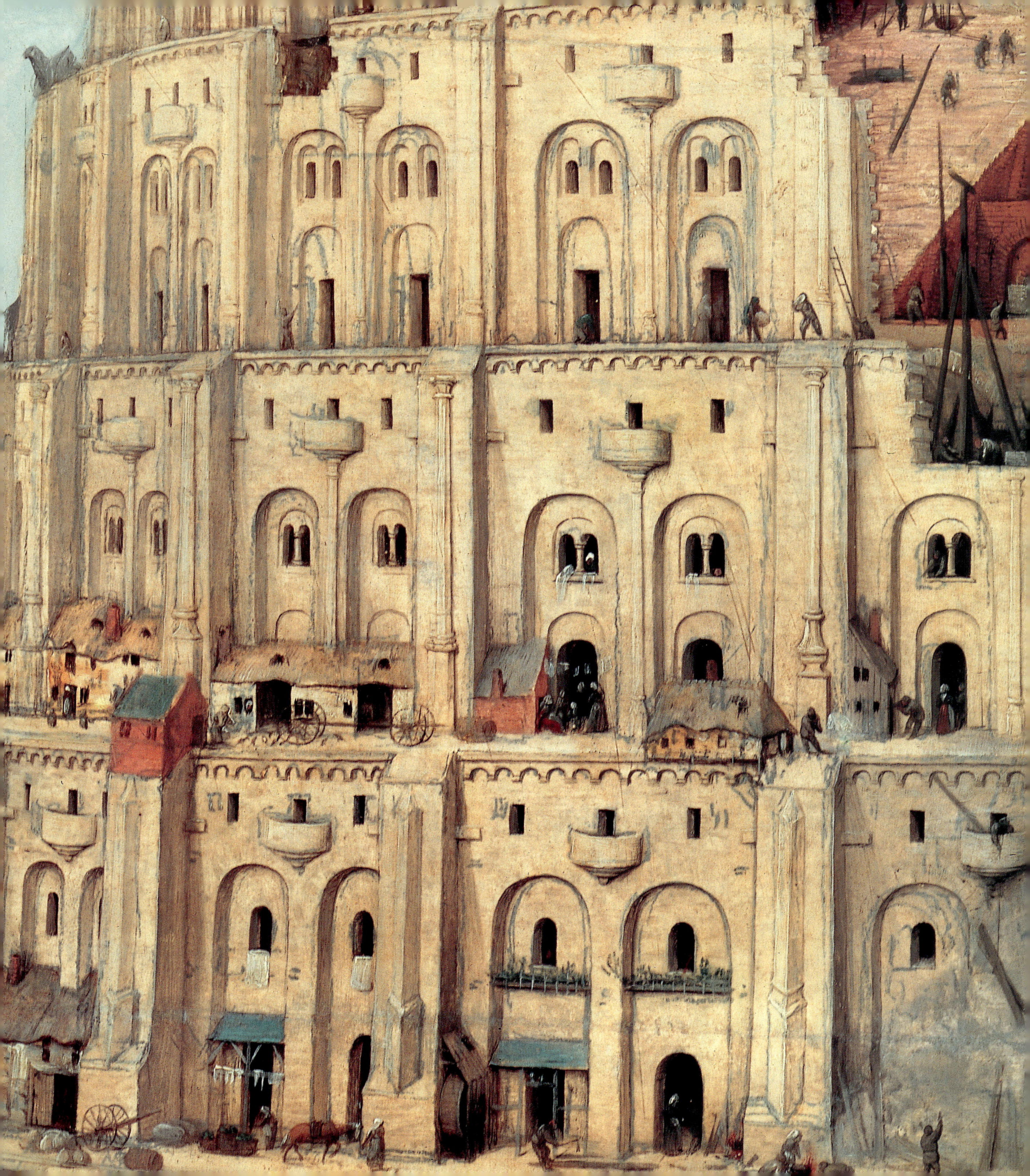

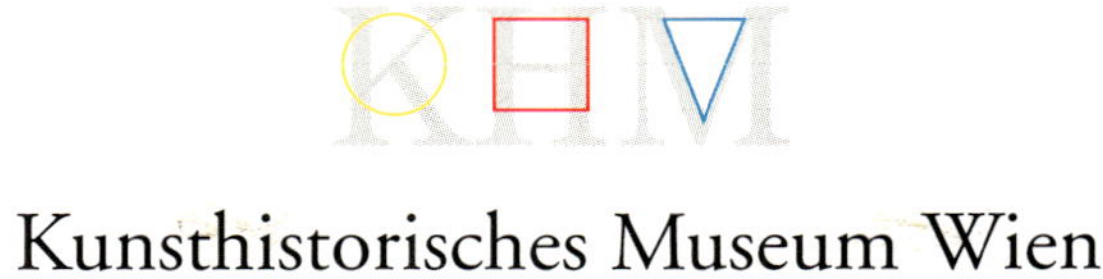

Kunsthistorisches Museum Wien

Pieter Bruegel the Elder
at the Kunsthistorisches Museum in Vienna

edited by
Wilfried Seipel

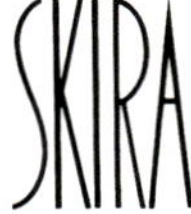

Media Proprietor and Publisher
General Director
HR Dr. Wilfried Seipel
Kunsthistorisches Museum Vienna
1010 Vienna, Burgring 5
Austria

Design
Marcello Francone

Layout
Eliana Gelati

Translation
Dekryptos, Brussels

Editorial
Karl Schütz, Alexander Wied,
Elisabeth Herrmann-Fichtenau

Photography
© Kunsthistorisches Museum Vienna

Abbreviated title
Painting of Pieter Bruegel the Elder
im KHM
Vienna 1997
ISBN 88-8118-320-x

Illustr. on the cover:
Hunters in the Snow, Detail

Illustr. on the book page:
Battle between Carnival and Lent,
Detail

Illustr. on Page 2:
Tower of Babel, Detail

Illustr. on Page 6:
Peasant and the Nest Robber, Detail

List of Contents

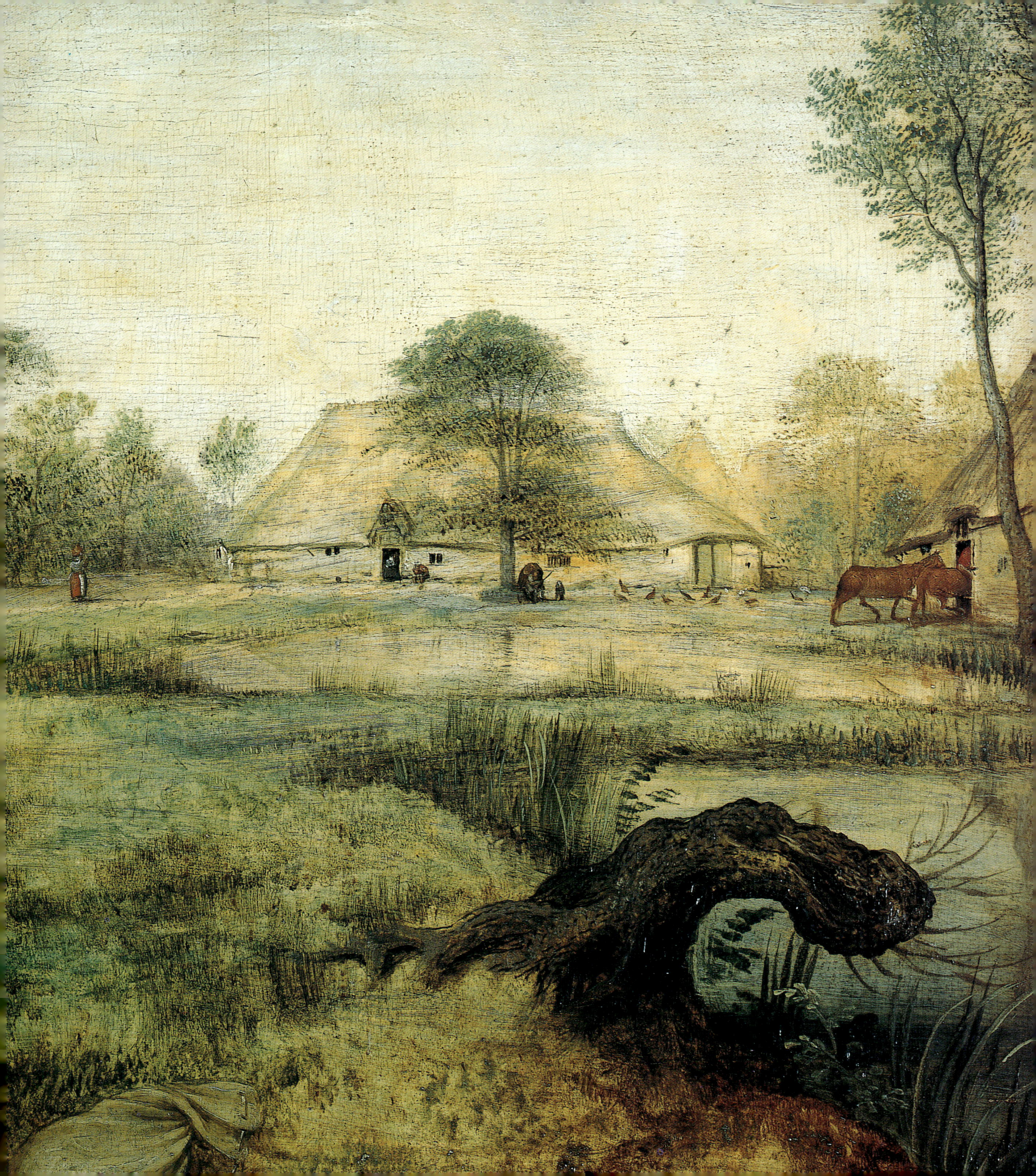

Preface

The great exhibition, "Bruegel – Tradition and Progress. A family of Flemish painters circa 1600", which opened in December 1997 in Vienna, was the impulse behind this first comprehensive monography of the paintings of Pieter Bruegel the Elder. In the hundred-year history of this museum, while there have been many treatises and catalogues devoted to the Flemish painting in general in our art gallery, it is astonishing that the paintings of Pieter Bruegel the Elder had never been examined in such a detailed and comprehensive form, even though most of our visiting public nourishes a particular admiration and ardent interest in this artist.

This volume is not intended to resume or take further all the scholarship and technical discussion that has grown up around Bruegel and has found expression in countless publications, large and small, important and not-so-important. Rather, our aim is to give to the visitor to our museum, and to the interested layperson in general, a lasting impression to take away with them. It is a publication that, thanks to its particularly careful design, and especially to the photographic material recently produced by Hans Kräftner, is able to give the broadest possible picture of Bruegel's work, insofar as it is represented in the art gallery of the Kunsthistorisches Museum, which still has the most extensive Bruegel collection in the world.

Of particular importance, and quite within the terms of our objective of spreading an understanding of the works and Bruegel's importance to as wide a public as possible, is the text written by Klaus Demus. Its powerful language and lively descriptions radiate the enthusiasm of this unrivalled Bruegel specialist. Today, with his widely recognized interpretations, Demus propagates an image of Bruegel that goes beyond all of contemporary criticism's psychological and metaphysical readings with its immediacy, intensity and humanity (but also in its supertemporal message)and explains the fascination that this great painter, today more than ever, holds for whoever examines his work..

To round off and complete the volume is a catalogue of works and a detailed biography by Alexander Wied, in which the most important publications to date are listed.

I am indebted to Dr Elisabeth Herrmann for her invaluable advice at a difficult time, and to Skira Verlag, Milan and their colleagues who participated in this project for the successful realization of our long-cherished wish.

Dr Wilfried Seipel
General Director of the Kunsthistorisches Museum

Pieter Bruegel the Elder – an Introduction

Wilfried Seipel

Only four years after Pieter Bruegel's death in 1569, the famous geographer, Abraham Ortelius — to whom the world owes the first modern atlas, the *Theatrum Orbis Terrarum* (1570) — wrote in his *Album Amicorum* about his former friend: "No one, except from envy, resentment or ignorance of his art, would deny that the incredible Pieter Bruegel has been the most important painter of his century, even to the Mannerists. Why he was torn from us in his prime? Whether I blame the death which treated him as older (than he was) perhaps on account of the excellent skill which could be observed in this man, or whether I (accuse) nature which, compared with his artistic and imaginative, imitative ability, was afraid of being overshadowed, I find difficult to say". This judgement, which certainly could not have been made without the special friendship between Bruegel and Ortelius (who had numerous paintings by his friend), describes the stature of the painter in an admittedly flowery, but nonetheless impressive language.

One of the most important colleagues of the Bruegel family, the painter Peter Paul Rubens, was not alone in recognizing Bruegel the Elder's extraordinariness. As a friend of the younger son of Pieter the Elder, that is, of Jan Bruegel, he not only owned several pictures by the latter's father, but also helped decorate the grave in Notre-Dame-de-la-Chapelle in Brussels with a painting which represented the key bequest to Petrus. Today this is in the art gallery in Berlin.This grave, restored by Teniers the Younger, a great-grandchild of the Bruegel dynasty, in 1676, contains a grave inscription going back to his son Jan. Here, Pieter the Elder is described as a "painter of the most faithful zeal and most charming art", which "itself praised by the mother of all things, nature, is admired by the ablest artists and imitated in vain by his followers". In both eulogies the references to Pieter's diligence and artistry cannot be ignored any more than the continual emphasis of his power of representation as a match for nature herself. A painter's work is thus praised shortly after his death, yet the later evaluation and interpretation is characterized over the centuries not only by simplification, false judgement and over-interpretation, but also by disinterest and ignorance.What do we actually know, therefore, about this ancestor of one of the most significant dynasties of Flemish painters, and about one of the most important and greatest painter personalities in art history? The conventional biographical details on his life are scant, inconsistent and in no way convey the importance and status of Pieter Bruegel, a status which he already had in the 16th century. The *Schilderboek* by Karel van Mander (1548-1606) is one of the most frequently quoted sources. It is usually enlisted to reconstruct the year and place in which he was born, his upbringing, marriage and training, his death and legacy, as well as to confirm attempts to interpret the works also described and mentioned in this biography. Only comparable with his obvious model, the artist's Vitae by Giorgio Vasari, is the work which first appeared in 1604. These five hundred or so pages contain not only a theoretical didactic poem, an extensive commentary on Ovid and an "iconology", but also, and in particular, the description of the life of the Italian and north European painters. The utilization of the biographical details given here, but also the interpretations of Bruegel's works have decisively influenced the image of Bruegel and the evaluation of his works to date both in the scientific as well as particularly in the non-scientific discussion as creations of a crudely amusing painter, who as a peasant paints only peasants and their world, and whose farcical stories and graphically described adventures and love affairs recall for the reader the picture of a humorous, almost scurrilous joker and cheerful fellow. Only in the last few years, particularly in the treatise by Jürgen Müller on the *Mythos vom Bauernbruegel* (*Myth of Bruegel the Peasant*) published in the catalogue for the great Bruegel Exhibition of 1997 in Vienna, is this parody of Bruegel corrected. Müller follows a literary biographical topos and incorporates in the overall framework of a representation of Flemish painting in its rivalry with Italian art obviously intended by van Mander as a concept, where a rather unimportant role determined by crudeness and peasant cunning is assigned to Bruegel's work, compared with the Italian painting. So which details can be filtered out of Bruegel's life despite all the extras added later, the distortions, misconstructions and false interpretations determined by the spirit of the times? We are well informed about the date of death on the basis of the abovementioned grave inscription in Notre-Dame-de-la-Chapelle, at least in relation to the year. His date of death is designated by the majority today as 5th September, yet the year of his birth can only be reconstructed from a later biographical detail to within five years. The first guaranteed date from Pieter's biography comes from the register of St Luke's guild in Antwerp, from that guild of painters into which Bruegel was admitted as a free master in 1551. Since the entry age for the St Luke's guild was usually between 21 and 25, the date of Pieter Bruegel's birth can be placed somewhere between 1525 and 1530, but this is not definite, of course. Just as uncertain is Pieter's place of birth. According to the biography mentioned in Karel van Mander's *Schilderboek*, Bruegel "was born in an unknown Brabant village of the name 'Breughel', the name of which he has borne and left to his descendants". Since there are two versions of the location for Breda, — on the one hand, the present Dutch town of Breda, and on the other hand, the town of Brée today in the Belgian province of Limburg, which was also written in the Latin form as Breda in the 16th century — and one or even two villages by the name of Brueghel can also be proved for both places respectively, so locating it exactly is as good as impossible. Added to this is the way his name is written in the list of masters of St Luke's guild as "Peeter Bruegels". This could also be construed as a patronymic, whereby a place of origin by the name of Brueghel could no longer be implicitly assumed. The biographical clue to "Pietro Brueghel de Breda" obviously meant by the Dutch town of Breda is nevertheless found in 1567 with the contemporary Italian scholar, Guicciardini, who lived in Antwerp. Wherever Bruegel's place of birth may have been, his later career and his acceptance into the guild of St Luke in Antwerp in 1551 already mentioned concludes that he must by then have received a sound training which further shaped and fostered his undoubtedly existing talent.In Karel van Mander's biography there is a clue challenged, of course, by so many researchers, that Bruegel would have studied under Pieter Coecke van Aelst, a "courtier of Emperor Charles V". He had been a member of St Luke's guild in Antwerp since 1527 and we have proof that he had been in Brussels since 1544. The fact that the mention of Pieter Bruegel as his pupil is also found, of course, in a later biographical obituary to just this Pieter Coecke from the year 1628, just as the clue likewise given by van Mander to the later marriage of Pieter Coecke's daughter to Bruegel, should therefore have greater force of expression than is granted of late to the topos of an artist's biography, a biography which van Mander takes for granted, despite all the obviously stylistic and pictorial differences between both these painters and their works of art. Some support for the thesis of a possible teacher-pupil relationship between Pieter Coecke and Pieter Bruegel could, of course, be provided by the fact that Coecke had not only been a painter but also a kind of "universal artist" working just as much with sculpture, architecture and tapestries as he was making a name for himself as publisher of a Vitrus translation which appeared in 1539. Would that first teacher and mediator of humanist educational content not be suspected even in him, whose knowledge even for Bruegel must be assumed which, as far as can be reconstructed, is confirmed both in his paintings as well as in his later circle of friends? Coecke was therefore perhaps less of a teacher of painting technique, and more of a fatherly friend and humanistically-trained discussion partner. In the end he was also to give his daughter Maria in marriage to Bruegel. From the obituary to her father, we know from her that she was "often carried in Bruegel's arms". The model for Bruegel's landscape art, according to Konrad Oberhuber's research (1980), could also be found in the work of Matthjis Coeck (circa 1509 to 1548) who was heavily committed to the Netherlandish tradition, and whose brother, the famous publisher, Hieronymous Coeck, was later to duplicate Bruegel's drawings. Nevertheless there is much that remains uncertain and speculative here. We stand on safe, even if not contemporary ground, with the details provided by the case files from 1606 on the production of an altarpiece in Mecheln for the glove-makers' guild of this town. Bruegel was responsible, in teamwork with Pieter Balten, for the construction of both the winged exteriors of the altar with portrayals of two saints worked in grisaille. Based on the details of the case Minutes, 1550/51 emerge as the years when it was finished, therefore shortly before Bruegel's acceptance into the St Luke's guild. Unfortunately these works have not survived, as there is no work at all from the period before 1552 which can be attributed with certainty to Bruegel.After his acceptance in to the guild of St Luke in 1551, Bruegel left Antwerp after a short, but important interlude with Hieronymous Coeck and started his great Italian journey. Hieronymous Coeck was of decisive and impressive importance in publishing or duplicating prints after Hieronymous Bosch and other significant painters for the circulation of graphic works, and hence for the knowledge which we have today of the art of drawing of this period. This short stay in Antwerp probably also explains the fact that Bruegel was to return to Coeck again after his Italian journey. Even if attribution, identification and time of production of so many drawings which can be associated with Bruegel's Italian journey are not always certain, the approximate route of his journey and the most important places he visited can nevertheless be reconstructed in crude lines. Perhaps he travelled through France (Lyon) and Switzerland to Italy, but perhaps he also journeyed across the sea.A few details on his Italian journey can be reconstructed from later letters, for example that of the geographer, Scipio Fabius, from Bologna to Abraham Ortelius in 1561, in which Pieter Bruegel is still mentioned as the painter de Vos, who was obviously the travel companion or even the guest of Fabius in Bologna. Four works by Bruegel, two of which are gouaches with a view of Lyon, are mentioned in the inventory of the famous Italian miniaturist Giulio Clovio from 1577. A copperplate engraving of 1561 by Frans Huys, who was also responsible for transferring the Bruegel's exhibition pages on to copper and their duplication, shows a sea battle in the Messina Straits. One of the two earliest datable drawings by Pieter Bruegel from 1552 portrays a mountainous landscape with an Italian monastery. Whether this was in Italy or France cannot be established with any degree of certainty. The *View of Naples* preserved today in the Galleria Doria Pamphili can also be interpreted as proof of his stay in southern Italy. His stay in Rome produced *The Ripa Grande in Rome*, today in Chatsworth. It is dated 1552/53, when Bruegel had already returned to Rome again from southern Italy.The reproduction of seascapes assimilated in the later paintings of Pieter Bruegel with their breakers towering up and deep valleys of waves drawn so grandiosely and painted so convincingly, but also that of mountainous landscapes of far, diminishing horizons, of forests and steep valleys, of rocky crags and finely serrated mountain features, is the most impressive result of an encounter with nature experienced intensively during the Italian journey, as was to be imprinted on Bruegel's memory for later work. The significance of these impressions already seems to have occurred to Karel van Mander, who formulated the witty remark in the above-mentioned biography which is happily still quoted today in all the publications: "He drew many scenes according to nature, so that it is said that when he was in the Alps, he swallowed all the mountains and rocks and, when he returned home, spewed them out again on canvases and panels, so close was he able to come to nature in this and other respects". He should have returned to Antwerp towards the end of 1555, therefore the edition of the twelve engravings of the *Large Landscape Sequence* by Hieronymous Coeck, who displayed great publishing activity in his publishing house, "To the Four Winds", can be proved as from 1555. It was not just the large sequences of drawings which emerged for these printing works at the beginning of his first great creative period. Bruegel was also made intensively familiar with the world of humanist ideas already known to him from his period of apprenticeship with Pieter Coecke. The well-known geographer, Abraham Ortelius who, together with the cartographer, Mercator, was decisively to shape the conception of the world at that time, associated with each other here, along with the famous Cardinal Antoine Perrenot de Granvella, Archbishop of Mecheln, one of the great art collectors not least of Pieter Bruegel's pictures. Granvella was Governor of the Netherlands and Philip II's counsellor and presided over the Dutch Council of State until 1564. It can be concluded from a letter by this Cardinal that the prices of Bruegel's pictures rose considerably after his death, which the appreciation of his paintings at that time impressively confirms. The only picture which can still be assigned with some certainty today to Granvella's collection is the *Flight into Egypt* of 1563, now in the Courtauld Institute in London.Granvella's passion for collecting Bruegel's works is all the more noteworthy, since the Cardinal, as a representative of the political establishment, would probably have had little understanding of the hostile attitude of the great master towards Philip II and the Spanish oppression of the Spanish Netherlands associated with his name. The fact that this attitude of Bruegel, on a par with that of the oppositional nobility, was generally known could be inferred, if researched with care, from Karel van Mander's biographical details on the painter's last instructions to his wife. From his death bed he instructed her to burn drawings which were far too biting and satirical for fear that after his death "something unpleasant could arise" for her from them. Granvella had, of course, already been removed by the King in 1564 at the request of the Regent, Margarete von Parma, since he had become unacceptable as a "hardliner" to the increasingly stronger aristocratic opposition. In August 1566 there was a notorious iconoclasm which ravaged the interior decoration of cathedrals and churches. In 1567 Duke Alba marched into Brussels at the head of a strong army and set up a reign of terror which was to last until 1573.So back to Pieter Bruegel and his collectors. Amongst them in particular was the wealthy businessman, Nicolaas Jongelinck, who was Cardinal Granvella's confidant. A guarantee is documented by him from 1566, which he gave to the City of Antwerp for a friend in the form of his collection of paintings. Along with a painting by Albrecht Dürer, there were sixteen paintings in all by Pieter Bruegel in his possession, among which were *Christ Carrying the Cross* and the *Tower of Babel*, as well as the complete series consisting of six paintings of the *Seasons*, three of which, just as the first two mentioned above, are today in the Kunsthistorisches Museum in Vienna.An entry in the marriage register of the church of Notre-Dame-de-la-Chapelle in 1563 is one of the less certain biographical details of the life of Pieter Bruegel. The marriage of Pieter Coecke's daughter, Maria, to Bruegel (already mentioned above and described by Karel van Mander) is documented with it, according to the statement made by van Mander: "Finally, when the widow of Pieter Koeck was living in the end in Brussels, he fell in love with her daughter whom he, as he recounts, had frequently carried in his arms, and took her as his wife". Whether Bruegel's love affair with his house maid, who had disliked his mother-in-law, likewise cited by the biographer, finally tipped the balance for the move from Antwerp to Brussels, can no longer be elicited with certainty. The last six years of Bruegel's life in Brussels were his most fruitful period, both with regard to his family and his creativity. In 1564/65 his oldest son, Pieter the Younger, was born. In 1568 Jan (the Elder) was born, and both sons were artistic personalities who continued their father's great tradition in the following decades and who were to lead Flemish painting to new heights. Among the most famous paintings of this last creative period of Bruegel are *Christ Carrying the Cross*, which appeared in 1564 and today is in Vienna, and in particular the six paintings comprising the sequence of the *Seasons*, which we have already mentioned in connection with the collection of the banker, Nicolaas Jongelinck. The *Conversion of Paul* and the *Suicide of Saul* appeared in the years thereafter (both paintings now in Vienna).No paintings are known from the last year of his life, only the archive notice that the Spanish soldiers quartered in his house are to withdraw and financial compensation is to be handed over to him. Perhaps an illness which finally led to his death was the cause of this alleviation of his living conditions. The instructions already given to him some time beforehand by the City of Brussels to document the excavation work for the canal between Brussels and Antwerp, probably did not come to fruition.Thus the life of one of the great personalities of art history came to an end, the course of which, despite the fragmentary record of so many biographical details, reflects the image of a creative person equally committed to society and art. However the basic mental attitude, the religious conviction and the political commitment of Pieter Bruegel are measured and interpreted, — and the range between the topos of an amusing peasant Bruegel obsolete in the meantime as regards an artist philosopher committed to the trends of humanism, even of the Roman Stoa, is wide —, his works and the explosive force assembled in them of the expressiveness of his drawings and paintings remain in the end the message felt until today of one of the greatest painters of our time.Through his creative power formed on the basis of his own experience, his own impressions and adventures, Pieter Bruegel was to become the great poet of the portrayal of landscape, nature and mankind in equal measure. Beyond all the psychological and iconological interpretations, and superseded by biographical and contemporary historical assumptions, the surviving paintings by Bruegel form a cycle, even an epic poem of human existence in their helplessness both in nature and in the course of world history which seemingly cannot be influenced. The *Tower of Babel* as the symbol of the failure of human striving after consistency, even perfection; the inescapable fate of the children in the Bethlehem scene of horror; the sun's course elapsing as a cycle and the cycle of growth and decay in nature determined by it and eternally repeating itself; these are among the great narratives of art, not just in Flemish painting. The historicizing portrayals of the history of salvation which have become icons of the history of redemption, the message of the Old and New Testaments, are only seemingly in contrast to the encyclopaedic reproduction of games, proverbs or festive customs. *Peasant Wedding Feast* and *Peasant Wedding Dance* and the *Fall of Icarus* are all just variably weighted facets of Pieter Bruegel's one, all-embracing concept of nature. He understood how to reconcile mankind with this history and nature around him in his paintings as no-one before him (and hardly anyone after him) has done.And finally, the fascination emanating from Pieter Bruegel's paintings and the impressive increase in the numbers of visitors captured by a Bruegel exhibition, cannot perhaps just be explained from the viewer's longing. They also seem to be better understood as regaining their own position in the world, in nature, in these pictures themselves. The love of the small things and events of existence only seemingly losing itself in the detail never, of course, obstructs the view of the whole, of the context. In Bruegel's portrayal of people, multiplicity has come to terms with the homogeneous oneness of nature. The individual is lifted up in a great whole behind and above everything.

On the Bruegel Paintings in the Kunsthistorisches Museum, Vienna

Wilfried Seipel

It is generally acknowledged that the Kunsthistorisches Museum in Vienna has the most extensive collection of paintings by Pieter Bruegel the Elder in the whole world, as well as almost two dozen pictures by Jan Bruegel the Elder, his younger son. The history of the Kunsthistorisches Museum's collection cannot be separated from the history of the museum's painting gallery, the formation of which owes a great deal to two collectors in particular: Rudolf II and Archduke Leopold Wilhelm.

Although the oldest parts of the gallery of paintings probably go back to Emperor Maximilian I, it was Emperor Rudolf II who first laid out the ground floor of the gallery with an imperial restraint that veiled a collector's passion, but also with great artistic understanding. It could boast on the one hand the most important and most extensive collection of paintings and water colours by Albrecht Dürer of the time, and on the other the paintings of Pieter Bruegel the Elder, eight of which can probably be proved to be in our collection today. The provenance of the paintings by Pieter Bruegel that Rudolf II brought into the gallery had two particularly important sources: the estate inventory of Archduke Ernst, the elder brother of Rudolf II, from whom the Emperor inherited the works of the Flemish masters, and the cash book of his private secretary, Blasius Hütter, which fills in important gaps in the estate inventory.

Archduke Ernst, who had been appointed Governor of the Netherlands in 1594 in order to restore peace there in those restless times, had little political success. The imperial collections, however, were to be greatly indebted to him as a collector, not just of paintings, but also of tapestries, automatic clocks, board games and books. His particular interest, however, lay in contemporary painting. From the cash book of his private secretary, Blasius Hütter, painstakingly maintained between October 1593 and March 1595, it can be estimated how amazingly extensive was the stock of paintings he had bought. Of particular interest to us here is a memorandum of 5 July 1594 that shows that the Governors of Antwerp had given the Archduke six paintings representing the *Twelve Months*. As Klaus Demus has convincingly proved, there were originally six paintings comprising a sequence of seasons here, three of which are in our Bruegel collection today: *The Gloomy Day (Early Spring), The Return of the Herd (Autumn)* and *The Hunters in the Snow (Winter)*. The *Spring* picture is missing, *Haymaking (Early Summer)* went to France after Napoleon plundered pictures from our collection and finally landed in the Lobkowitz collection (Tchechen). The *Summer* picture, *The Wheat Harvest*, is today in the Metropolitan Museum, New York. The fact that the pictures of the seasons were originally owned by the Antwerp banker, Nicolas Jongelinck, who handed them over to the City of Antwerp as a guarantee together with other paintings by Pieter Bruegel and was probably no longer able to redeem them, has already been mentioned above.

Along with the pictures of the *Seasons* in our collection, the *Conversion of Paul* as well as *Children's Games* and the *Peasant Wedding Feast* also come from the estate of Archduke Ernst. The date of purchase and the purchase price are both listed for all these pictures in Hütter's cash book mentioned above. Thus 160 guilders were paid for the painting of the *Peasant Wedding Feast*, 538 guilders for *Children's Games* together with two other paintings, and the relatively high sum of 320 guilders paid for the *Conversion of Paul*. Whether the portrayal of the procession to Calvary in the manner of Bruegel likewise mentioned in Archduke Ernst's inventory corresponds to our *Christ Carrying the Cross* cannot be proved with absolute certainty. The entire estate of Archduke Ernst – books, paintings and objets d'art – was brought to Vienna after his death, and thence some of the most valuable paintings reached Emperor Rudolf II in Prague.

Even if an inventory compiled in the lifetime of Emperor Rudolf II has not come down to us, a connection can still be established between those paintings by Pieter Bruegel whose provenance is described in Archduke Ernst's above-mentioned estate inventory while Karel van Mander's comments provide information about another part. Thus, in his *Schilderboek* on Pieter Bruegel he writes: "Some of his most important works are now in the possession of the Emperor, that is to say, a large picture representing the tower of Babel, full of fine details, [...] two further pictures that represent the procession to Calvary, make a very convincing impression and are enlivened here and there with comical scenes, [...] finally a Conversion of Paul in a very beautiful mountainous landscape". From the details in Hütter's cash book we are able to conclude that the *Conversion of Paul* was acquired by Archduke Ernst and handed over to Rudolf II. The *Children's Games* had likewise been bought from Archduke Ernst and is in our collection today, even if it is not mentioned by Mander as being in the possession of Rudolf II. It is generally acknowledged that the 16 paintings in total by Pieter Bruegel comprising Nicolas Jongelinck's guarantee also included the *Tower of Babel*, which is mentioned both by Jongelinck and by van Mander and is attributed by the latter to the collection of Rudolf II. The *Battle between Carnival and Lent*, however, is mentioned with no reference to the collector, Emperor Rudolf II. Only in later inventories are the *Peasant Wedding Dance* and the *Peasant and the Nest Robber* mentioned. The paintings of *The Storm at Sea* and *The Slaughter of the Innocents in Bethlehem,* still wrongly attributed to Pieter Bruegel in various publications, can today be ascribed to Joos de Momper or Pieter Breughel the Younger.

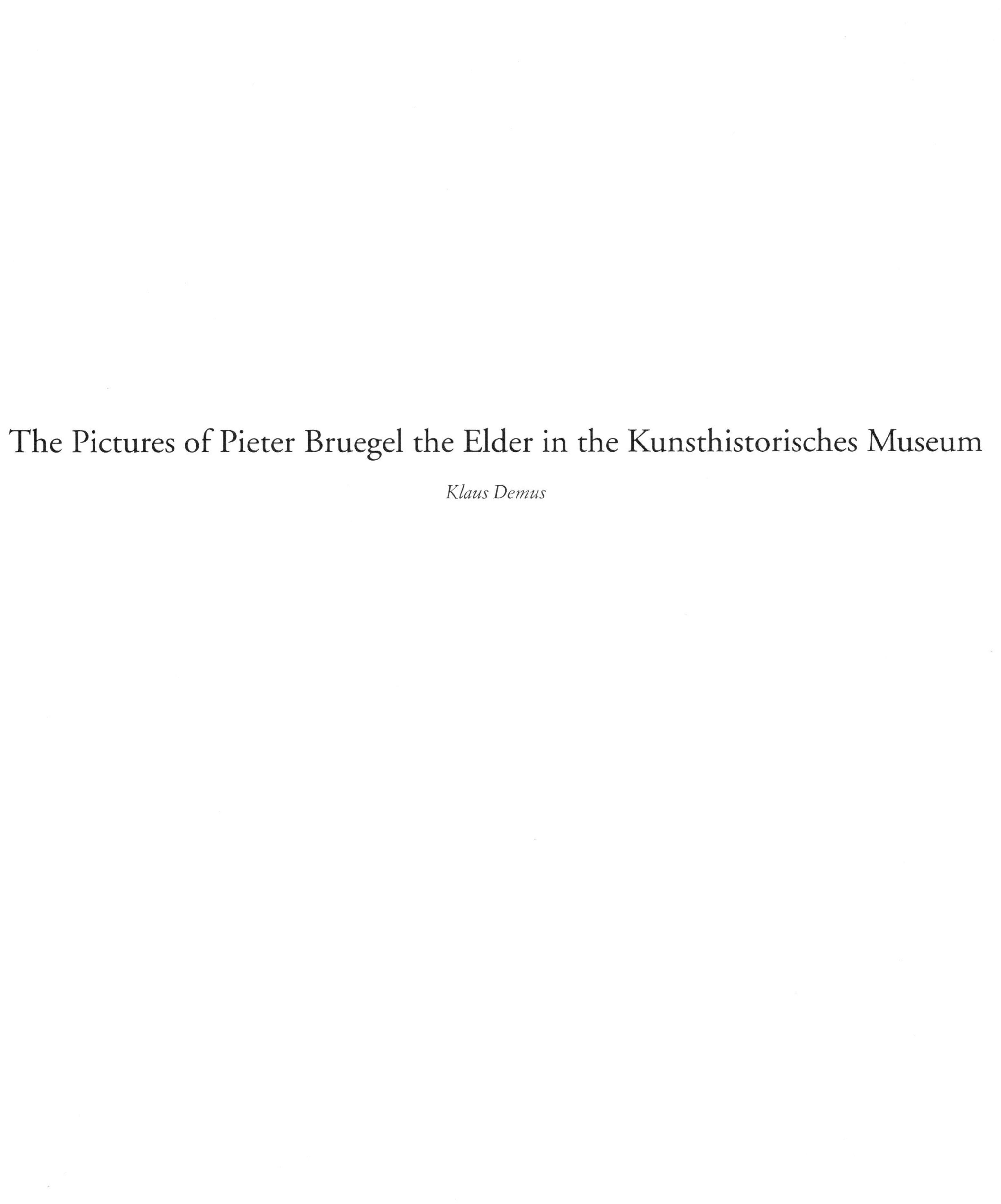

The Pictures of Pieter Bruegel the Elder in the Kunsthistorisches Museum

Klaus Demus

Battle between Carnival and Lent
1559

Signed below left on a stone: "BRVEGEL [V and E linked] 1559"
Oak, 118 × 164.5 cm
Probably Rudolf II; taken from the Treasure Chamber into the Gallery in 1748;
Inv. No. 1016

Despite considerable losses, the Viennese gallery still holds a dozen original paintings by Pieter Bruegel the Elder. This wealth may be attributed to Emperor Rudolf II's passion for collecting. In 1600 it was already considered impossible to obtain any more of Bruegel's works, so much had the Emperor captured for himself. The plundering of Prague in 1648 and Napoleon's art thefts in 1809 provide an official explanation for some of the gaps, but many works fell victim to the centuries-long disregard of Bruegel. The whole collection is discussed below.
Along with *Children's Games* and the Berlin picture, *Proverbs*, *The Battle between Carnival and Lent*, dated 1559, belongs to a genre of encyclopaedic portrayals devised by Bruegel. Sebastian Brant, Erasmus of Rotterdam and Rabelais had also observed the "human menagerie" with a cool, ironic eye, cataloguing it. Bruegel, in his own time, observed these human activities objectively from above, but his vision was not that of the Literati and must be energetically defended against a widespread tendency today to impute moral satire or even religious or political partisanship and criticism to him. Bruegel's paintings do not contain allusions to be discovered and deciphered. On the contrary, Bruegel created his own didactic, pictorial form, in order to be able to express directly and without allegorical digressions his deeply-held views of man and the world. To do this he cloaks himself in humour, but never holds a negative attitude, managing to combine occasional criticism with a love of humanity.
In the "encyclopaedic" group of pictures of 1559/60, Bruegel shows an insatiable interest in the never-ending variety of shapes and forms offered by peasant life, which was to be his "signature" world. He captures a myriad of everyday and not-so-everyday things, hardly ever repeating himself. Their form seems to attract him just as much as the things themselves. He shows the same dual interest in human outward appearances, exploring the wide range of morphological types and personalities. He manages to veil his humorist's eye with a winning sophistication. The fact that all this realism is brought into an unmistakable Bruegel-style form makes him interesting to us. Bruegel's powerful expressive style, an artistic phenomenon of the greatest significance, is outwardly that of both a great humorist and an epic poet.
The theme is custom represented in his "Sitz im Leben" (place in life). The brilliant humorous idea of the three "encyclopaedic" works was to represent the diversity of the subject through an objective as well as "natural" "list" . The gaze is thus a survey of the natural world which appears as a "world theatre". The setting — the market and church squares of a town — is divided into contrasting sectors like a Mystery Play stage: the church on the right, the inn on the left are the antagonistic halves of the scene in which all the customs of Carnival and Lent are represented as a live event, spilling into the narrow connecting streets.
The idea of antagonism is once again brought to the fore as both a real and a "symbolic" theme in the Shrovetide play (performed by a carnival brotherhood) that gives the picture its title: Prince Carnival (the corpulent pancake woman) and skinny Lent confront each other in a joust. The picture is a genuine source of forms of the custom and, according to folklore research, the costumes and processions are portrayed down to the minimum details. Nothing is arbitrary. Folklore also provides the key to all the other scenes.On the "Carnival side" the Shrovetide play, "The Dirty Bride" (gypsy wedding), is being performed in front of the "Blaue Schuyt" (Blue Boat) inn. It is a popular subject that has many forms, like the ancient drama of brothers fighting and recognition of the king's sons (Urson and Valentine, Wild Man) staged not far away, in front of the "Dragon" tavern. Just round the corner the children are emulating the adults in "The King Is Drinking!". Processions of lepers and cripples begging, traditionally fixed in the calendar year, show the

important position occupied by the fringe element in urban society, institutionalized in custom. In the distance, in the narrow street, the Count and Countess Halvasting's procession can just be made out along with a fire, perhaps the burning of the Winter straw doll.

Lenten customs and traditions take up the right half. After a Lenten sermon the faithful stream out of the church wearing mantles and carrying their chairs. They bear the ashen cross on their foreheads, like Lent. Nearby, old crockery is being smashed in a game of catch according to a spring custom and children are playing with spinning tops. The bakery shows yet another custom: as if in reproach for being late with spring cleaning — the woman on the ladder is making up for lost time, washing the windows — a "bogeyman", or rag doll, sits in the upper storey window in mockery. The scenes on the right in front of the church, where "Healing" is shown and exvotos and switches are being sold, are devoted to Christian duty. Here the sick, and even the dying (details considered too shocking had earlier been painted over), the blind and cripples begging in front of the church door, are given alms. In contrast to the waffles being cooked on the opposite side, the Lenten food of fish is being sold at the market fountain and the "pure" drinking water juxtaposed with a lighthearted moralizing tone with the trash-eating pig. Bruegel's "literalness" of description occasionally reaches the point of verbalizing the scenes and objects, an articulation he was able to demand from the well-informed observer of his time in that era of sayings and proverbs. Thus the scene at the centre of the picture becomes the key to the whole simply by this kind of verbalizing. What is the couple seen from the back stepping into the picture, led by a fool, looking for? According to the saying quoted in Sebastian Franck's "World Book": "Shrove Tuesday (on Ash Wednesday!), carrying their torches and lanterns on a bright day, shouting loudly that Shrovetide is upon us." This was how Bruegel the humorist composed. And he directed as in Shakespeare's plays: the different seasons shown in either half of the common stage: a tree losing its leaves on the left, coming into leaf on the upper right, is "symbolically" stated, jokingly imitating the medieval method of representation. Through the diversity of these features, the picture, wonderful in itself as a vivid compendium, is a miracle as a work of art, not only in design, but above all in the intention of its central idea.

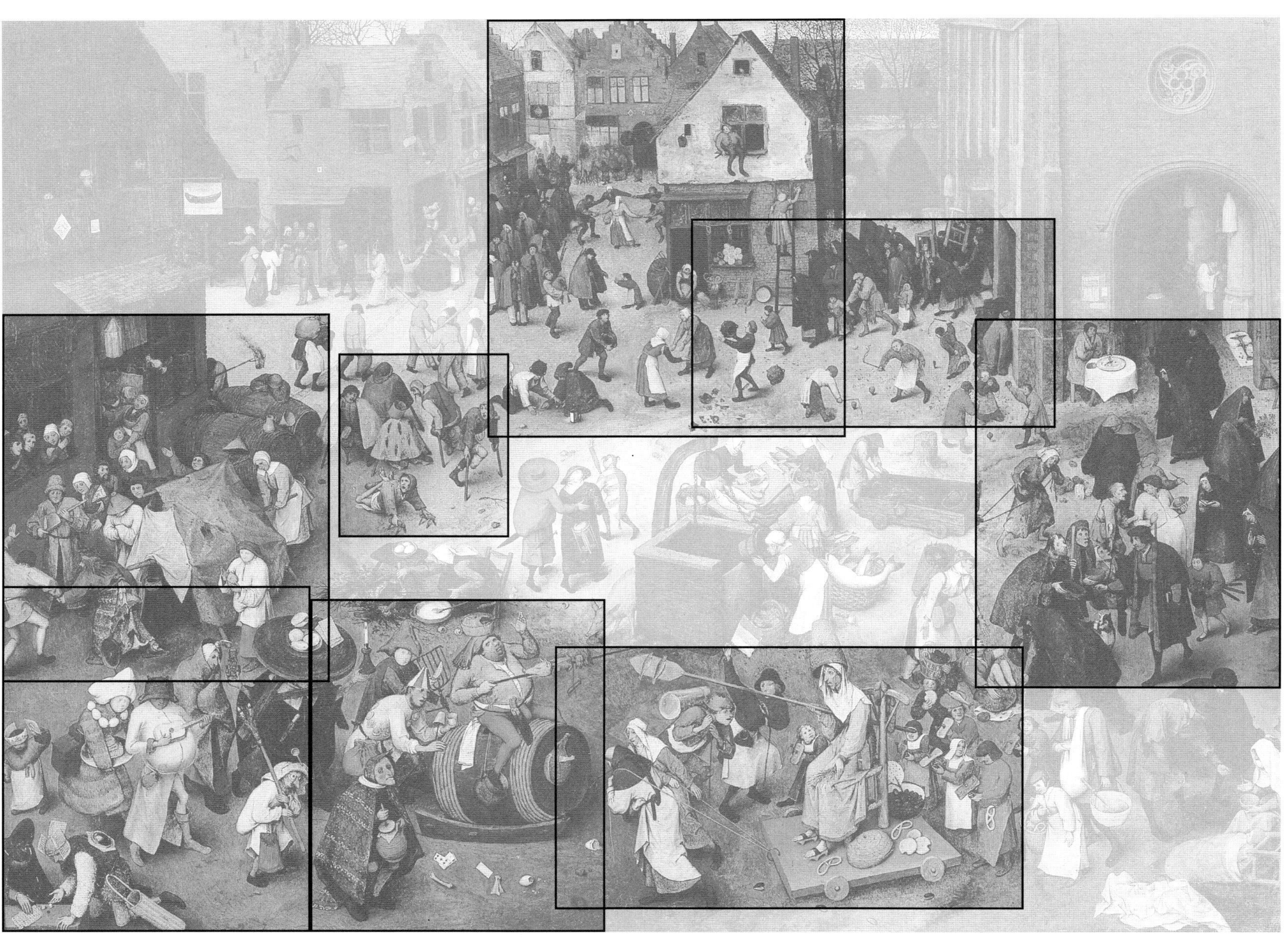

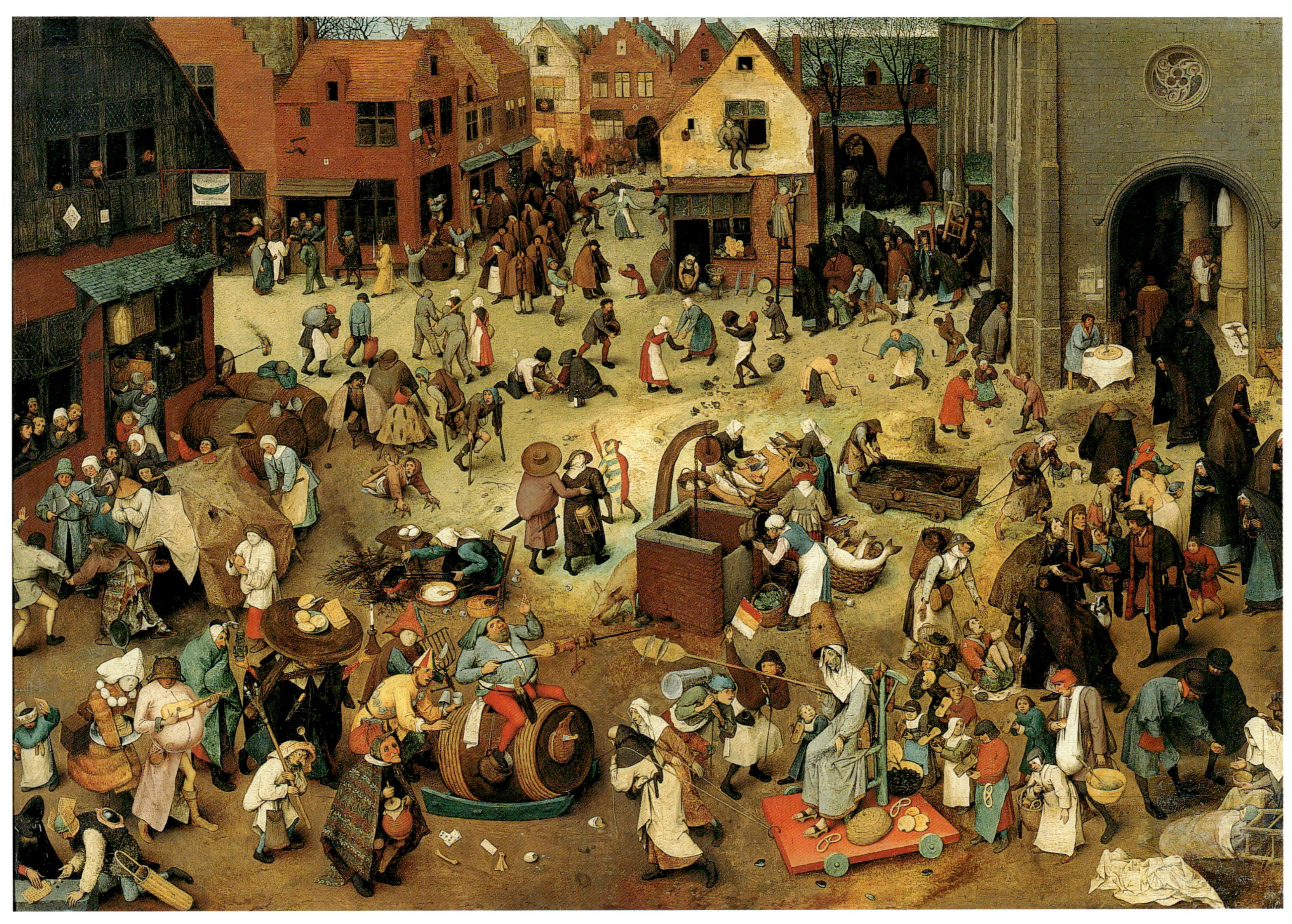

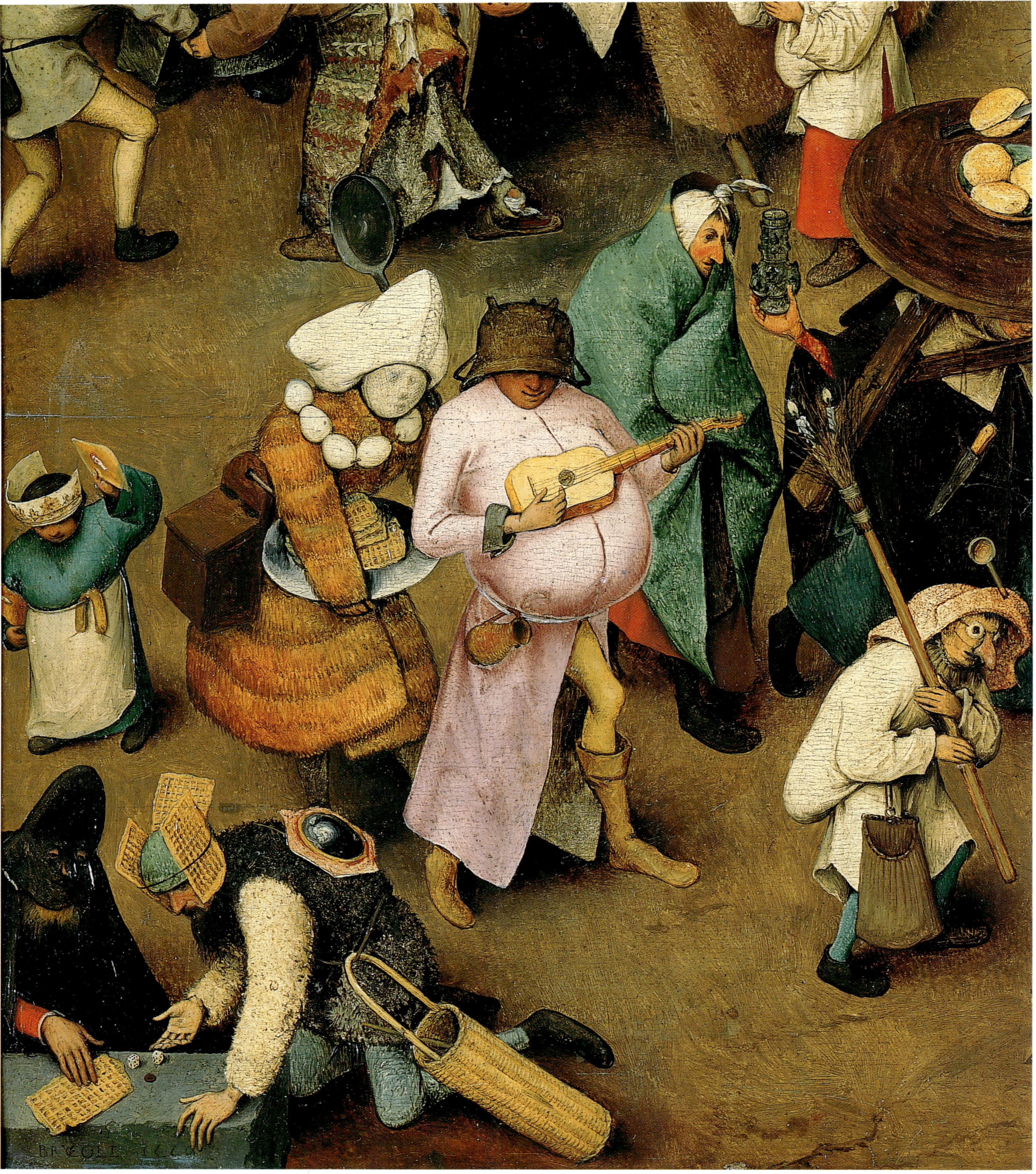

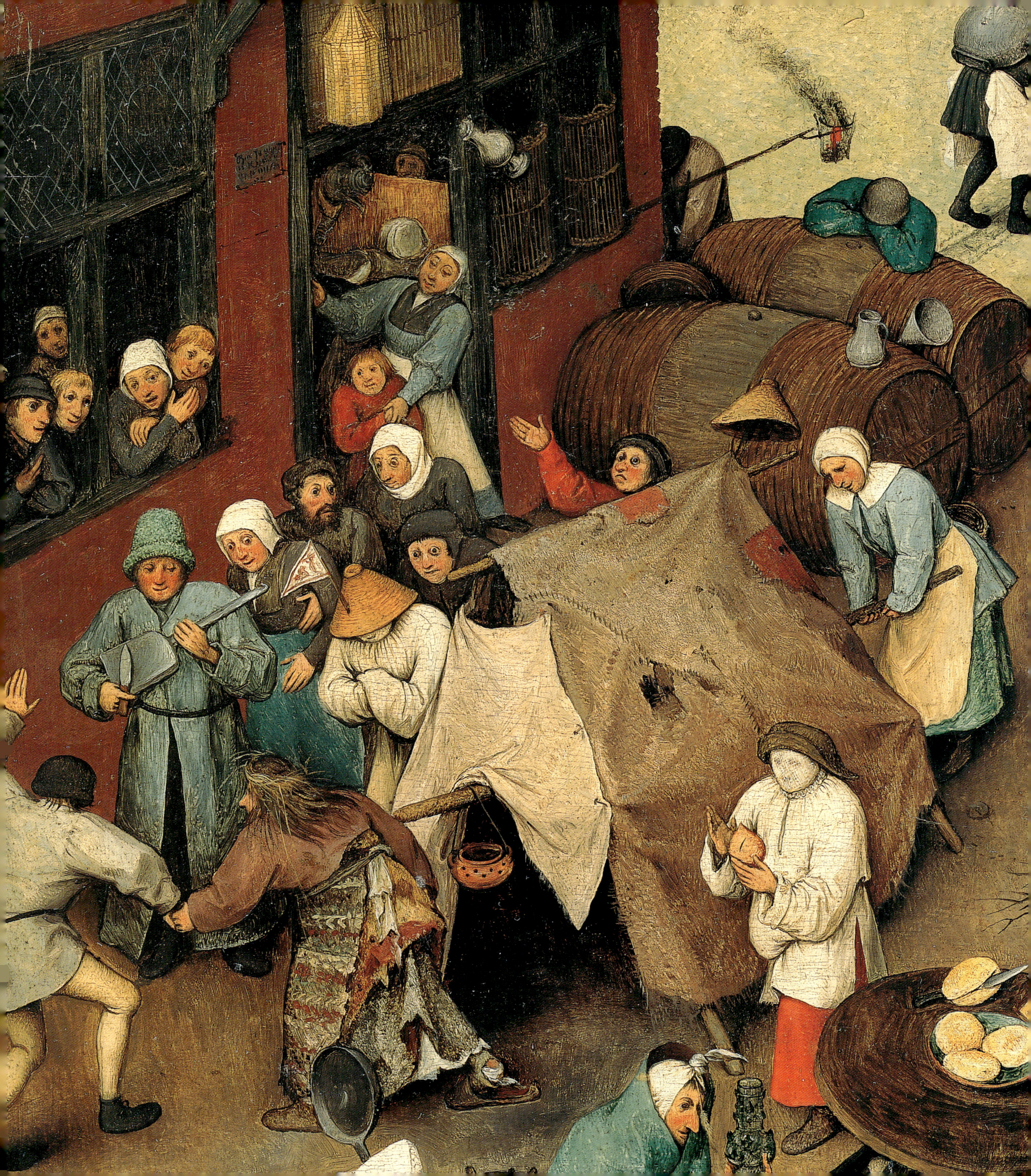

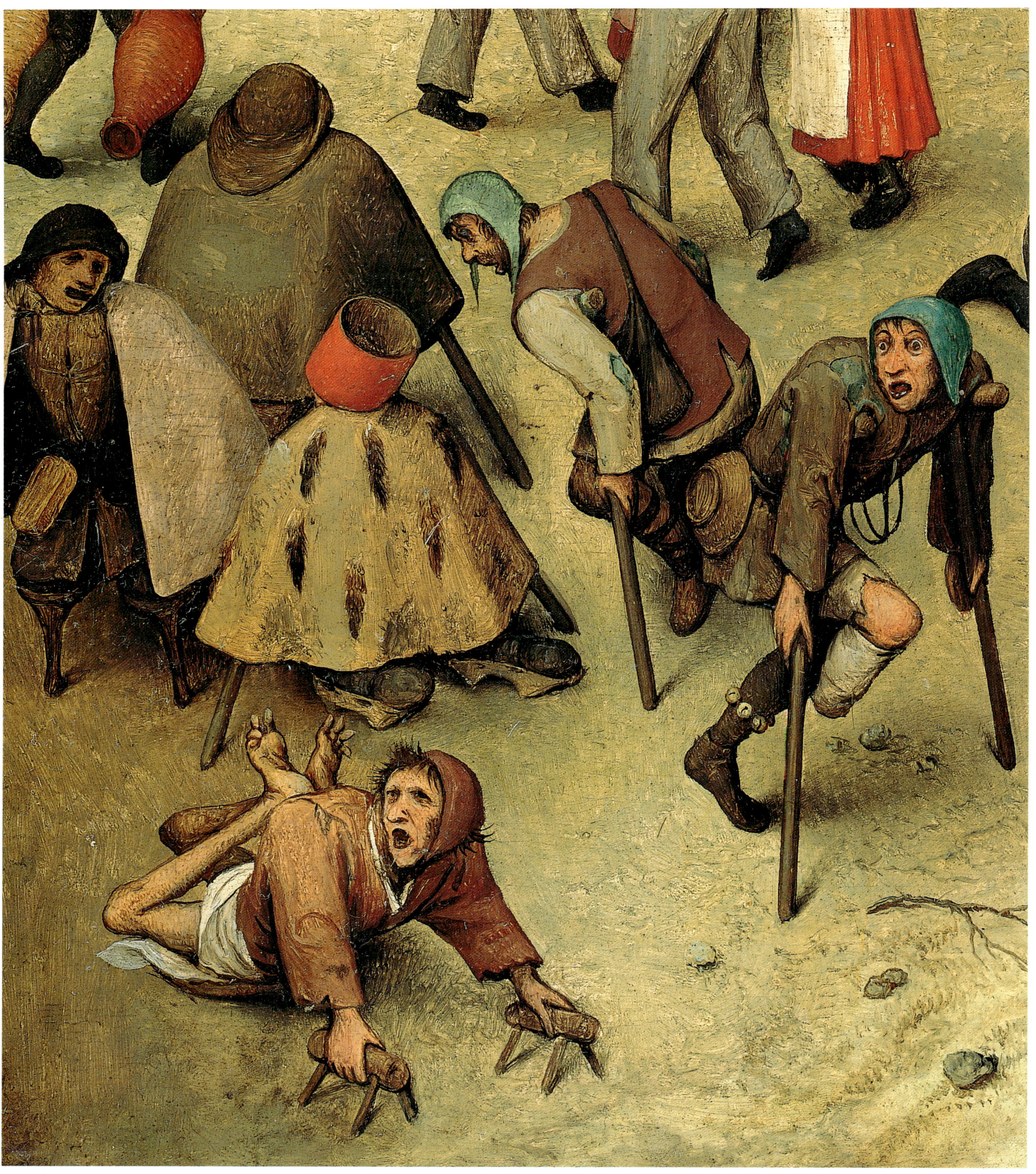

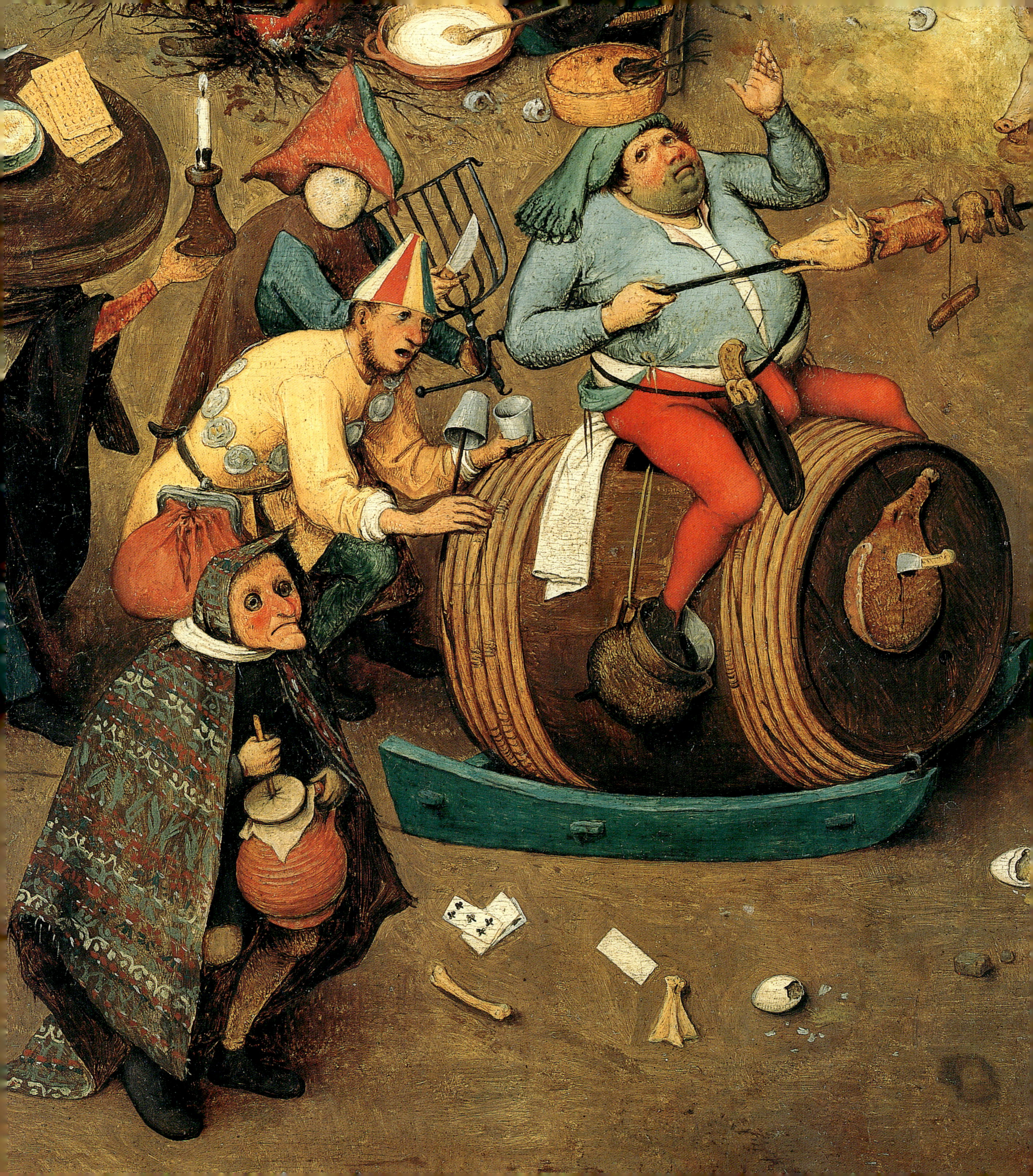

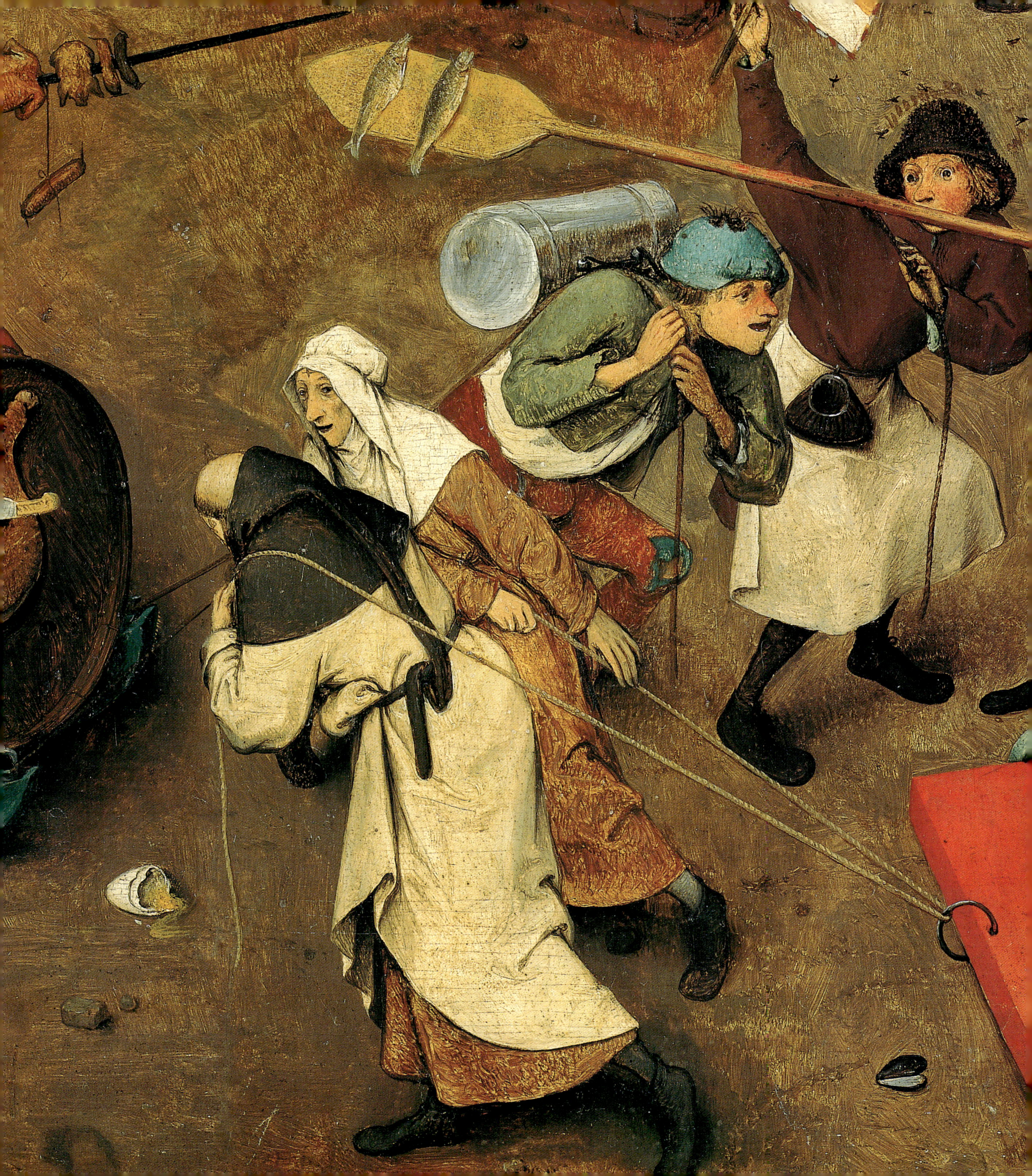

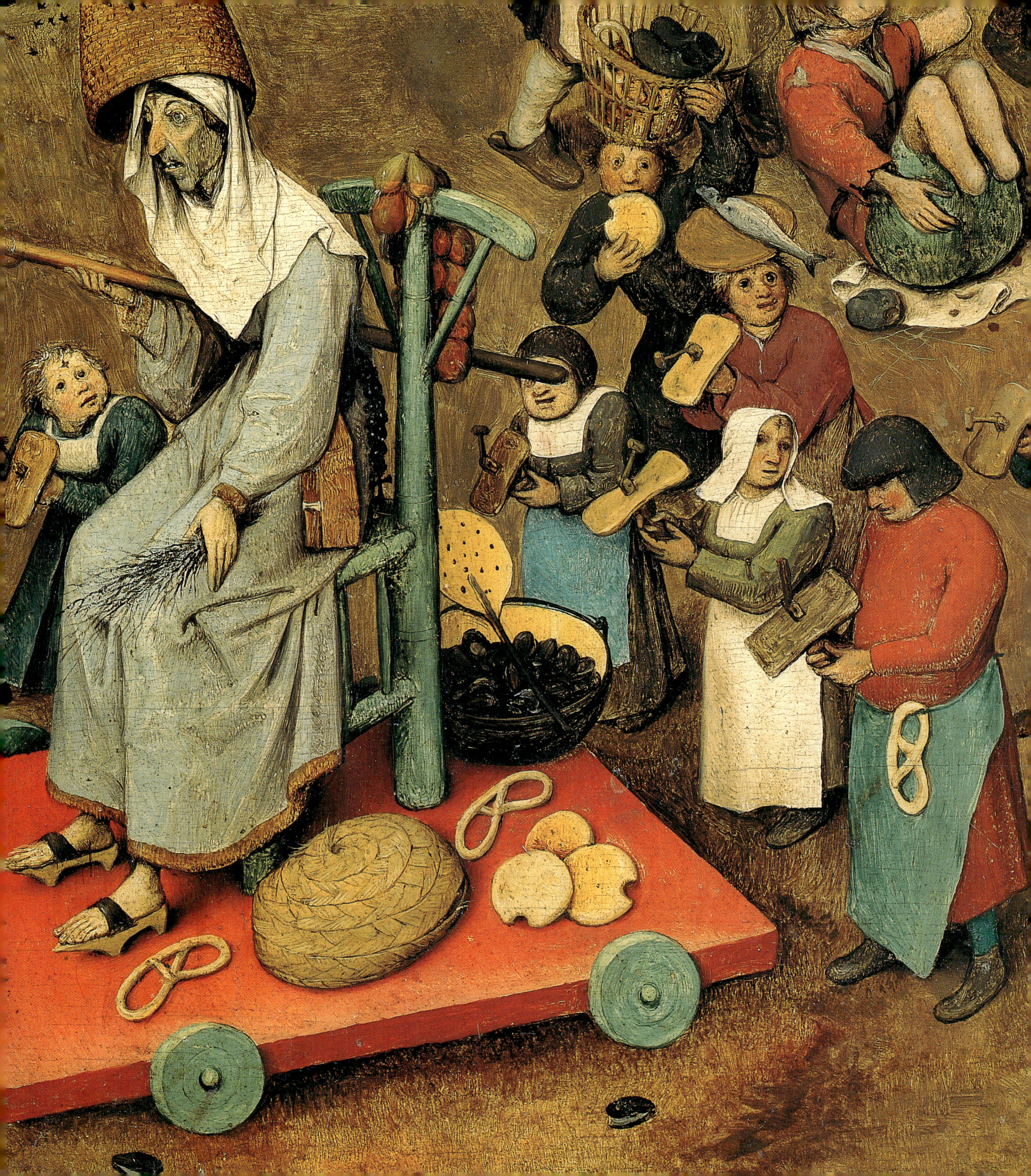

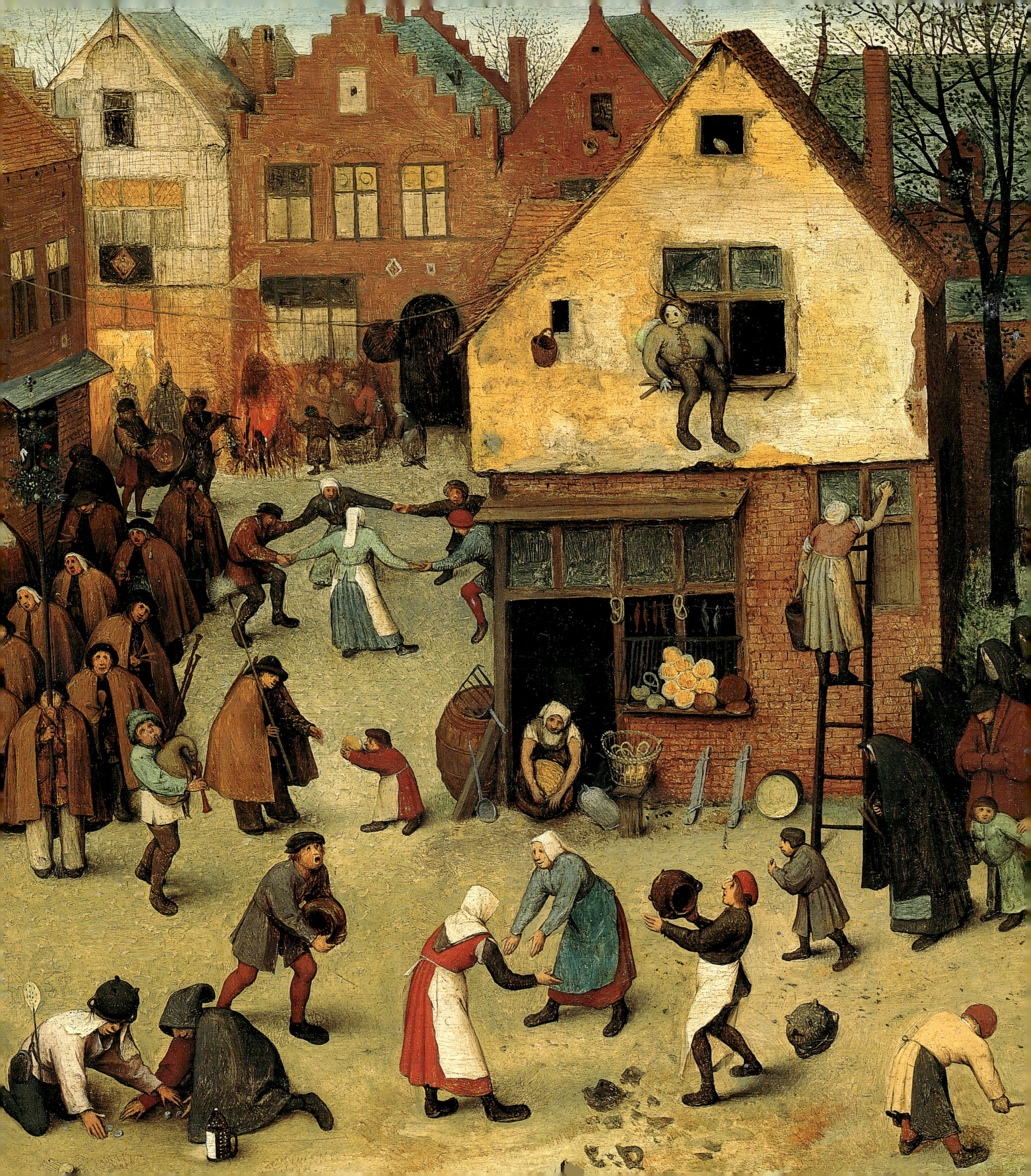

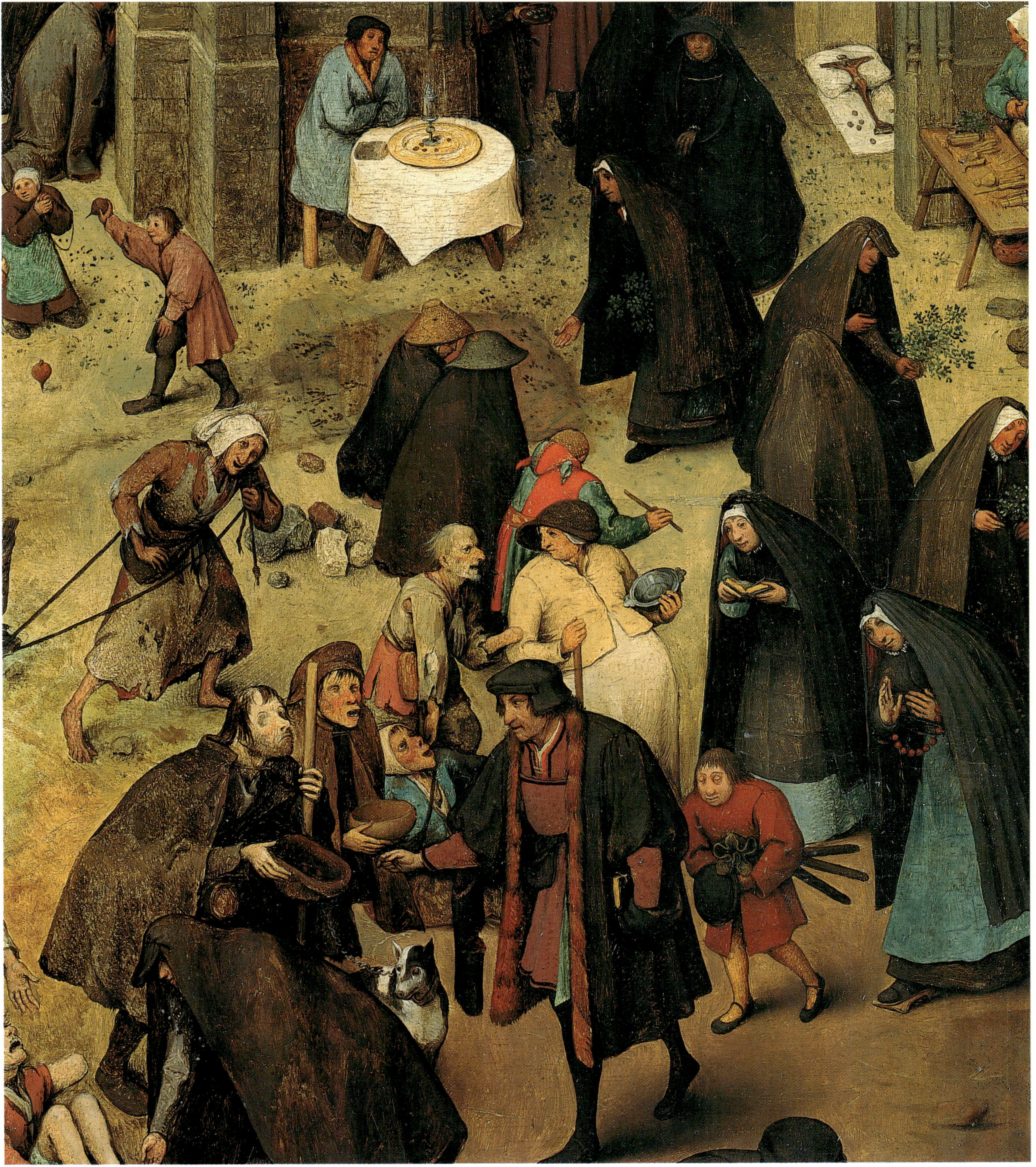

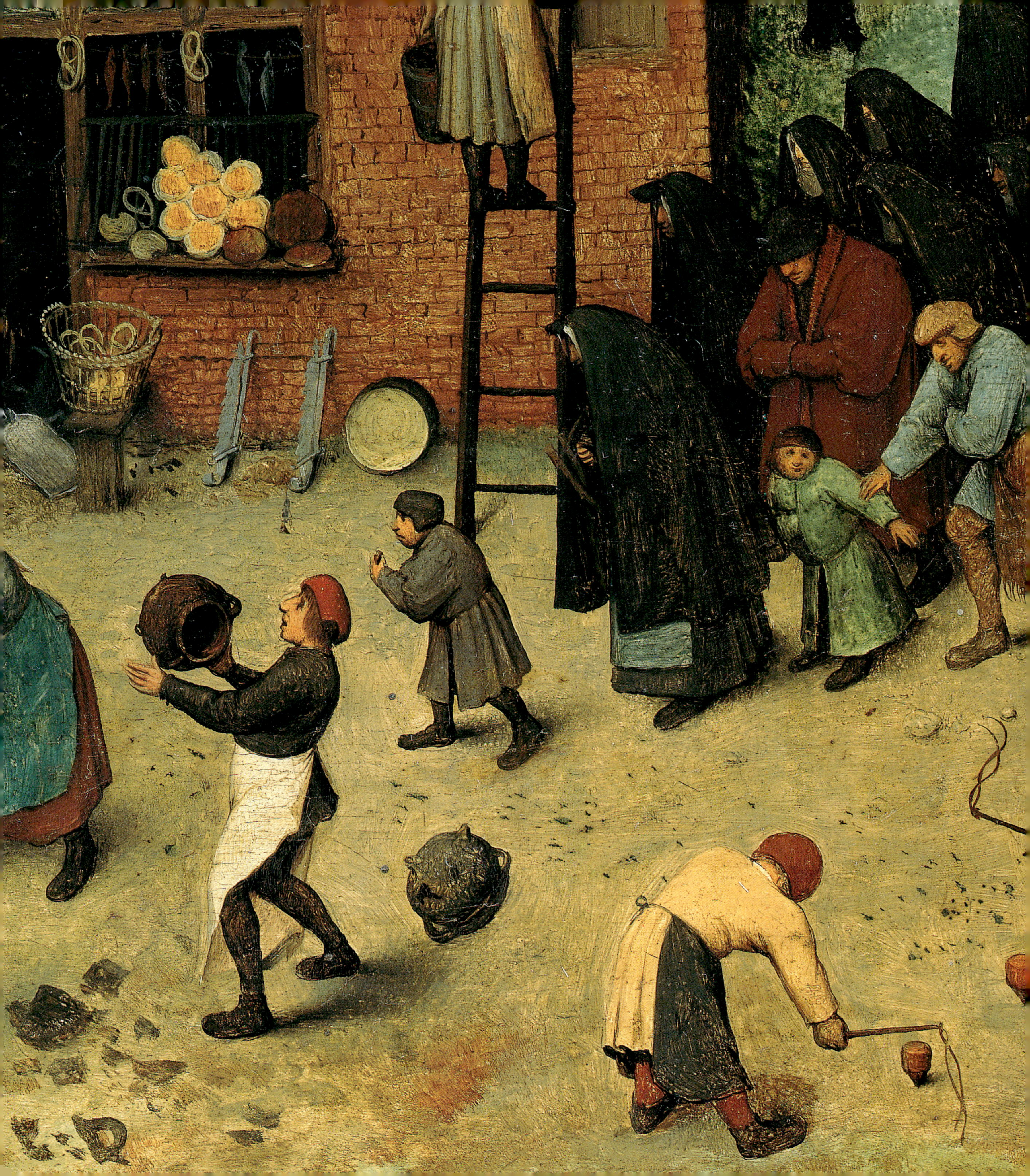

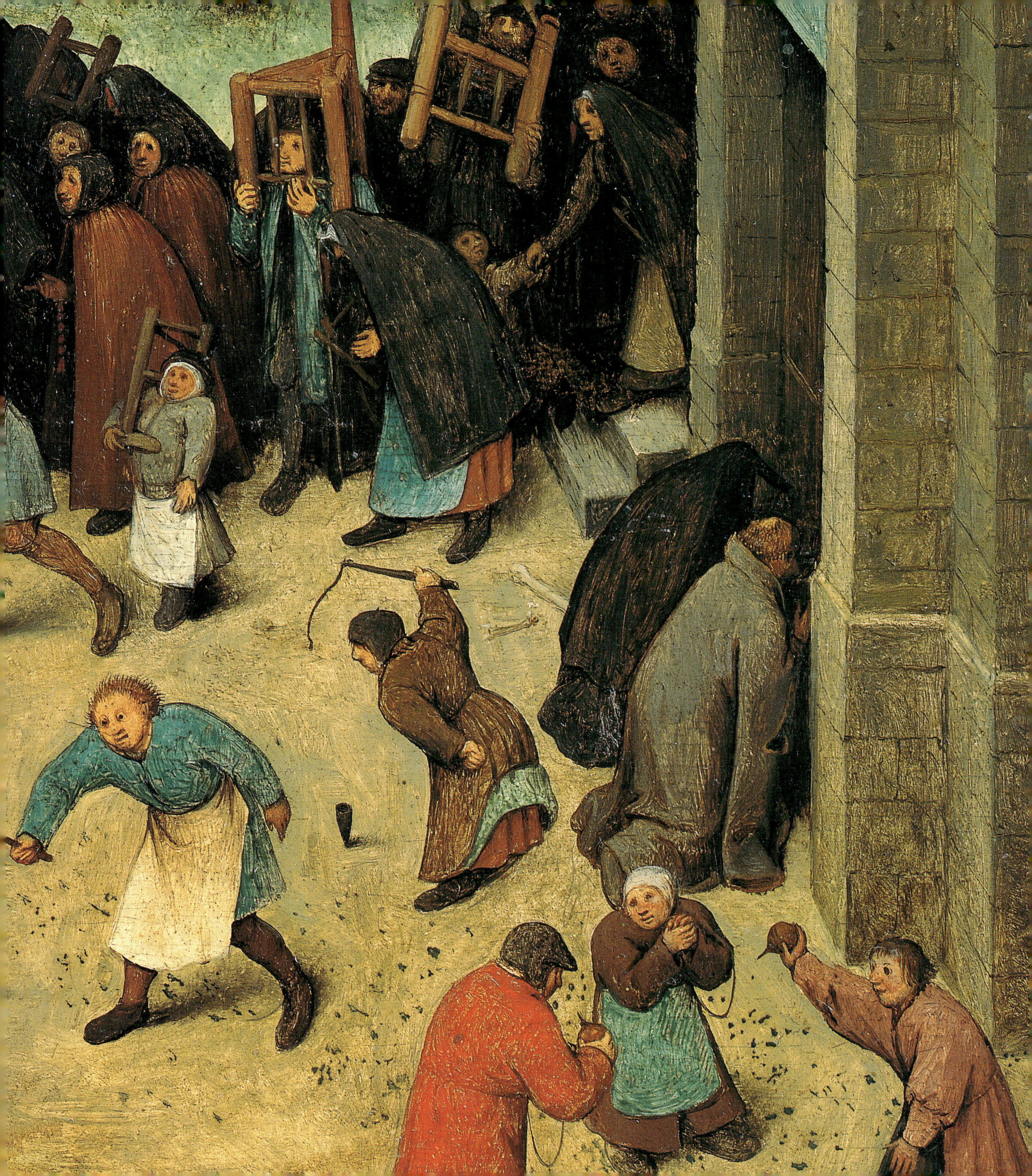

Children's Games
1560

Signed below right on the beam:
"BRVEGEL 1560"
Oak, 118 × 161 cm
Acquired in Brussels in 1594 by Archduke Ernst; Inv. No. 1017

More than 230 children are playing the ninety more or less easily recognizable and identifiable games, many of which are still played today (or were until a short time ago). Adults, with two necessary exceptions, have been excluded, and the whole town appears to have been given over to the children. The main square with the town hall, the long street and the outer area opening out into meadows, with trees and a river for the country games: all this can barely contain the inexhaustible activity. Once the observer has assessed the place and ascertained the picture's theme, there is nothing for him to do but, remembering his own childhood, recognize and list the games by name one by one — and nothing is repeated. This is an amusing and interesting exercise because knowledge that is not often called on is tested. It is also amusing because the remembering is bound up with reliving the experience, so that there are no limits at all to putting oneself into the picture to do so again and again. And it is interesting in a higher sense because the full effect of recognition is only achieved by saying the name of the game, making clear its practice or meaning. Since most of the games have a number of different names, depending on the geographic region, period in time (generation) and dialect and/or language (in Bruegel's time we are dealing with the vernacular and Latin), this task should not be underestimated, and it imbues the picture with a significance that goes well beyond mere entertainment. It lies, as so often with Bruegel, in aiming at the word that completes the picture, at the language involved in its "interpretation" which is only fulfilled as "knowledge". (Anyone who is familiar with the lists of children's games by Froissart and Rabelais and his brilliant translator, Fischart, gets the higher joke that Bruegel delivers "carriage free" by means of this lively representation to his public with whom he shared a taste for that sort of "world knowledge". Lists such as these have been drawn up for the games in our picture, spirited Flemish descriptions and their equivalents in German and English. Alongside the "technical" descriptions, there still survive some older, vividly expressive variants, descriptions and idioms. We should consider these as the natural complement to Bruegel's graphically humorous account and form.) Pictures and words — these should suffice, presented in such abundance. Unfortunately, some critics have got it in their heads that this cannot be the meaning of the picture; they believe that, clearly, the artist wanted to express something else, something deeper, with his portrayal, and this something is to be deduced from the metaphoric value of the children's games in vogue at that time. To be precise, the common denominator is human folly, which drives all human activity just as if it were a children's game. Thus, it would be essential to realize in particular that "Standing on your Head", "Blowing Bubbles", "Riding a Hobby Horse" and the like refer to sinful, imperfect human behaviour with respect to the Christian rationale, morality and faith. Therefore, Bruegel wanted to reflect human folly in the example of the children's game, and this meaning may be revealed and deciphered by accurately analyzing even the most seemingly harmless of games. We believe that this and any other dissembling approach will very soon be forgotten as ridiculous, though it had to be mentioned, however, since it is current. In the trio *Proverbs*, *Carnival and Lent* and *Children's Games*, conceived as three variations on the theme "Figurativeness and Literality", we find Bruegel's idea of a didactic role for painting for the first time, in the form of encyclopaedic paintings to be studied. He did not develop this idea, and, astonishingly, never repeated himself, either generally or in detail. His entire work as a painter was to be a chain of ever new didactic forms of expression being constantly rediscovered. He demanded this of himself as an artist — we can only note with wonder — for Bruegel's characteristic is this: he was as much an artist as an author. That is to say, a genius with a good measure of understanding and insight ("Wise is he who knows much about nature") which he applied to reality on the whole, nature and humanity and both as a coherent "world". Thus the world was as "legible" to him as a book; he possessed a kind of "wisdom of the eye" that spurred him on to a universal form of expression in his work. Since painting can only speak by showing, and its "message" has to spring from its perceptibility, Bruegel developed his own artistic form. This form does not achieve its didactic goal either in an abstract manner, such as the medieval symbolic language of art, or by allegory using standard examples and types; rather, it is based on the task of fully representing reality, a task which since the Renaissance has become a standard one even in northern Europe. Bruegel used various possibilities to translate his view of the world "into a pictorial language" or "to speak by metaphor", achieving a new representation of reality, remarkable for its intensity and accuracy.That period in time provided him with the basis for this. Motto, proverb and emblem were extremely fashionable and the interest in this interweaving of words and pictures pervaded every social stratum. The 16th century spoke in pictures as no other and its "speaking" graphic art was not just the book illustration, pamphlet and emblematic art. Only painting inasmuch as "high art" avoided this blending and combining of the spheres found in commercial art. It therefore had no formulae to offer Bruegel, not even an artistic genre or pictorial category. He had to create the possibilities for his "message" himself then. One of the first of these was the didactic, encyclopaedic work with its closed factual world, as extensive and complete as a specialist dictionary, tangible as a thousand-fold arsenal and inexhaustible in detail as a raging torrent of forms. The hero is the people, inasmuch as the creator of a second world compared with nature, purely human in language, custom and play. The desire for reality of the artist who faithfully creates a likeness yet again is as monstrous as with Rabelais. Bruegel here, however, lacks a method implemented in a virtuoso manner, spicing up the real, even distorting it into something monstrous: the fantastic element, the unbridled grotesque, supreme stupidity. Bruegel's interest in the monstrous relates with almost manic accuracy to the Being-exactly-like-that of reality, and he is absolutely dependable in his reproductions, perhaps the most faithful expert folk culture has had. But as a humorist he is at the same time the great formal artist for whom the inventory as well as the menagerie of the world is a source of endless amusement.

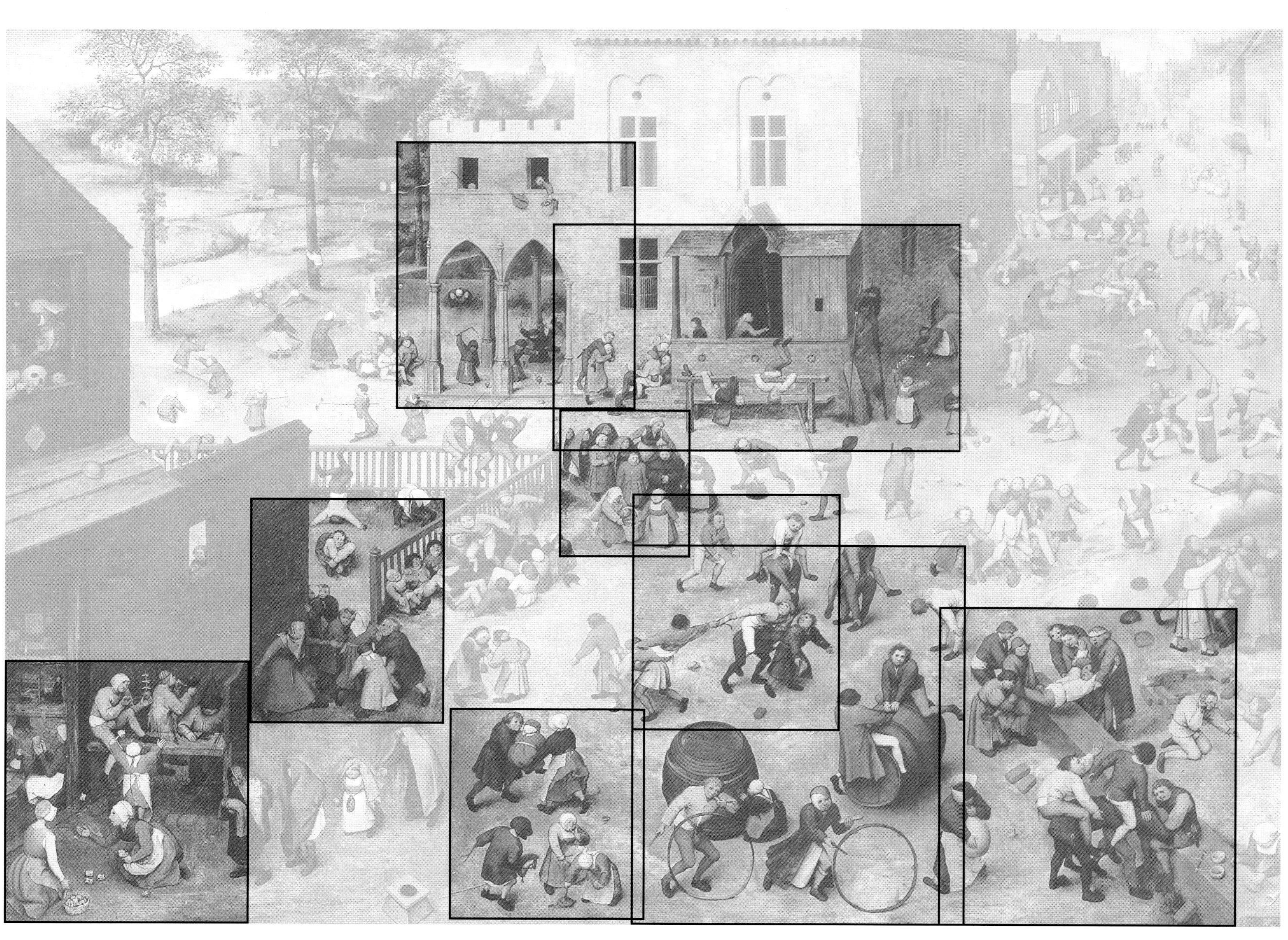

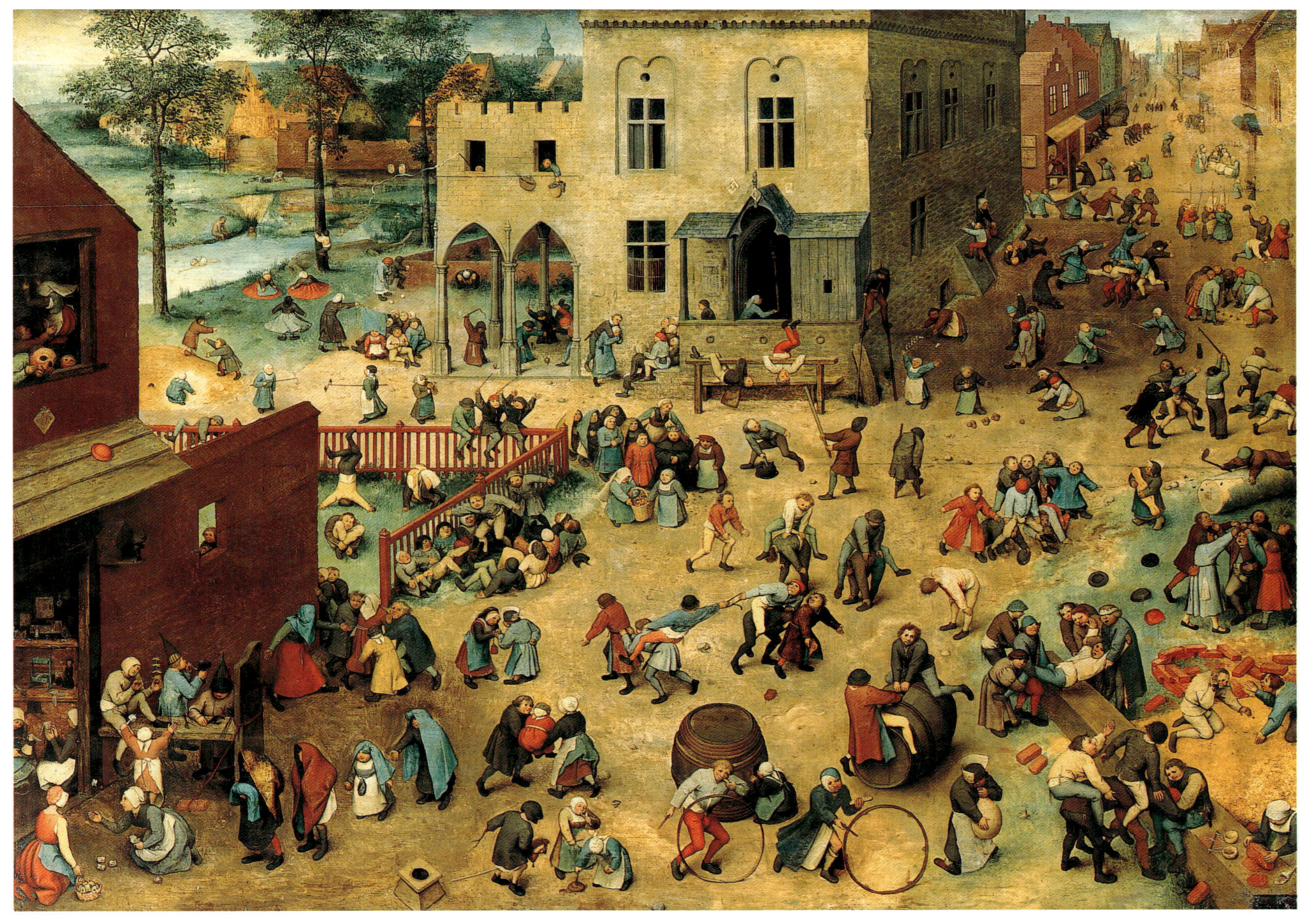

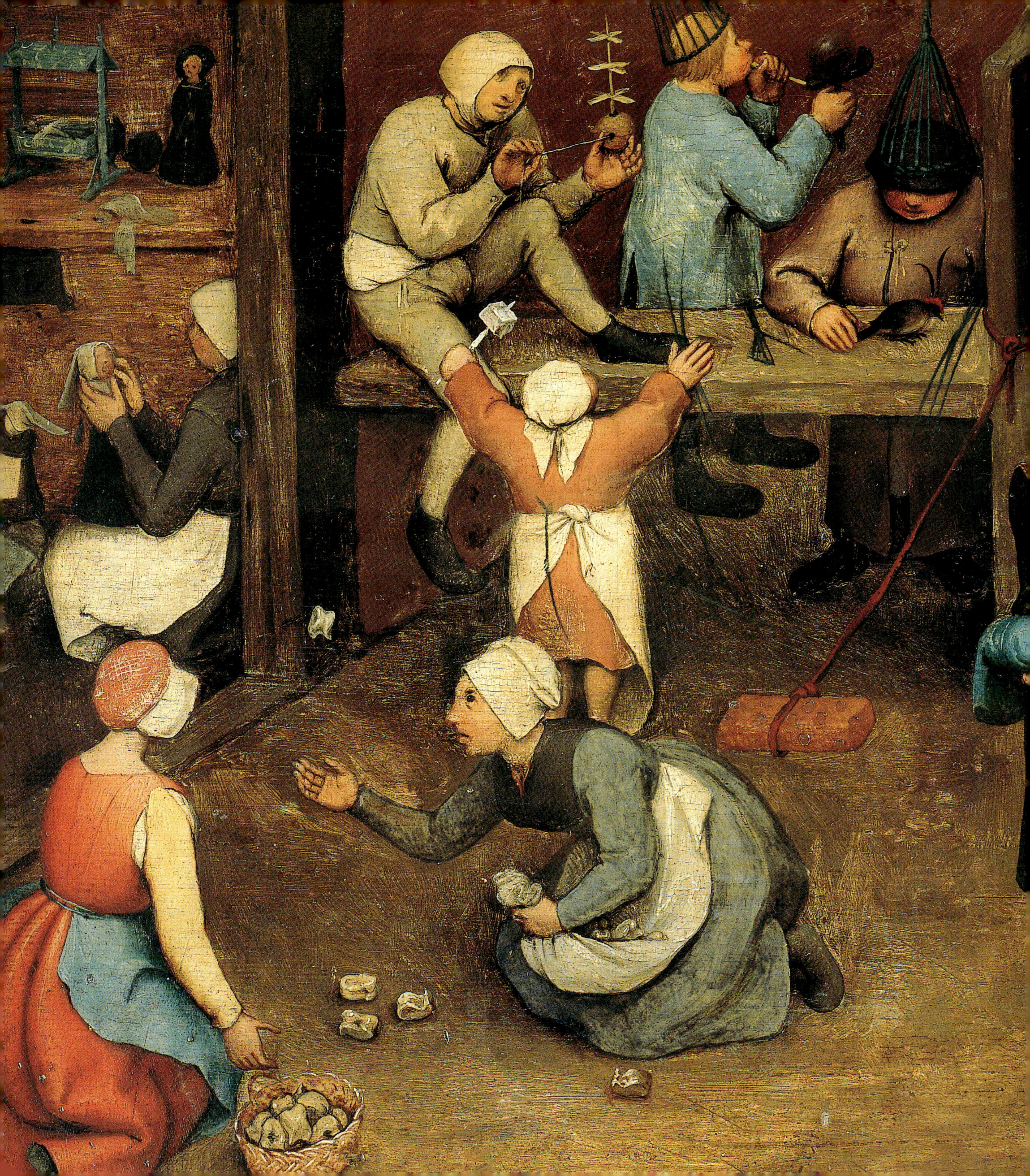

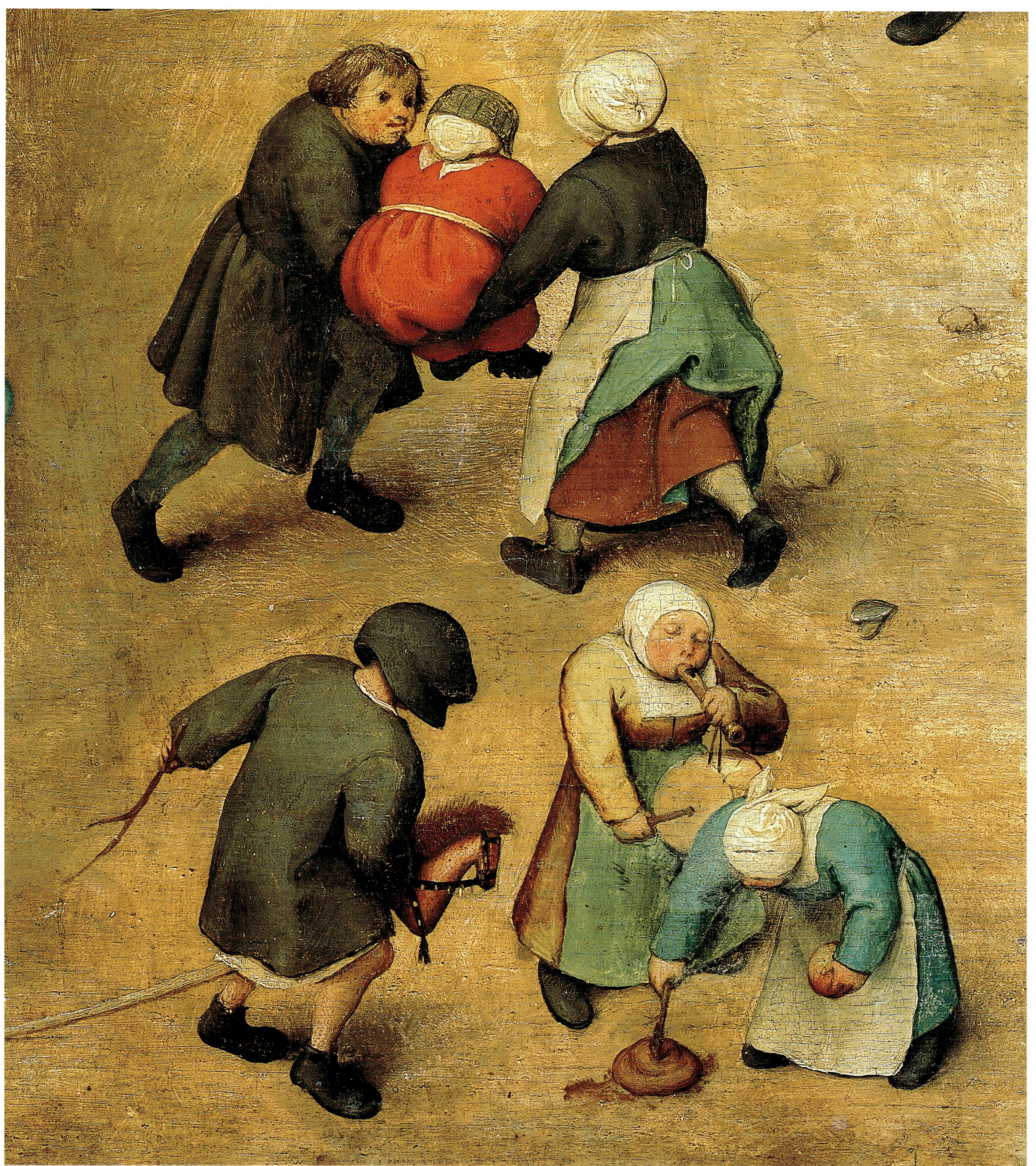

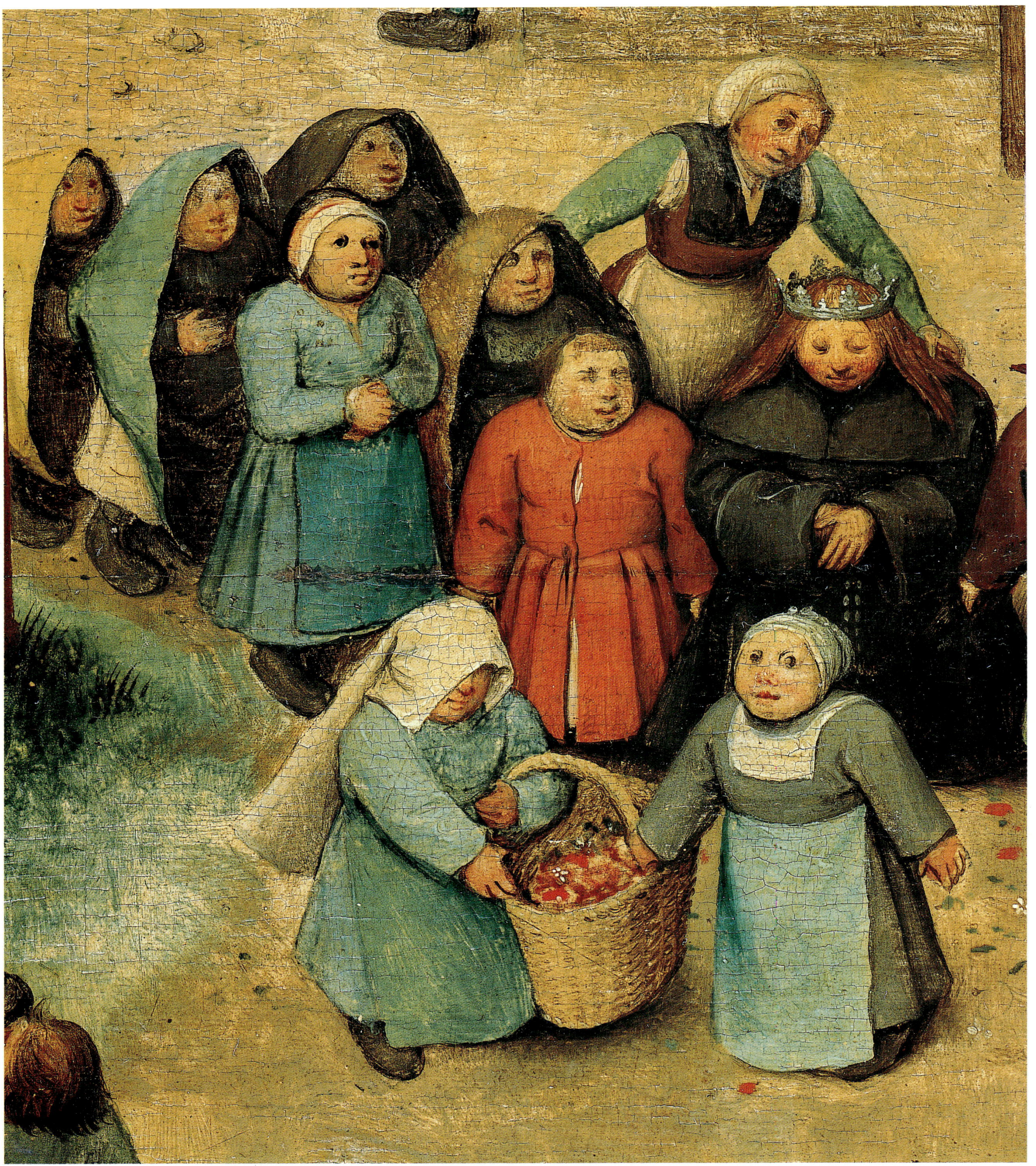

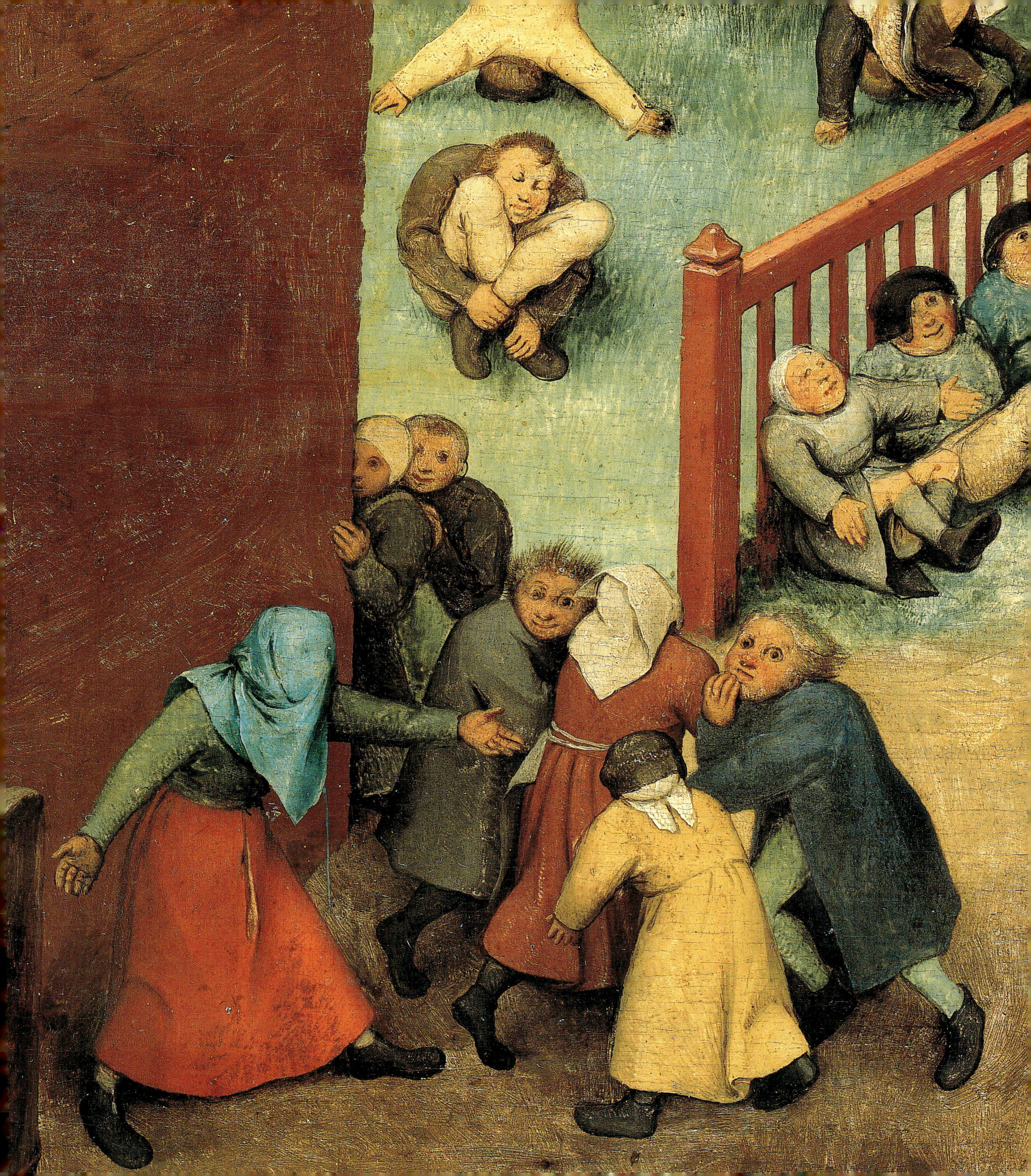

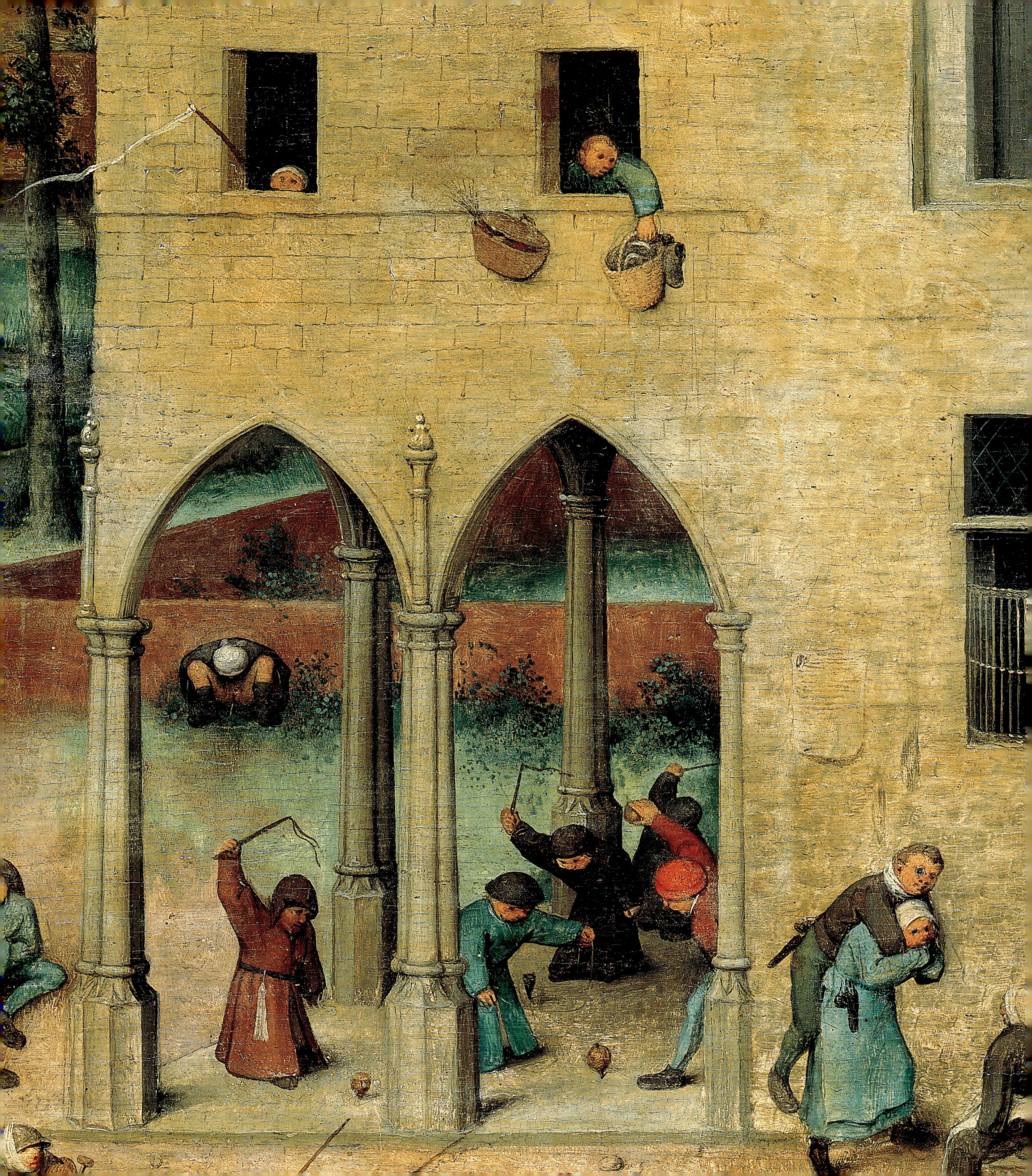

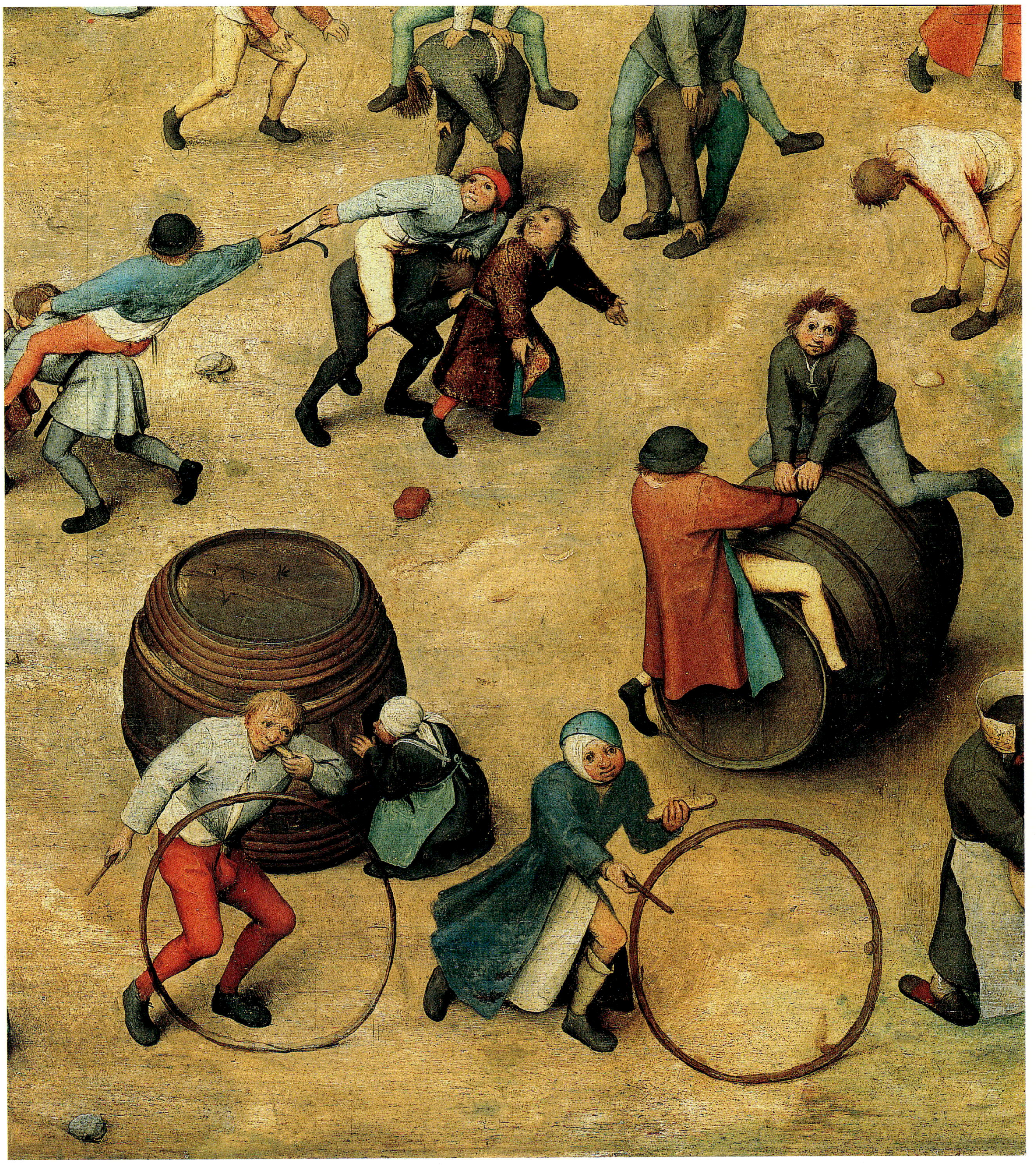

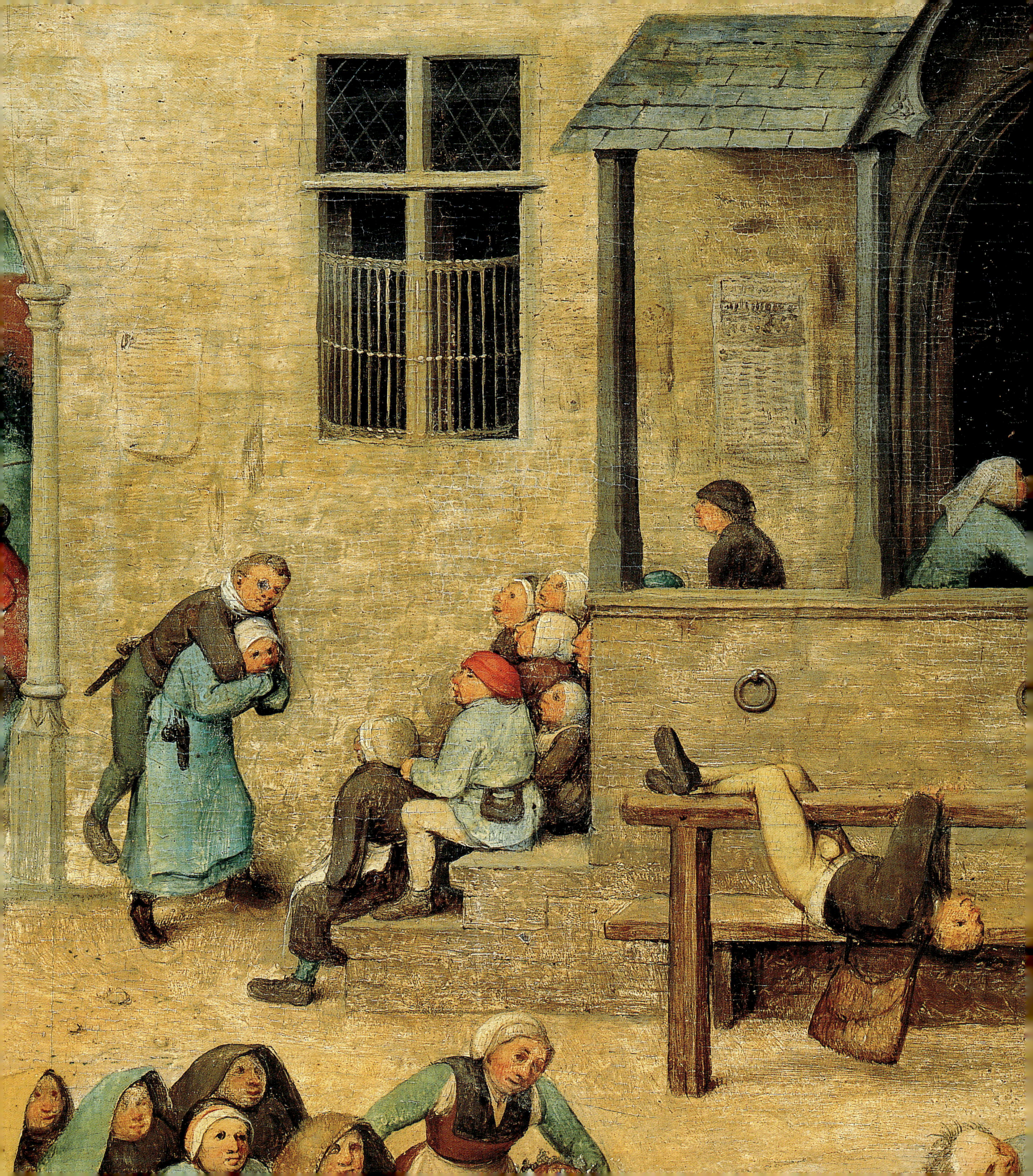

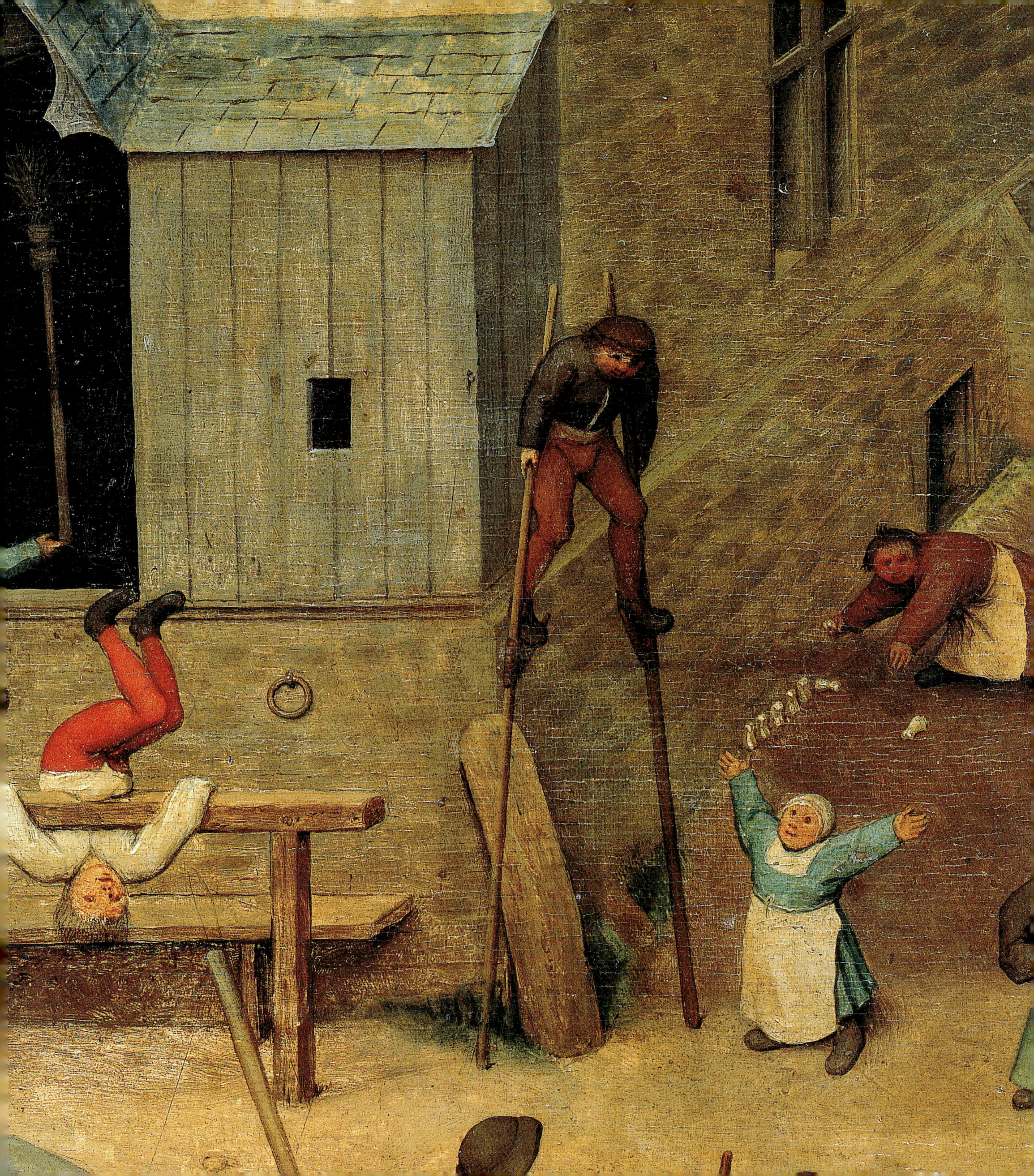

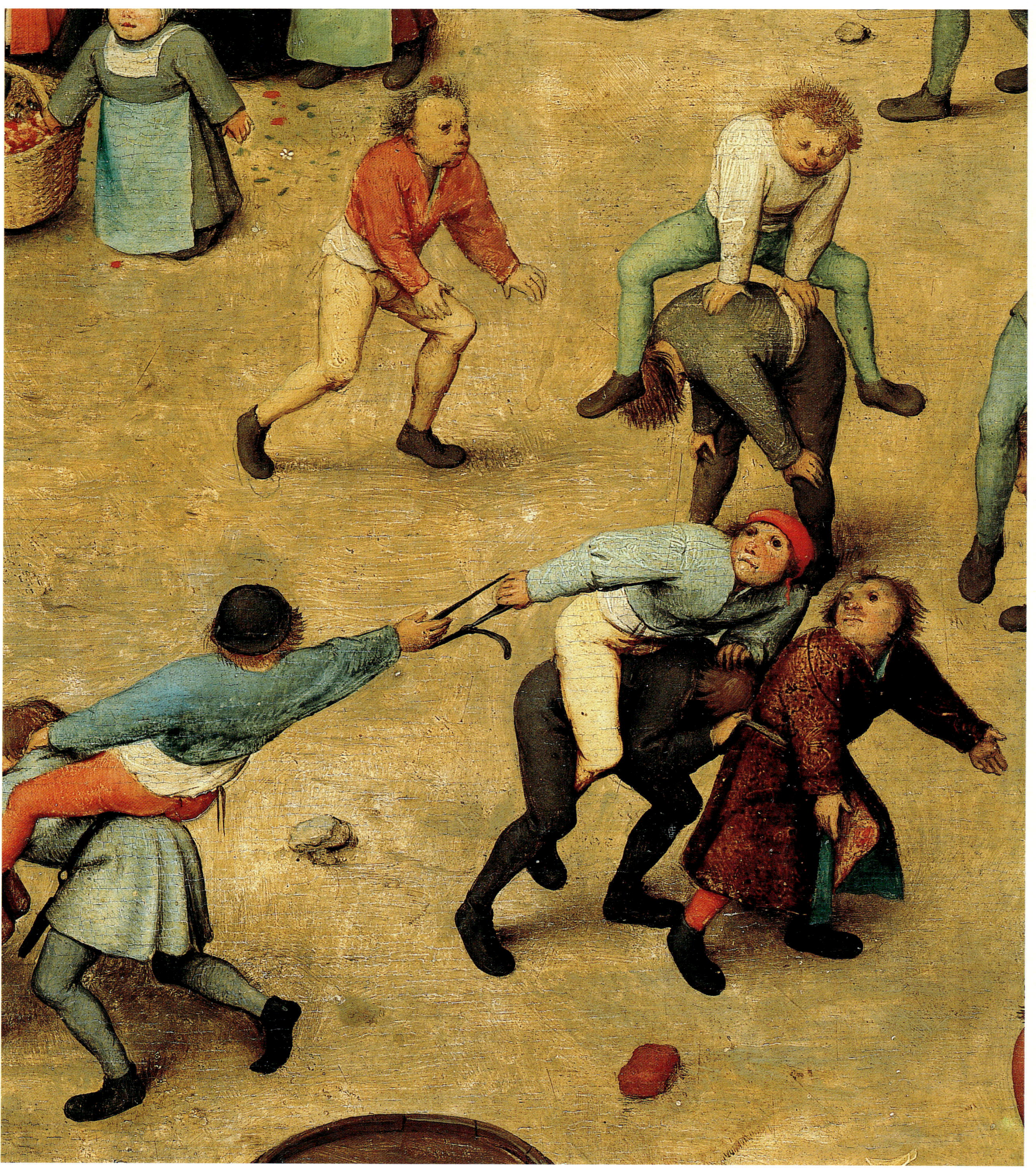

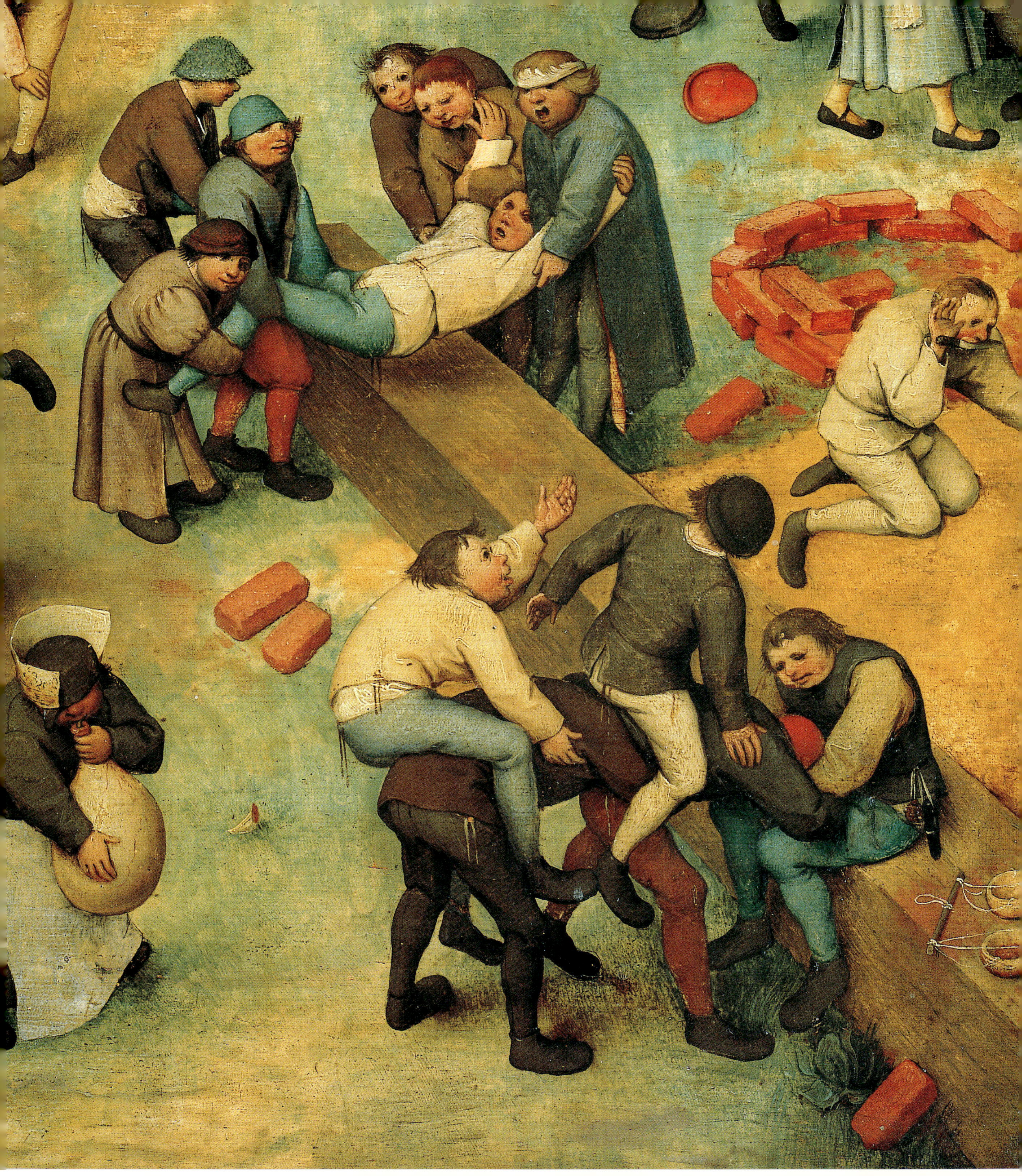

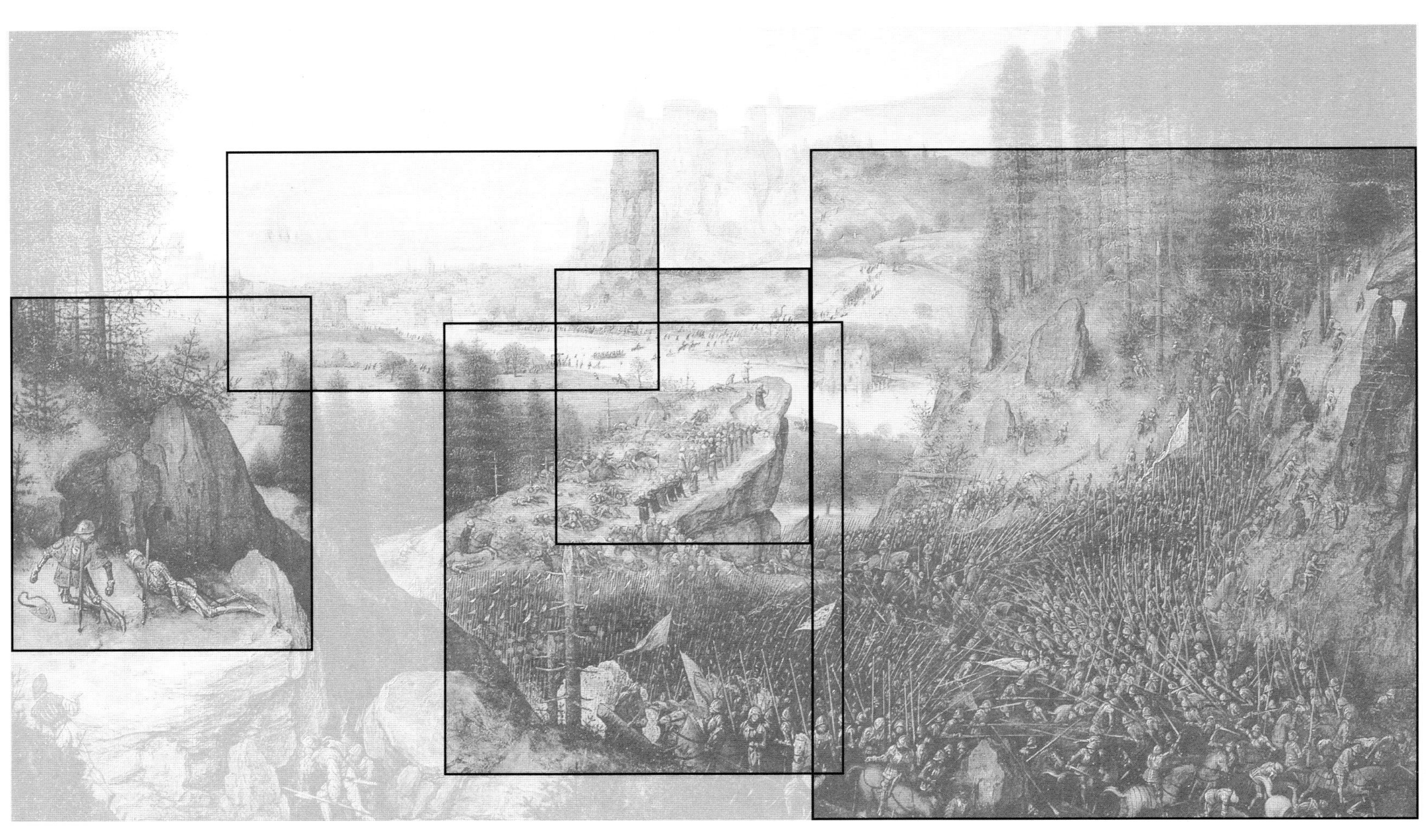

The Suicide of Saul

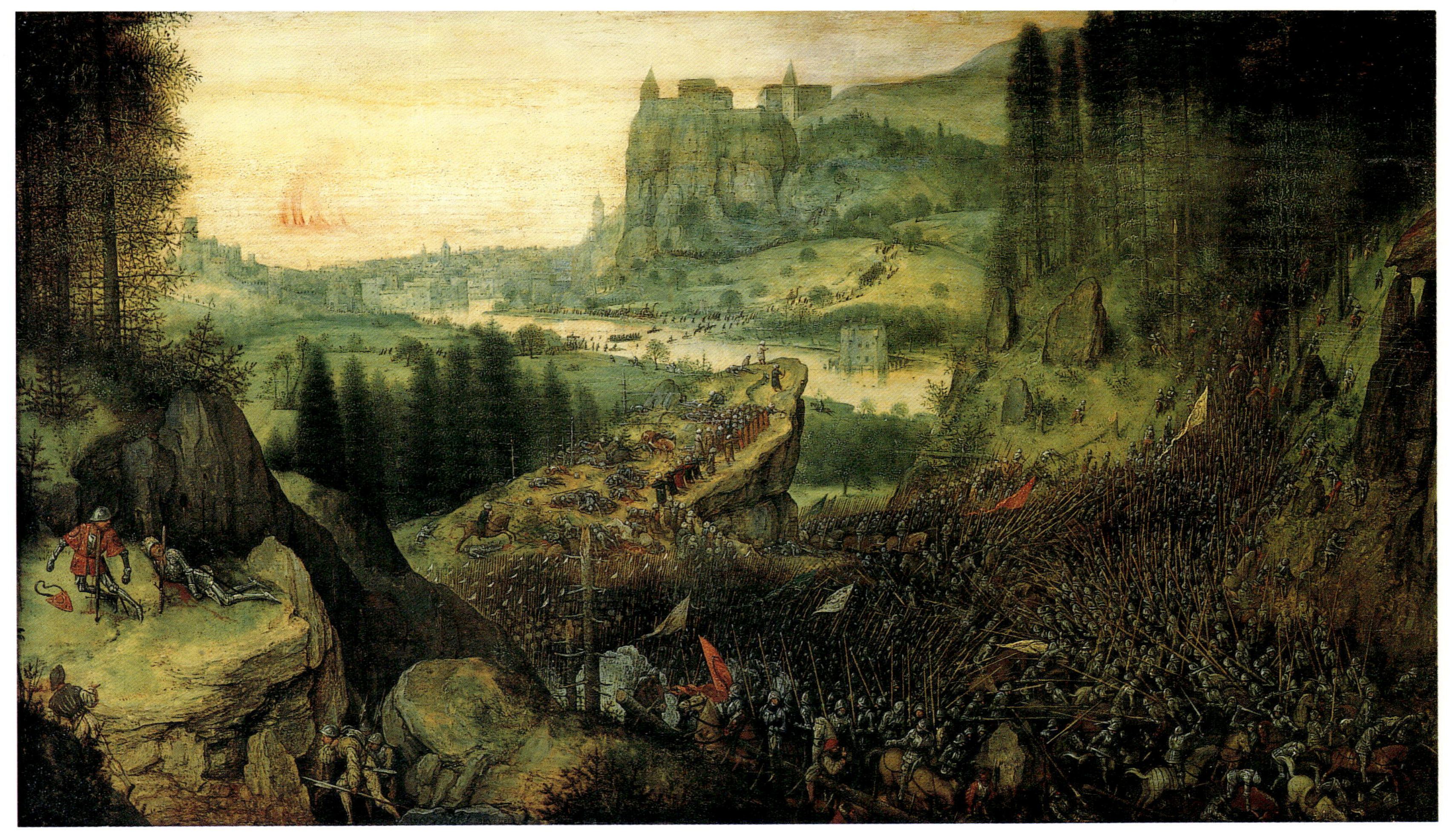

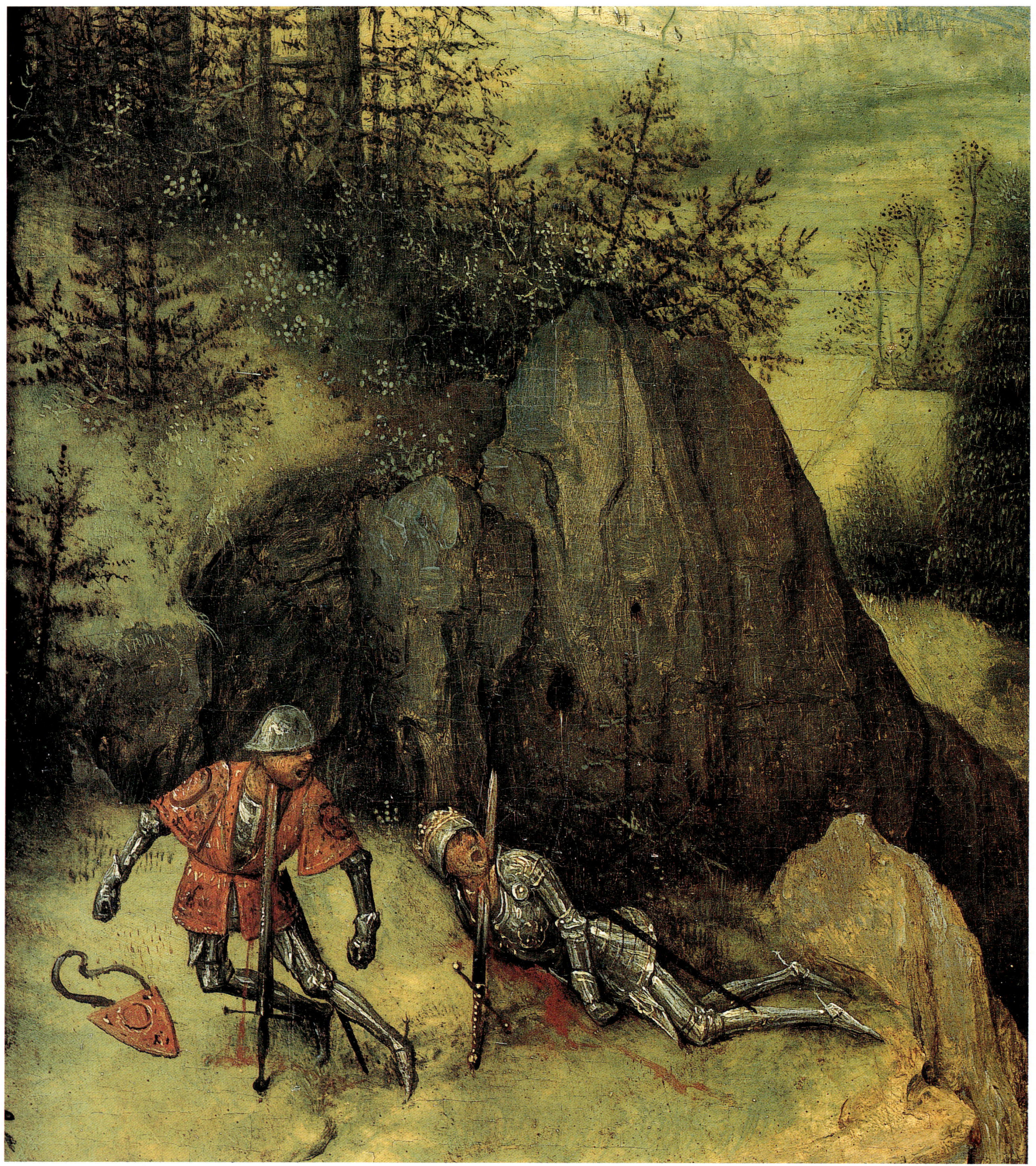

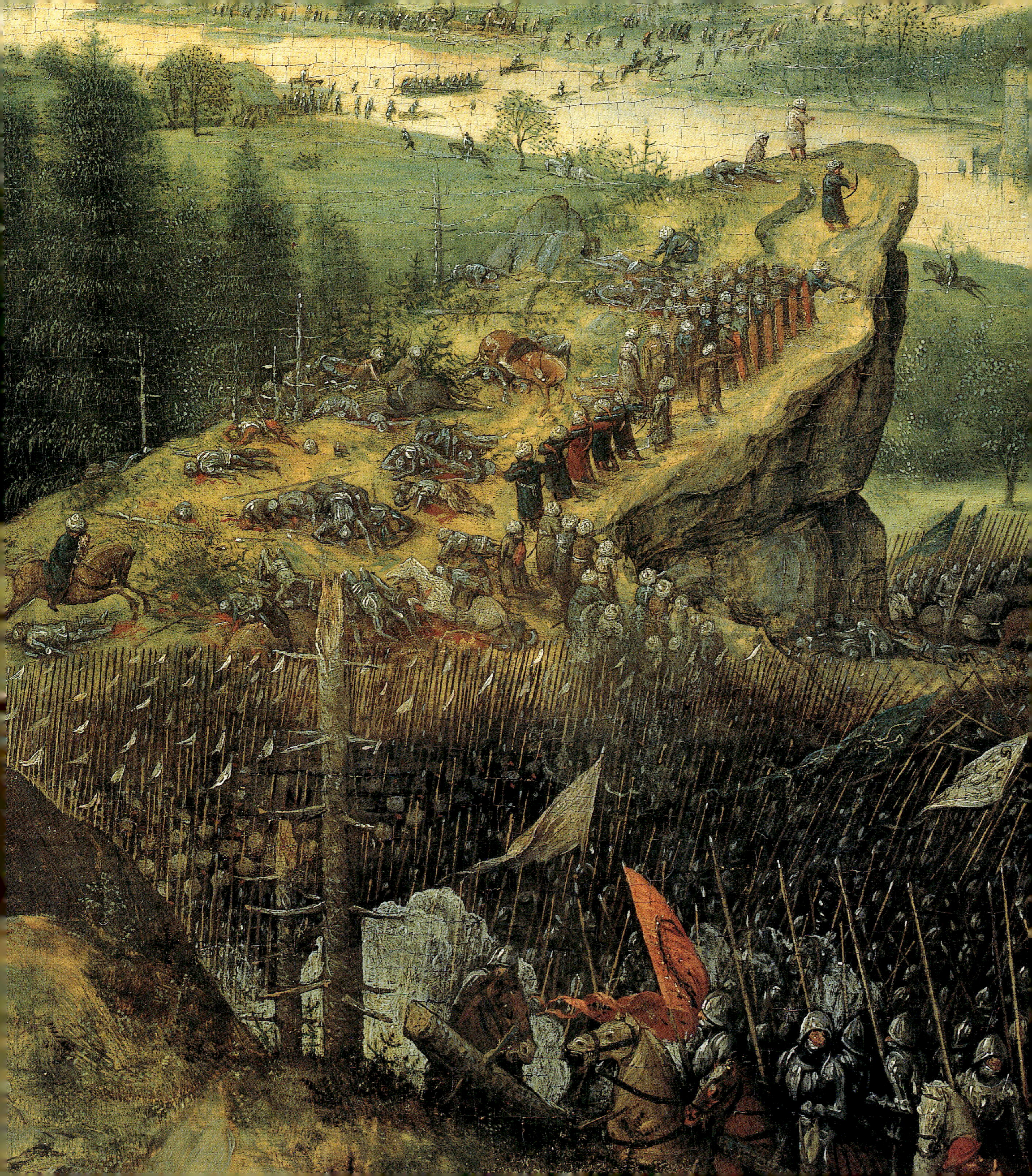

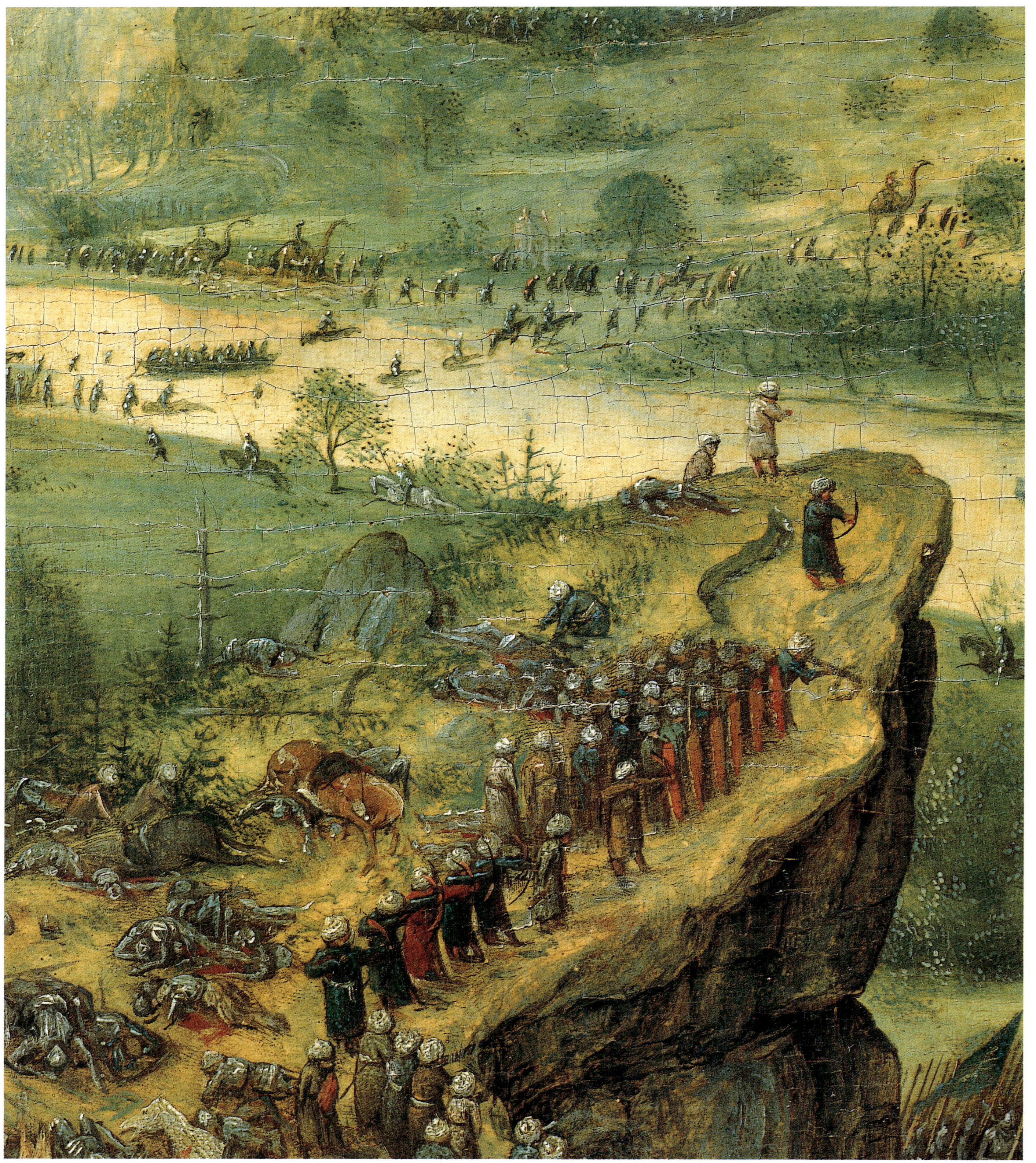

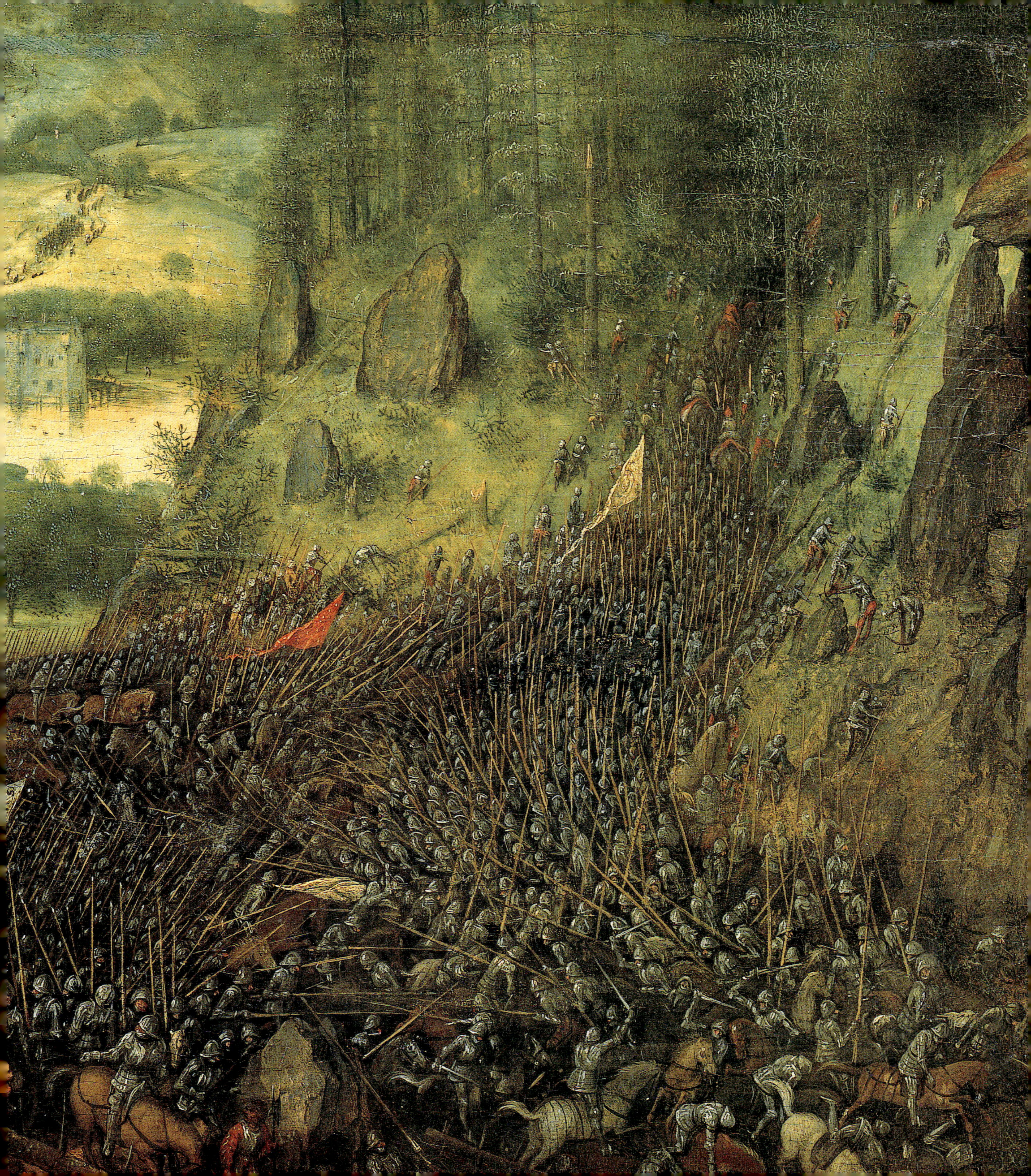

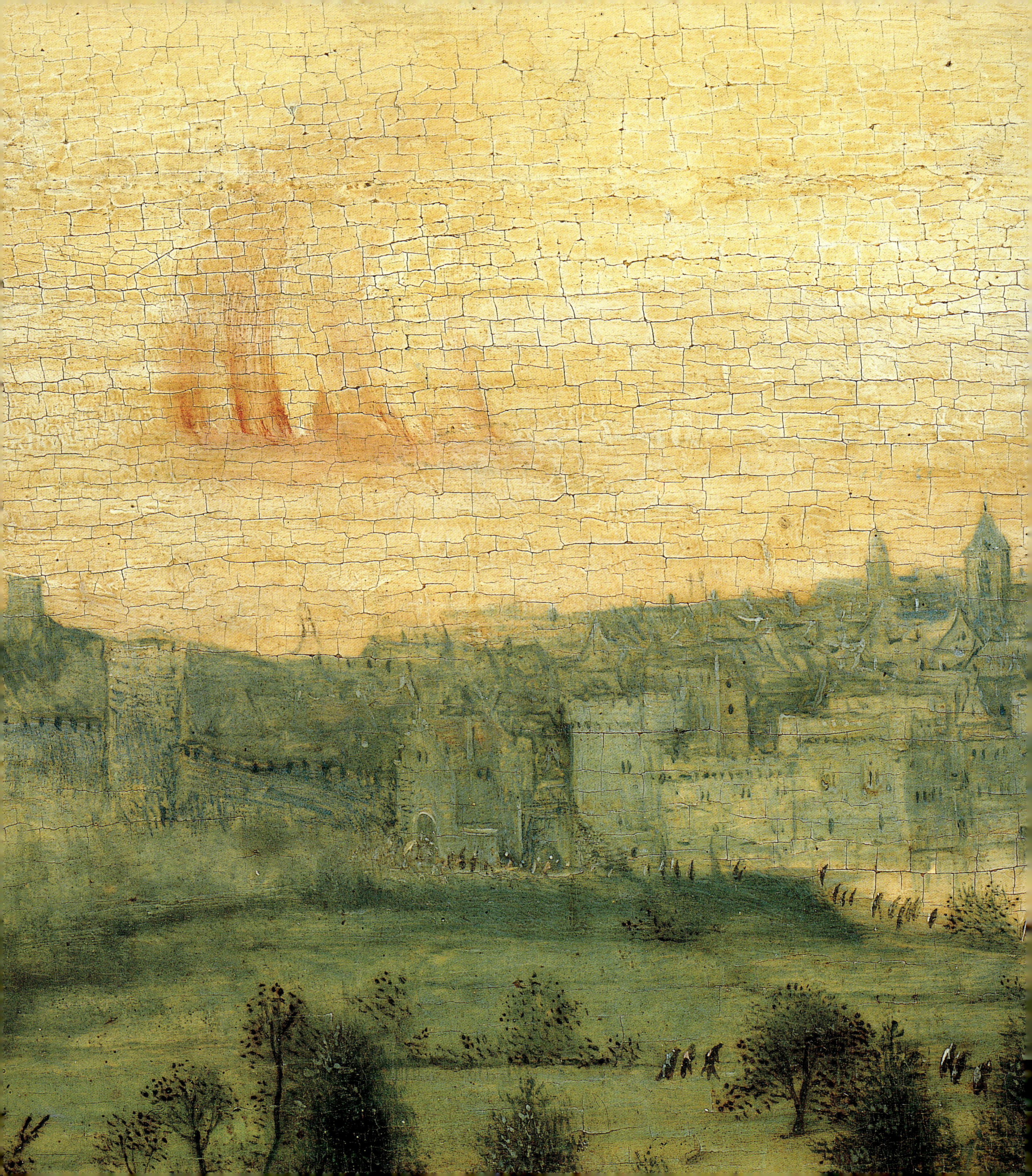

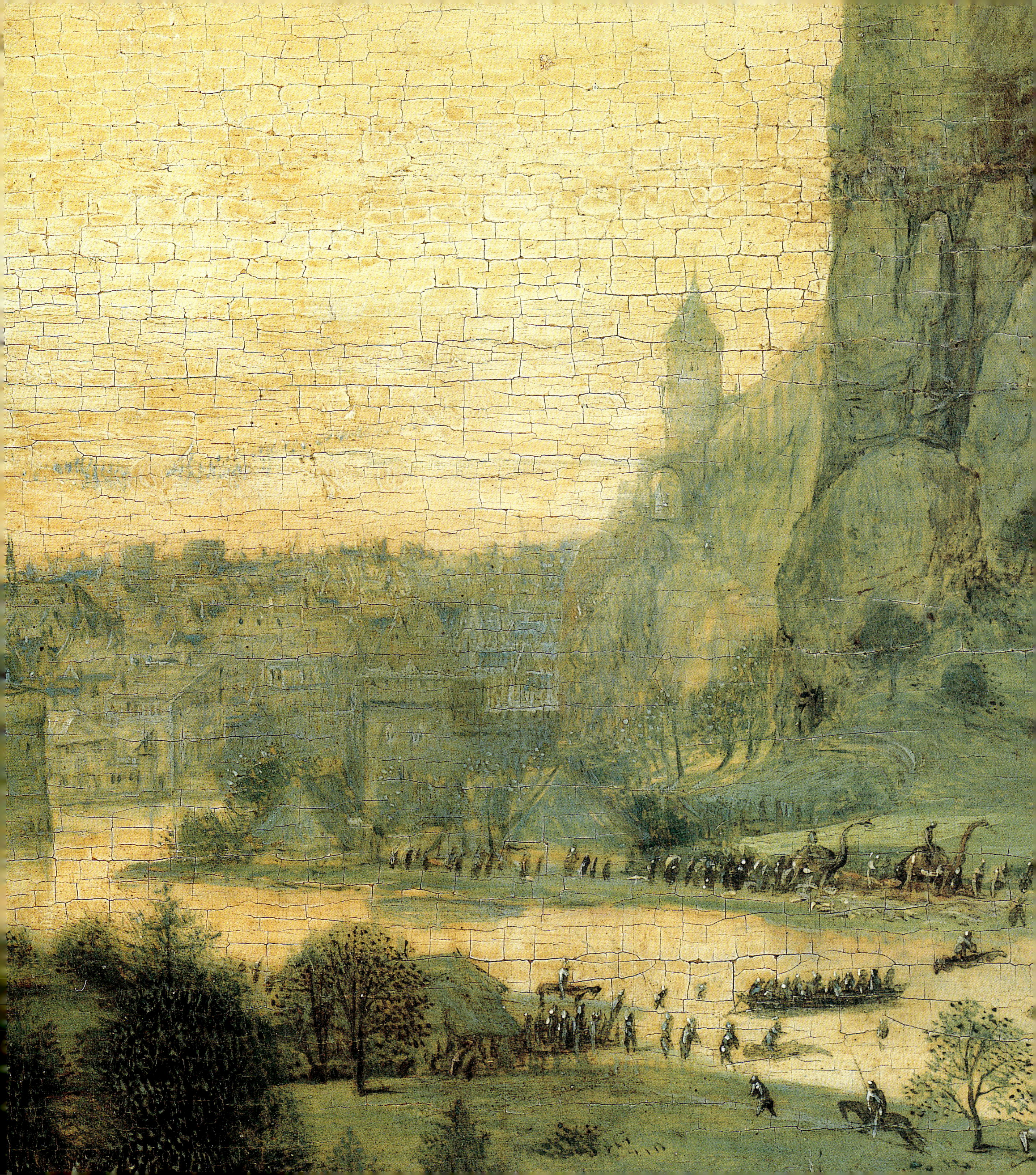

Tower of Babel
1563

Signed at the bottom on a block of stone: "BRVEGEL. FE. M.CCCCC.LXIII"
Oak, 114 × 155 cm
1566 Nicolas Jongelinck; probably became the property of the city of Antwerp in the same year; Rudolf II; Inv. No. 1026

Bruegel's large *Tower of Babel* is one of his most brilliant works. The almost inexhaustible opulence in the portrayal of the tower, more still, the abundance of ideas symbolized in it, have no equals in painting. Not least, however, is the set of forms that speaks. This theme had never before been conceived on such a large scale and the work represents the absolute pinnacle of the artistic imagination. Its meaning, however, lies in the fact that it shows, points out. It is a didactic work.
The question is, on what subject is it based? "Pride Punished" or "Architectonic Marvel"? In other words, can the as-yet unfinished tower be finished according to Bruegel's scheme or not. Bruegel always allowed the meaning of the picture to speak for itself through the image itself. So what do we see? A colossal mass resembling a mountain has already outgrown everything that could possibly appear, reaching right up to the clouds; a town and harbour stand at a respectful distance from its foot, and there are also tiny workers and their machinery to show the scale (Bruegel the humorist even has them living on it, with their laundry hung out to dry and their flower gardens). Strangely, there is nothing threatening about this astonishing sight. Is something like irony involved? The compact, extremely broadly built, truncated conical shape cleverly built around a rocky mountain is, admittedly, lopsided, presumably through lack of skill, but it still rises up perfectly solid and stable.
The concern of many an interpreter that it may collapse or indeed has already is utterly unfounded. Indeed, the construction is peculiarly fragmentary or vague and there are more gaping holes at the base. But there are people everywhere working on the tower, conferring a realistic effect. Or was it the artist's intention to show us clearly the construction. The broadest view inside the tower is afforded precisely where the structure seems to have a colossal, gaping wound. But are the gaps scattered over the whole entity and the "delays" in the completion of the work not bleak signs that the work is not proceeding as it should? Similarly, the desolation seems to express the discouraging lack of coordination in the work underway in various sections of the tower, and how much has already been lost in the individual parts. Have the helplessly small workers, striking at the rocks with their pickaxes, ever been worn out by the strain of it? Does not the whole huge and chaotic building site speak of the monstrous mockery of this enterprise which has long since become helpless?
It would be wise to check the construction and design of the tower. In so doing, one comes across simply atrocious jokes, fascinating as artistic ideas, of the highest intelligence and with a figurative power that recalls Leonardo da Vinci. Though obvious, the underlying idea around which everything hangs, incredible to say has been too well hidden until now. Bruegel shows quite plainly the work's design and realization. The base of the tower is a bulging ring rising up to a ramp and slowly spiralling to the top like a snail. Retaining walls protect it, taking the whole weight of it. To reduce this weight to a minimum, without jeopardizing the solidity of the structure, a tip from Roman architecture was taken. In fact, the impressive complex of walls, arches and piers, which remains unchanging in order, ramp by ramp, is directly inspired by the Coliseum in Rome, as is the clever separation between the massive outer shell in ashlar work and the lighter, porous inner structure in brickwork, modelled after the honeycomb. (The reference should inspire confidence.) The painting shows the construction of arched and barrel vaults, and the hewing, transport, hoisting and placing of the ashlar, using every possible lifting device (there is even a crane with tread wheel). Bruegel surveys the entire range of civil engineering and architectural know-how *en passant* in a humorous, didactic manner, but with the greatest zeal in search of completeness. We are convinced that all the building problems can be overcome, as the plan demands. Do we still have doubts anyway?
We have now reached the fascinating point where

we can get a glimpse of the upper part of the core of the tower, of its inner structure, as if it were an open beehive. The spectacle revealed to us are fantastic technical and rational details. We can make out a system with a construction like an onion, made in layers, rising up with tapering, radial vaulted galleries overlaid with a hanging spiral. The overall effect is perhaps comparable to the chambers and blade wheel of a turbine. But how wonderful! It is, quite clearly, none other than the convex projection of the concavity of the internal structure of the Coliseum, with the vaulted galleries there rising radially outward and here flowing together inwards! It is a formal idea that as an operation has no equals. The exterior and interior of the same model, therefore, but brilliantly transformed, stretched from a funnel into the nautilus chamber of the tower! Is this structural idea, however, appropriate here? How does it continue upwards? There, a chaos of unconnected elements proliferates. Around the shell-shaped cylindrical core articulated into storeys cluster broad rings of walls, radial fan partitions, tilted planes. And we must ask: how is a connection possible between the multistoried structure of the interior and the spiral shape of the exterior? Should not the whole thing necessarily have the spiral structure?

There, the tower has revealed its secret. Bruegel the laughing architect has let the mask fall: the structure is intentionally impossible, a well-devised absurdity, immensely ironic for all its rationality. In fact, the nautilus and the multistoried structure, bulb shapes, fan work and tapering spiral with radial galleries: this is no architectural wonder, but the triumph of the artistic idea, which makes the tower itself state that not only could it not be finished, but it could never be built at all! And that is not enough: for the sake of stability, the builders have carefully placed all the "verticals", even the main axis, at right angles to the "horizontals". Since the latter rise, as required by the spiral shape, however, the tower was inevitably lopsided! It was therefore designed lopsided! Therefore, it follows that in accordance with the biblical myth, the *Tower of Babel* is the paradigm showing that all human handiwork must remain incomplete. It cannot be complete because an arrogant ambition reaches its limits here. The artistic theme, then, is the demonstration of the inability to complete, of the failure of man's — especially modern man's — much-touted rationality, precisely because of the senselessness associated with rationality itself. (Today we would call it a satire of technique.) At first glance, the tower as "mountain" seems to be rejecting the teeming activity of the people and their aims set against nature, deviating from its order. (Even the cloud says this, with its subtle symbolic overtones.) It seems so irrational, because the tower is the creation of man and not of nature, and it appears as such even to the eye. To whom is the tower's irony directed? To those who have high-handedly appointed themselves universal architects. But the tower is "not playing the game".

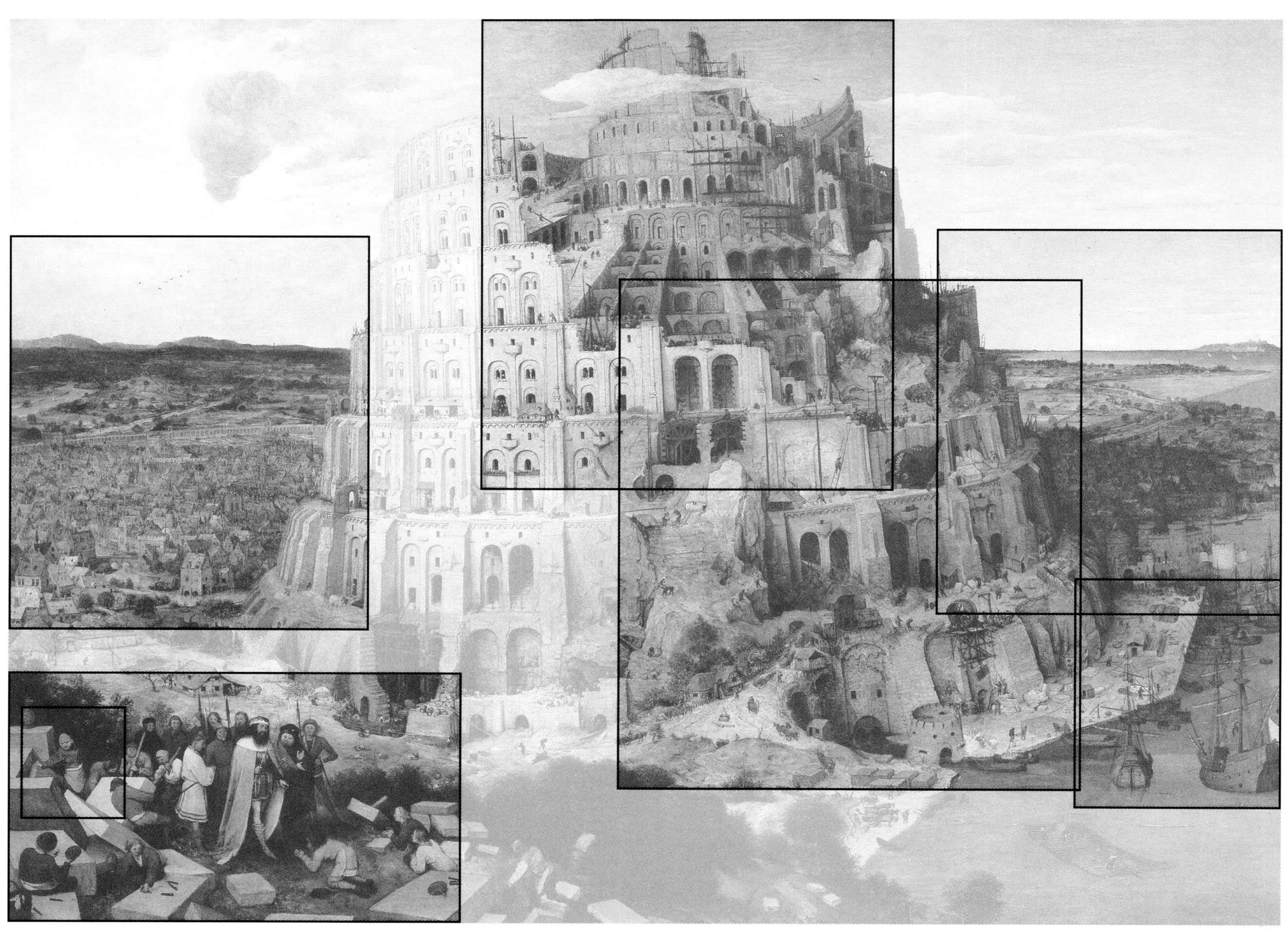

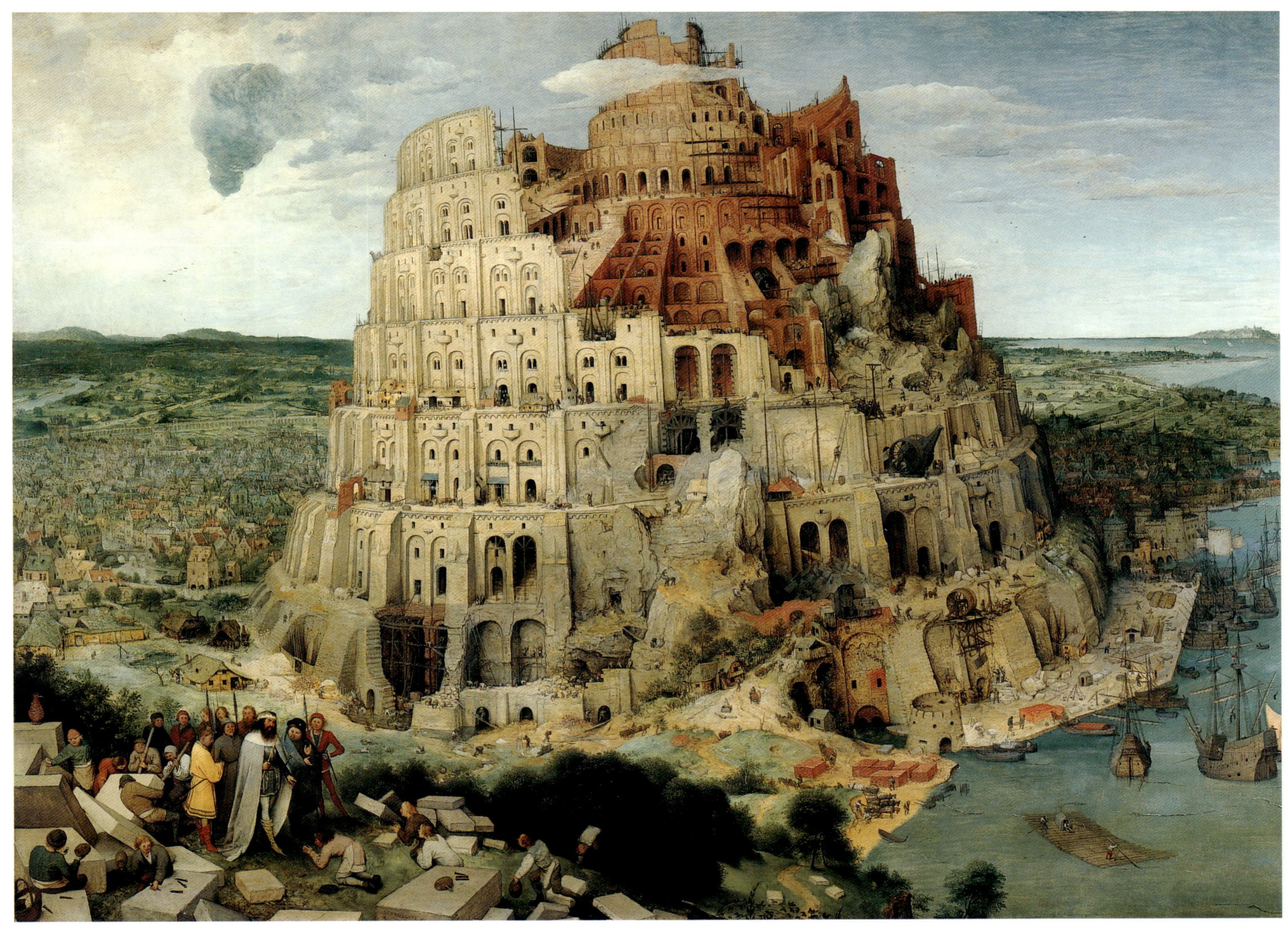

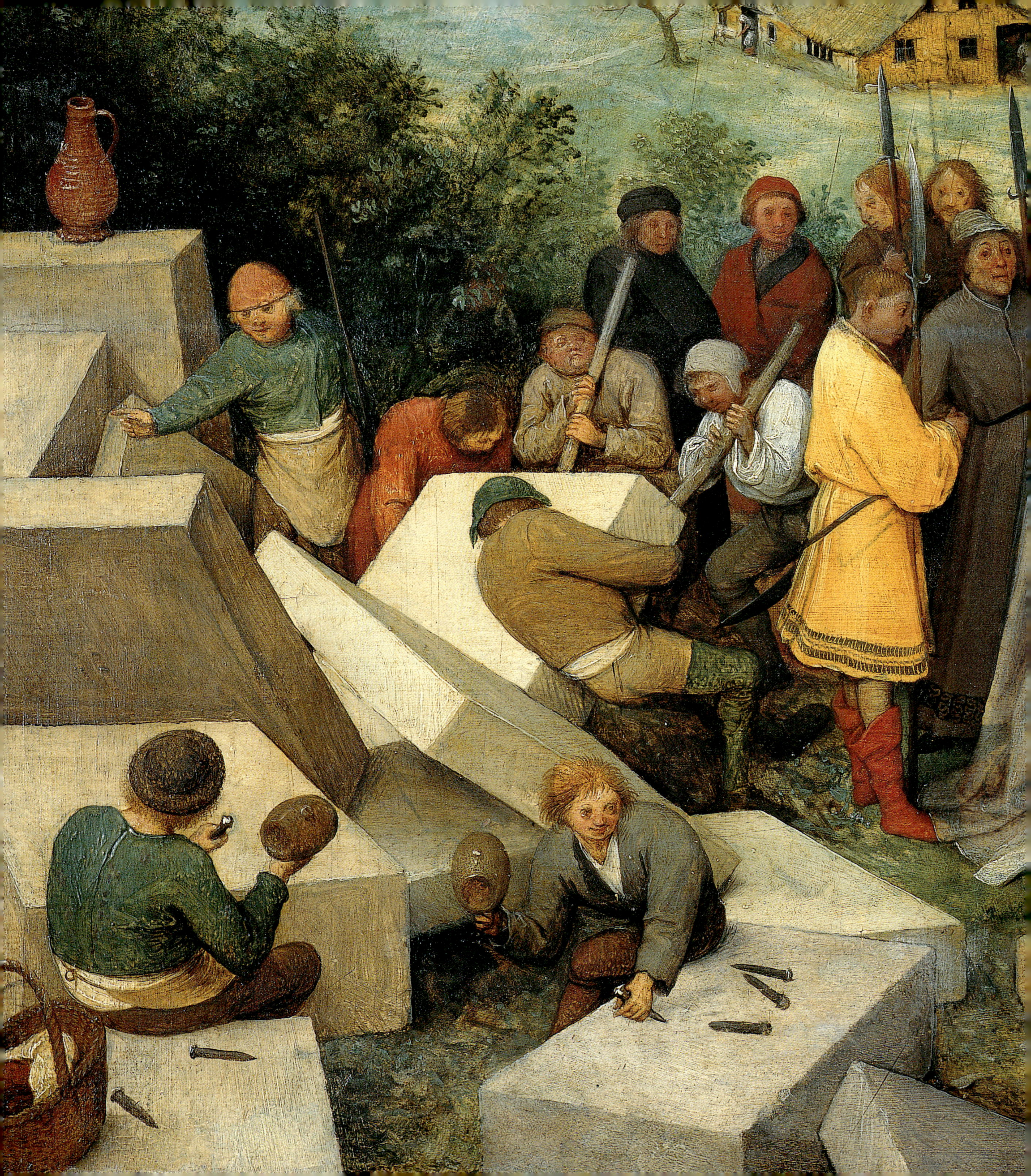

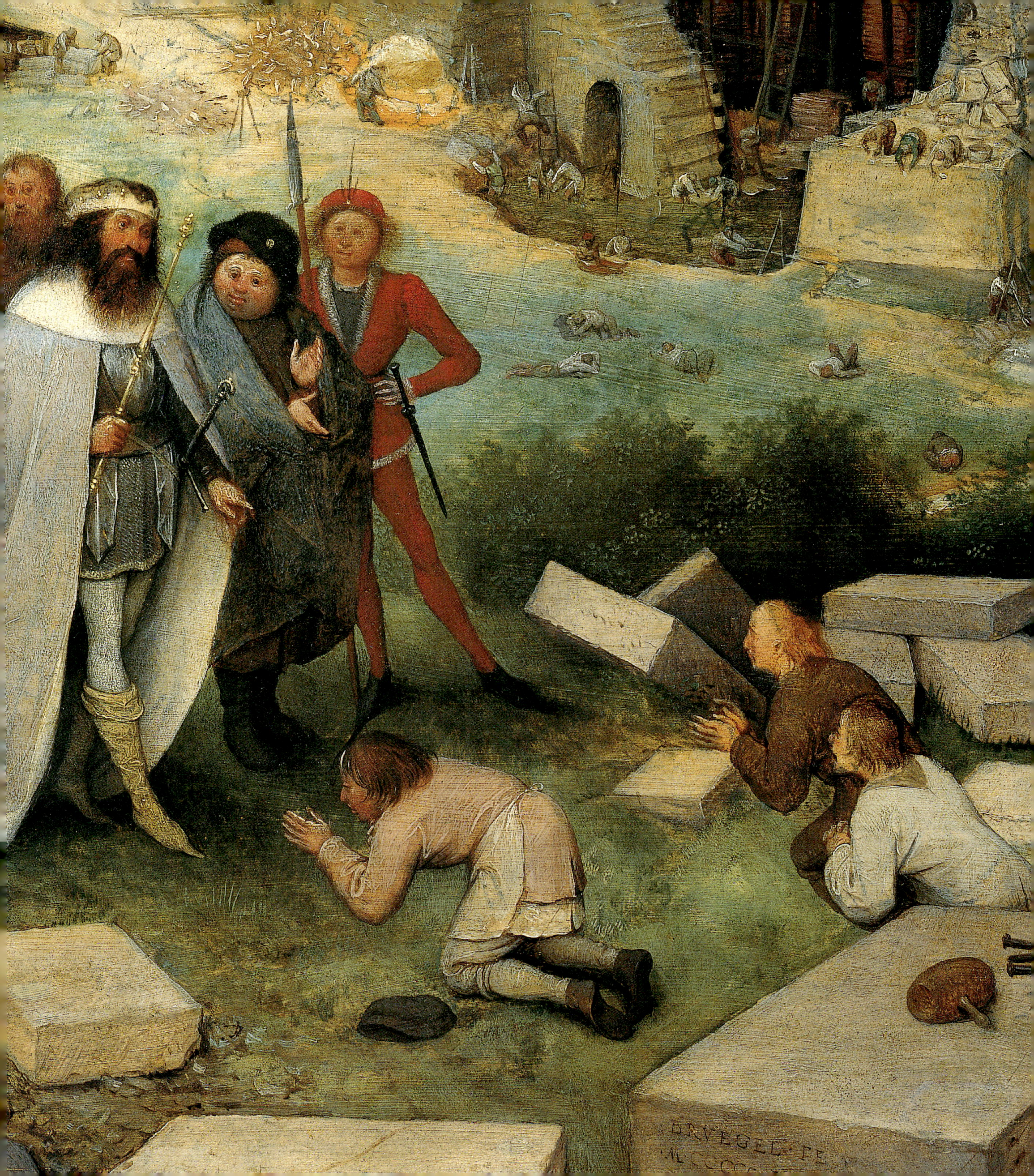
BRVEGEL·FE·

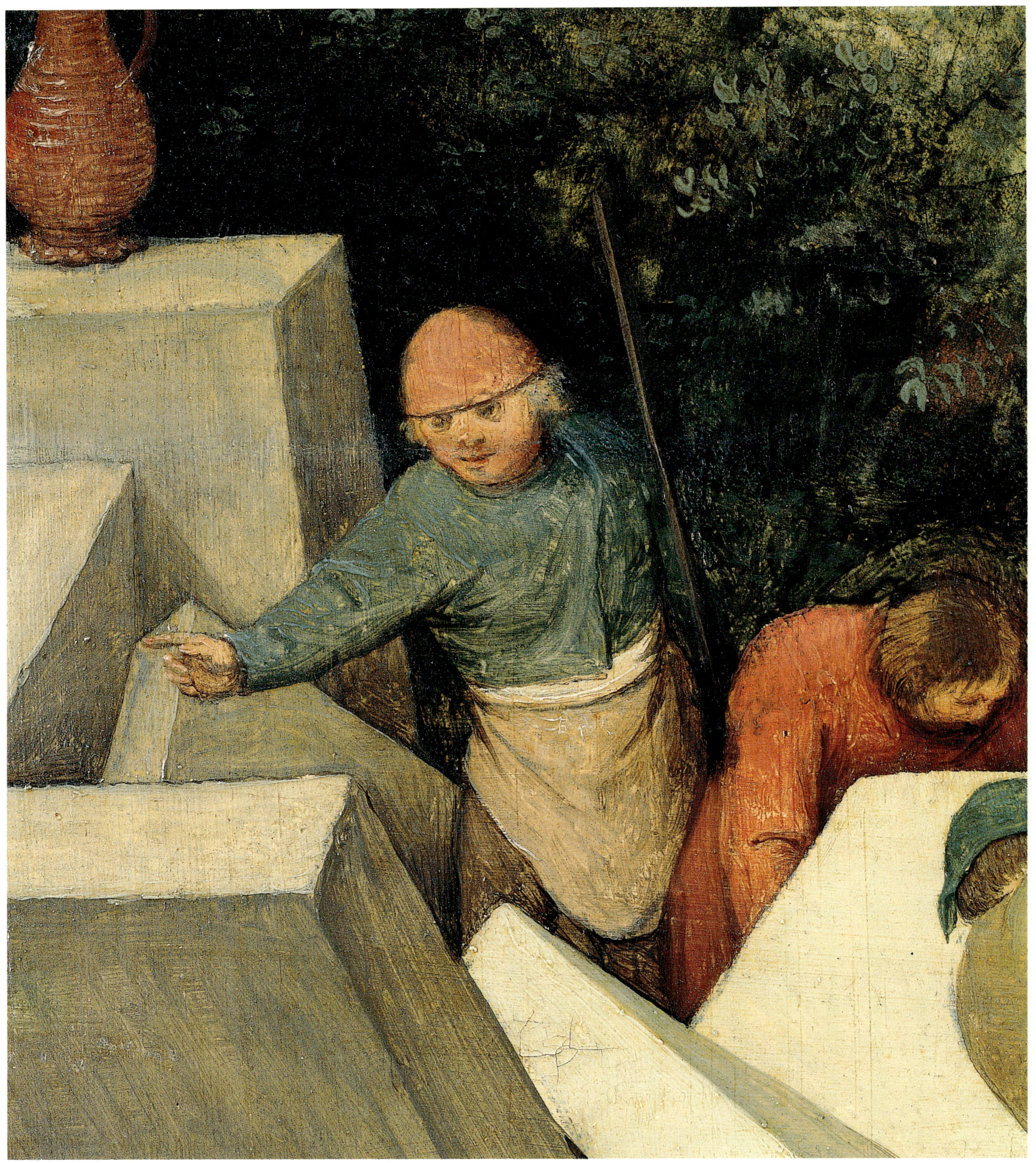

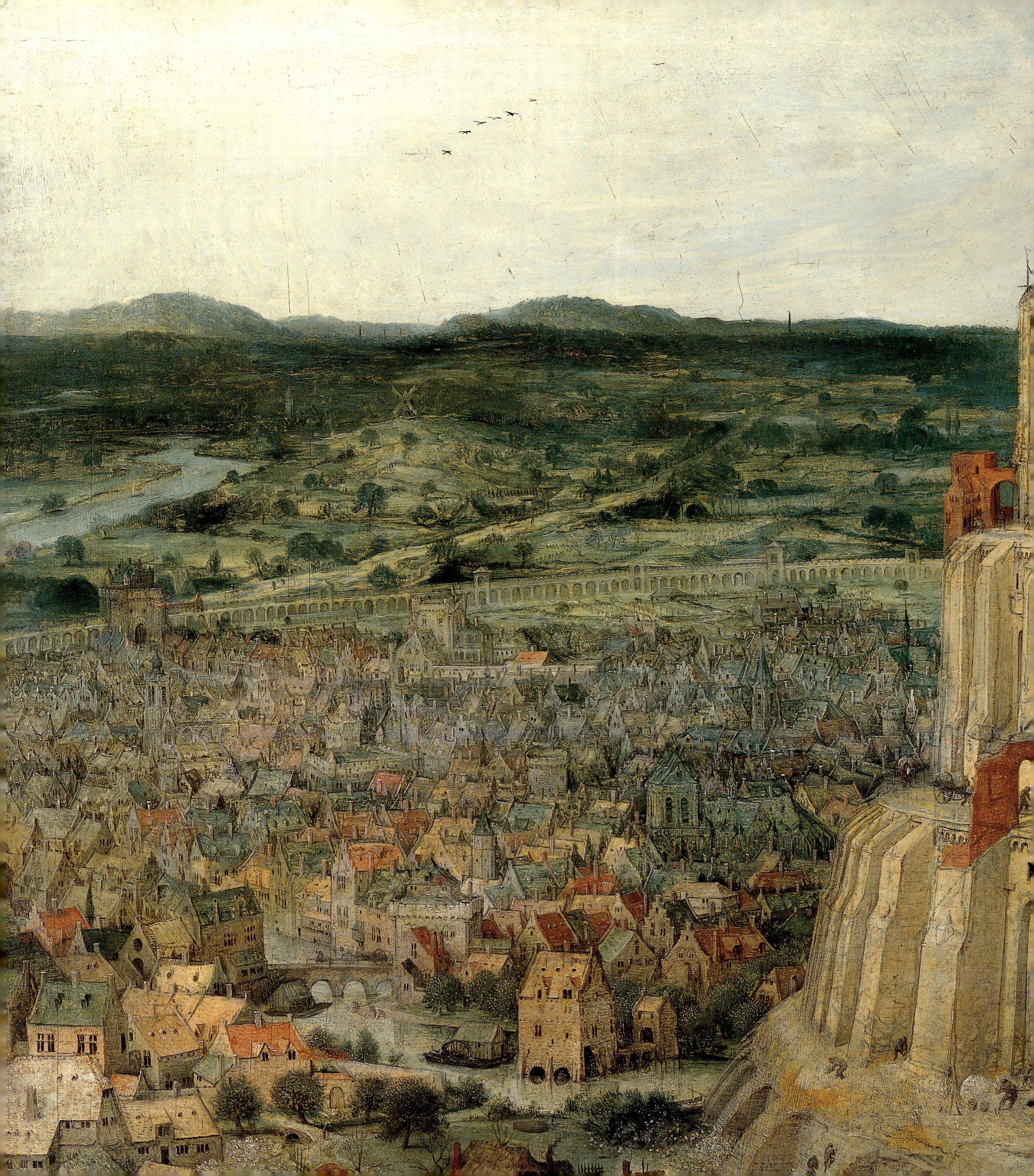

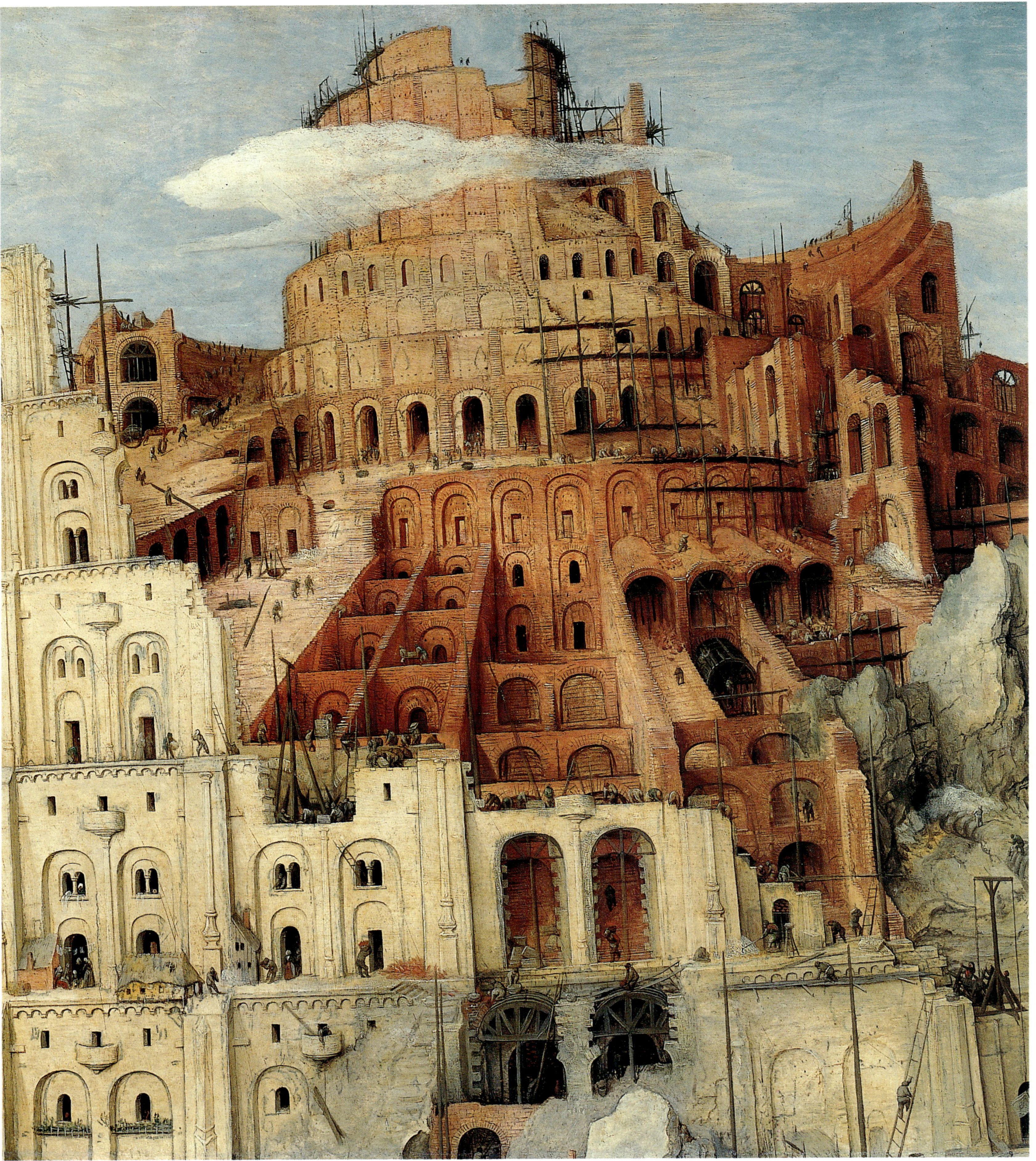

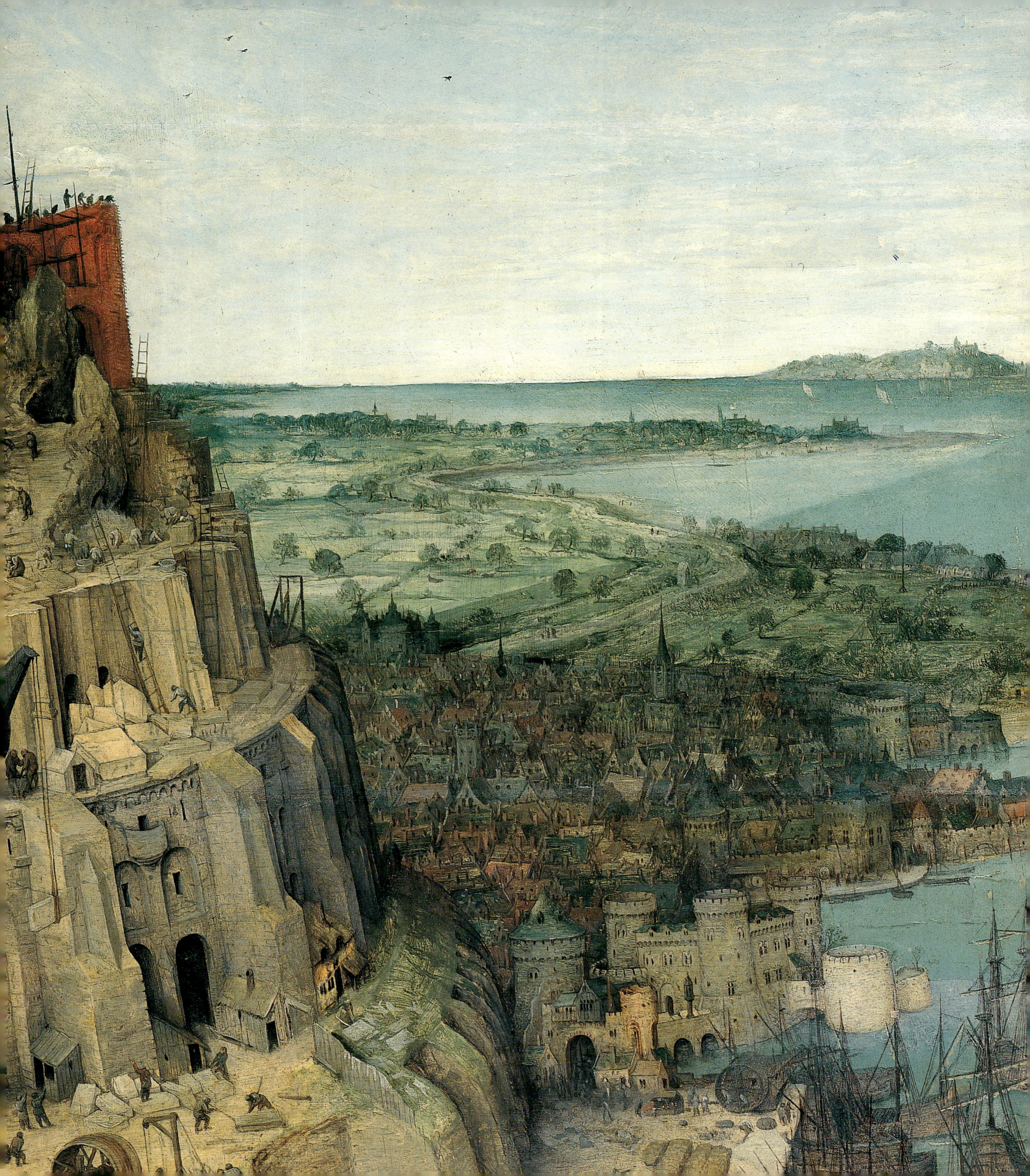

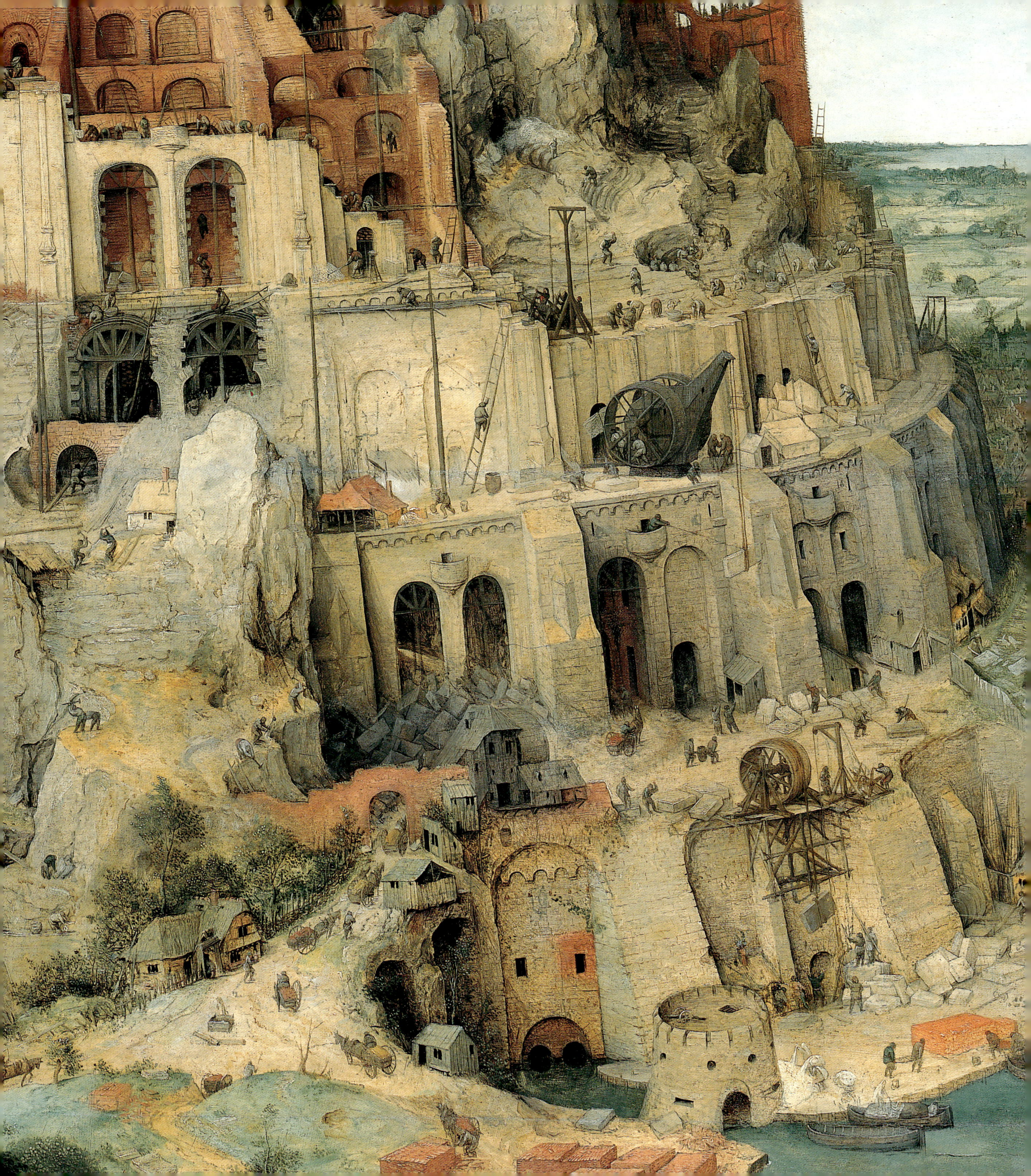

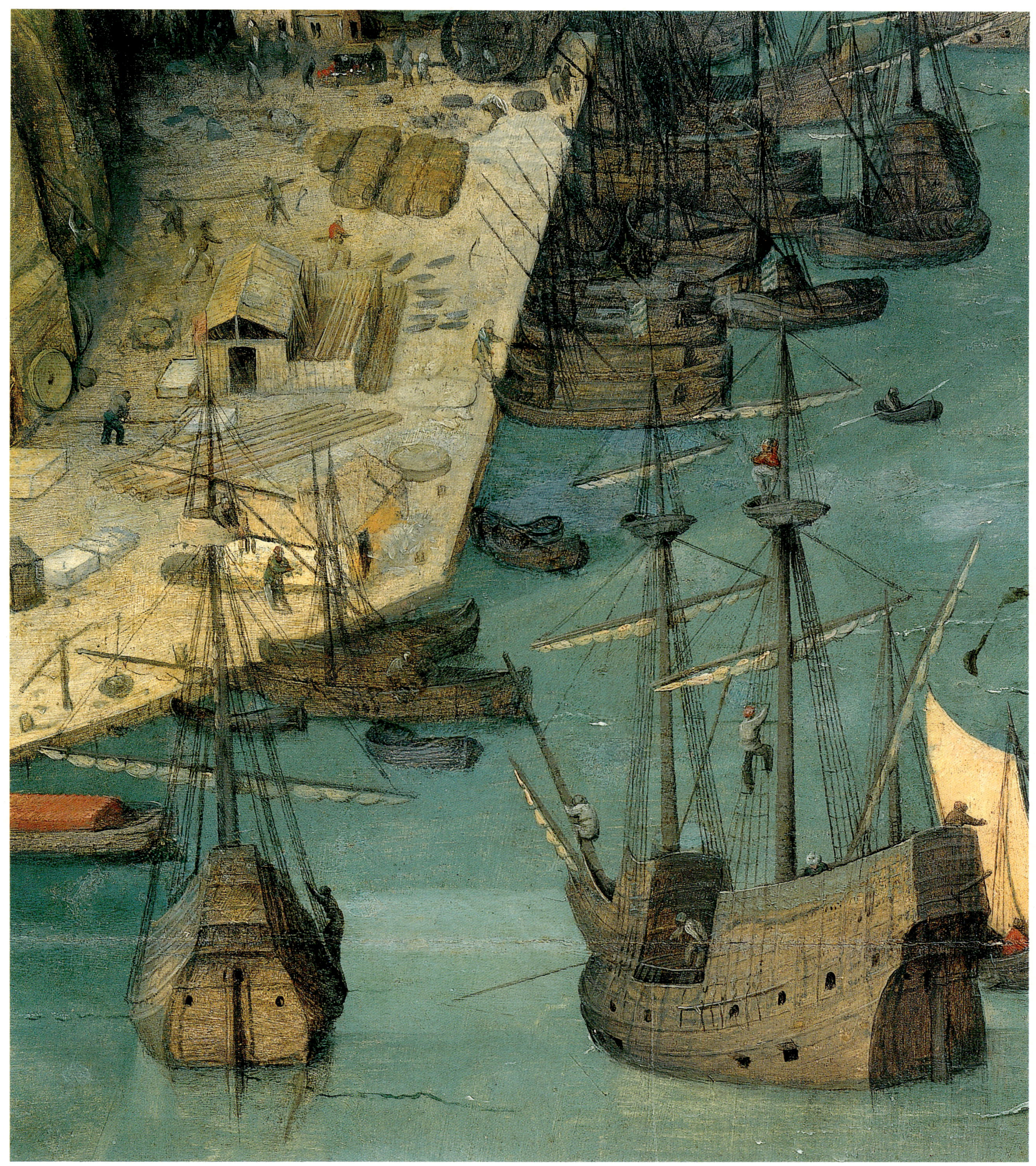

Christ Carrying the Cross
1564

Signed below right:
"BRVEGEL. MD.LXIIII"
Oak, 124 × 170 cm
1566 Nicolas Jongelinck; probably became property of the city of Antwerp in the same year; Estate of Archduke Ernst 1595?; Rudolf II; Inv. No. 1017

The theme of *Christ Carrying the Cross* is a tradition in Netherlandish painting that stretches as far back as van Eyck, continuing through to Bruegel and beyond. Bruegel was well aware of this tradition and expanded it in an extraordinary way, raising it to the level of an unrepeatable, unattainable achievement. In this painting as in no other does Bruegel's importance emerge for his role in perfecting the old Netherlandish tradition, opening up new avenues and developing areas new to art, as well as taking the old Dutch function of narration to its peak and conclusion. And he shows the way for later Flemish painting with his extremely concrete concept of nature.
Bruegel took for granted his entire composition, with its semicircular procession out of Jerusalem to Golgotha, and narrative and formal solutions and many details borrowed from predecessors. He merely widened the old framework, which consented the panoramic composition both in terms of the whole and in terms of the details that make it up. The view of the many-figured, scenically rich event between the points of departure and arrival becomes a view of the world as it is, infinite in the finite, for the profundity of the reality as well as the fullness of life.
Furthermore, instead of a fantastic account that simulates plausibility with highlights of real details but still cannot let go of the fairy-tale tenor and fantasy and the traditional exotic *topos*, a new, broader epic form emerges; it is almost limitless and dares to capture reality itself, even to take possession of it.
By the sole means of continuity Bruegel has welded together — and this is the extraordinary quality that places him amongst the great artists of the Renaissance — the two artistic eras, the Medieval and the one known as the Modern age. He narrates in the present tense, transports history into present-day experience and perceptions. He does not say, "Once upon a time", but lets reality live, imparting to this experience an immediacy of both a visual and an apparently commonplace nature. In the painting, we find images reflected in puddles and the effect of gusts of wind on a woollen cap which flies off a head. It is like a foreshadowing of the 19th-century epic, the narrative breadth of Tolstoy. The narrative process is presented in its entirety, analyzed and, with an infinity of individual details, each of which is proof of the originality of the observation and the accuracy of the representation, it is transformed into a unique event made up of a sum of elements that effectively goes beyond what the artist as such can bring together in the imagination. What is more, it assumes *genius*, the insight of the epic poet who invents and organizes.
In any case, Bruegel is not by any means a Modernist. To the contrary, while his 16th-century predecessors had already given to the genre style the theme of the history of salvation in a secularized or at least externalized form, Bruegel reinstated the seriousness of the religious subject in full. And not only: he offers the chance to analyze, dissect all human endeavour in light of this theme, so as to demonstrate that then as now it is equally blind, narrow, prejudiced and hopelessly "profane", incapable of perceiving not only the sublime reality but also any reality that is higher than the commonplace one before it. With the pointed humour of the narrative author, all the stock types, modes of behaviour, reactions that make the picture a truly inexhaustible source, present the crowd as a terrible menagerie. Only the few who in life as well have been isolated are highlighted: the poor and the different (the group of gypsies in the lower half of the picture, who are the only ones with the exception of the Begins in the righthand foreground and the group on the right with the self-portrait of the artist who look at and mourn Christ's collapse) and the children (whose parents, to the left of the wheel, hold them up in readiness for the blessed sight of the Saviour).
The strongest profession of faith in the divine in a profane world is, however, the group of figures highlighted and isolated in the foreground, showing the "swooning of Mary". The solemnly stylized

figured, archaizingly cited along the lines of a van der Weyden or van der Goes, are the only elements that symbolize the ideal. Even if the world moves ever in the profane, like a turntable around the winged axis, the grotesque needle of rock with the windmill on top (both elements are found individually in van Eyck, but only in Bruegel are they so brilliantly and humorously combined), the real focal point is with those people who are quietly grieving, the suffering, those who shun the blind, coarse and hopeless frenzy of the profane *vulgus* (what madness and cruelty combined is shown in the image of the "court jester" assigned to Christ inasmuch as he was the King of the Jews, and the leader of the group clustered around the cross; he is dressed in bizarre Jew's garb and plays the shofar — a caricature as the Messiah's herald. This is just one example of the brilliant exaggerations of the tradition stemming from Bosch.). It would be to misunderstand Bruegel, however, to accuse him (as has often occurred) also of being the "Ode" of the Horatian "profanum vulgus", the moralizing condemnation of the all-too-human, which he displays at every turn of the painting realistically and not without a sense of humour for the inveterate follies of the human menagerie. Children may have fun jumping in puddles; dogs may romp in the skinners' yards (with the piles of rams' horns) without having to call in the iconologists with their cries of "allegory" or "satire". And the waves of reaction stirred by Simon of Cyrene's arrest so that he could help carry the cross represent for Bruegel the epic artist, not the moral censor, a point of departure in the poignant development of a true-to-life human portrayal. Who, together with the iconologists, thinks he can discern an unfathomable double meaning in the fact that the confessors on the cart shake their crucifixes at the poor sinners Dismas and Gesmas? Would not their absence have instead been a flaw in the production? (Another example of Bruegel the humorist: he adopted the comic detail of the waggoner on the drawbar pulling up his legs when the wagon passed over a muddy area from a serious painting by C. Massys!) As the largest of Bruegel's pictures, it is the largest landscape of early Netherlandish painting. Its extent within the picture is remarkable and there is room for broad stretches of widely varying land forms; thus, it is a very natural landscape. As the beautiful summer day changes in the course of the procession into the "darkness of the sixth hour", the earth itself changes in appearance from lush radiance to bare wasteland, stripped of vegetation. Thus, Nature reflects the events of Good Friday, which are unanticipated and unnoticed by the profane humanity moving in its midst, but which will redeem and save man. This is the real, the sublime theme of the work.

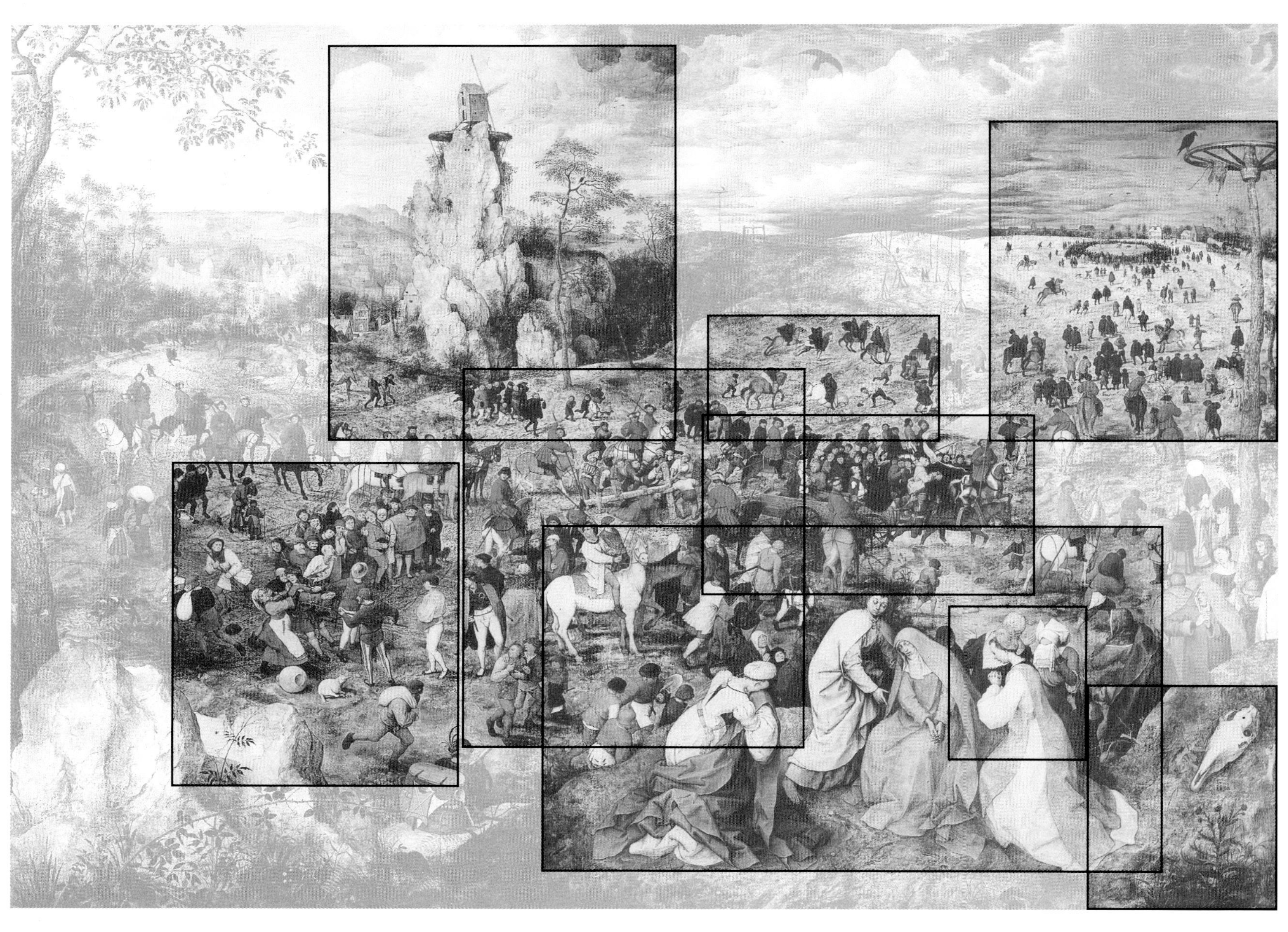

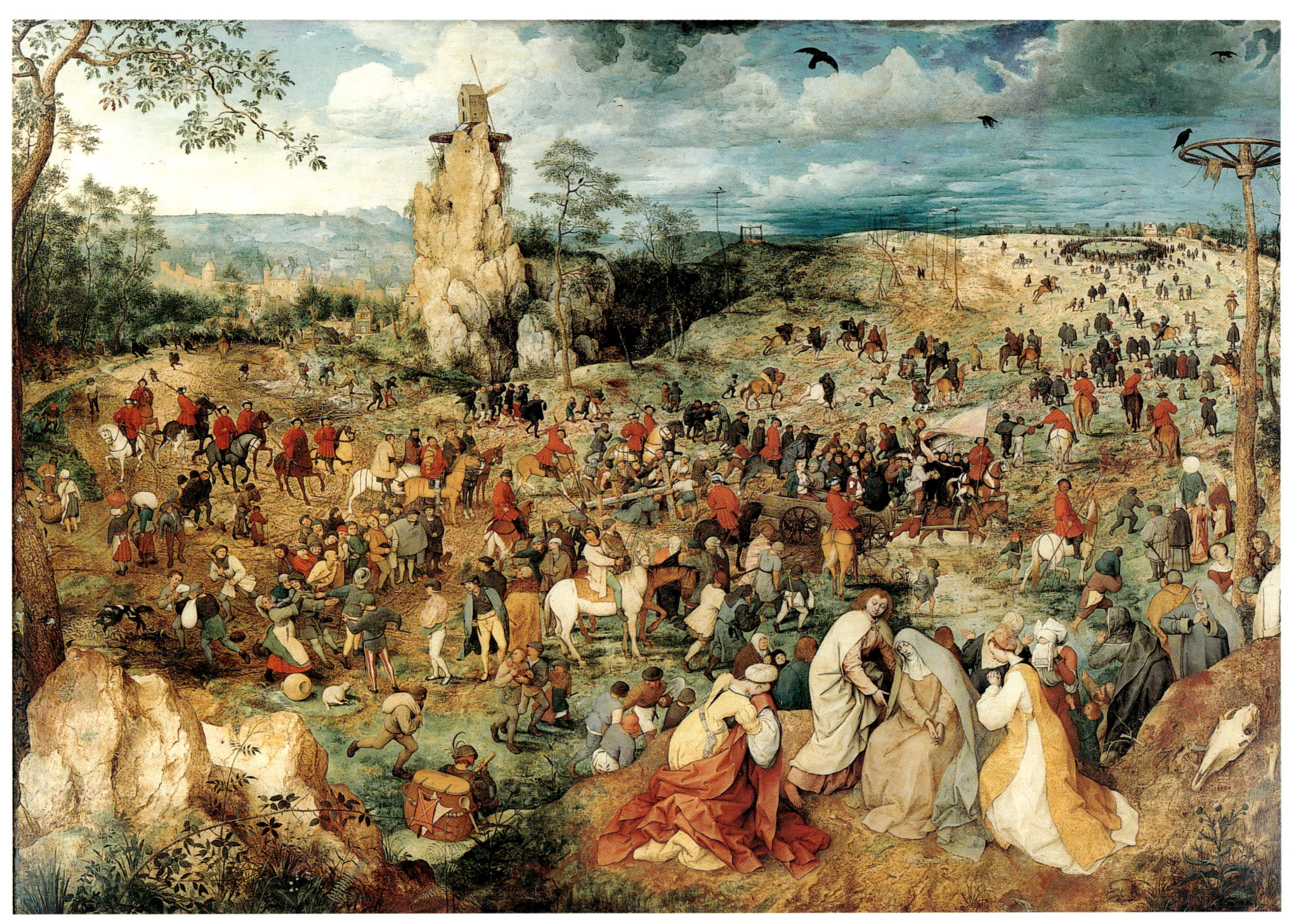

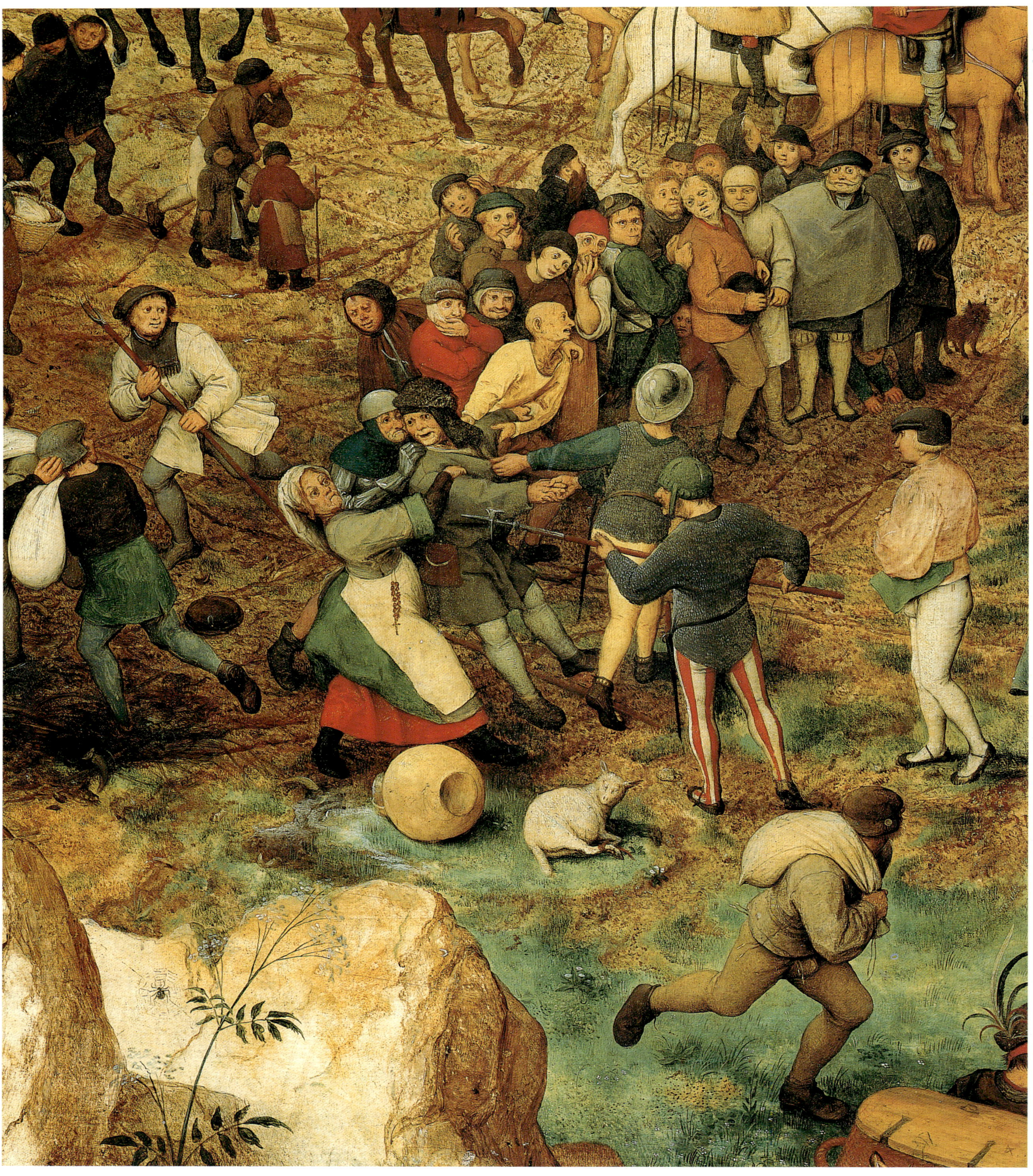

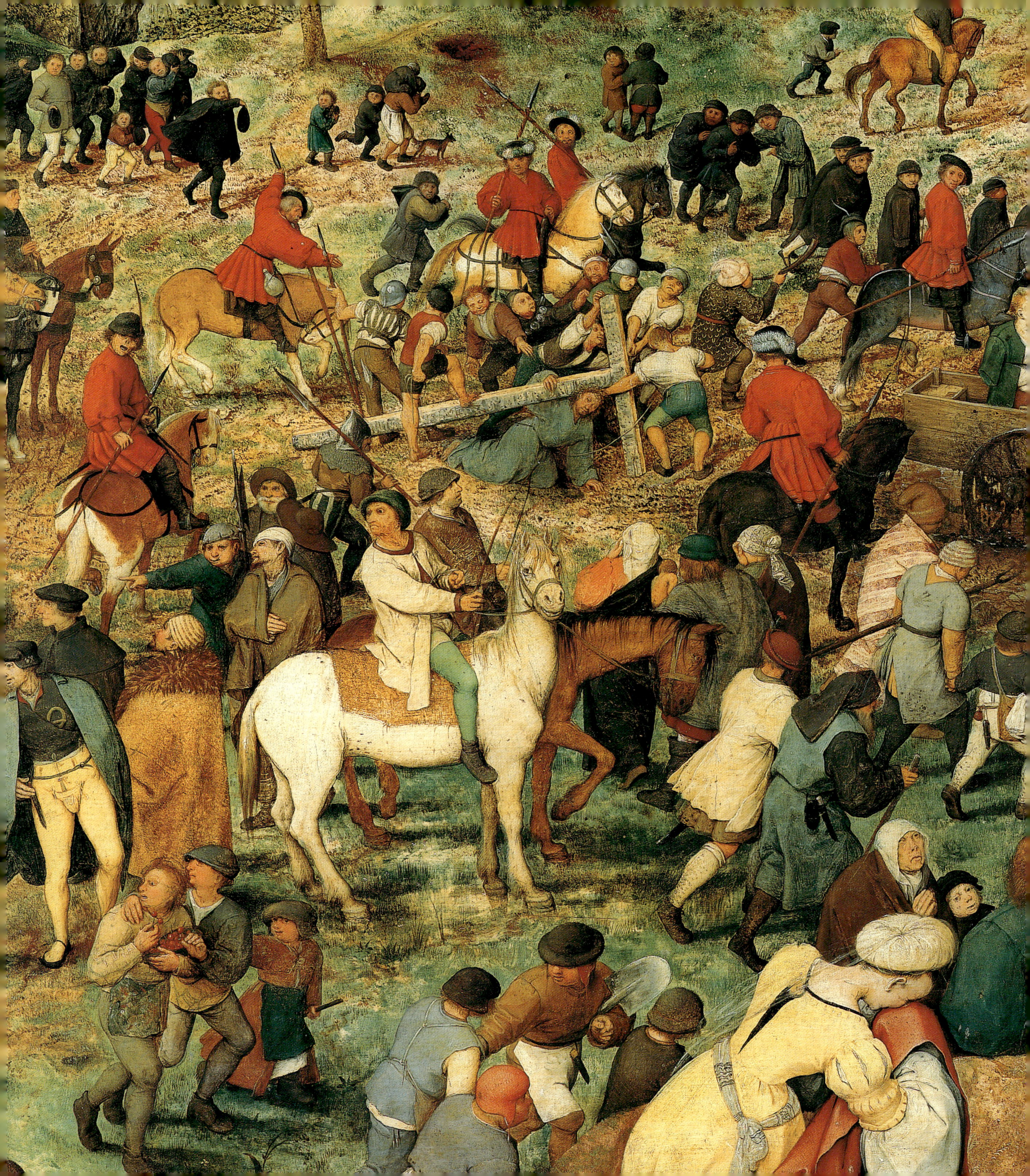

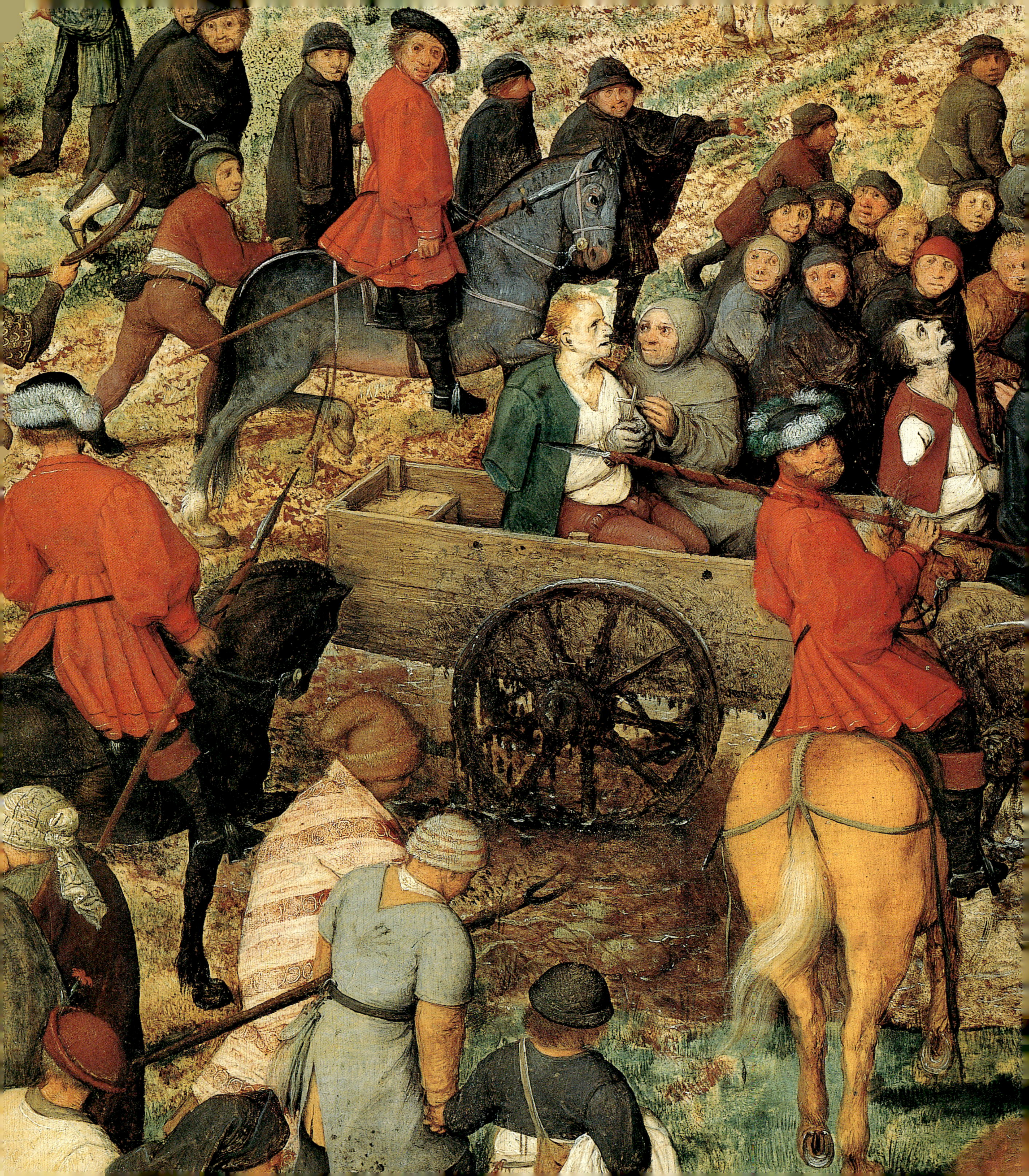

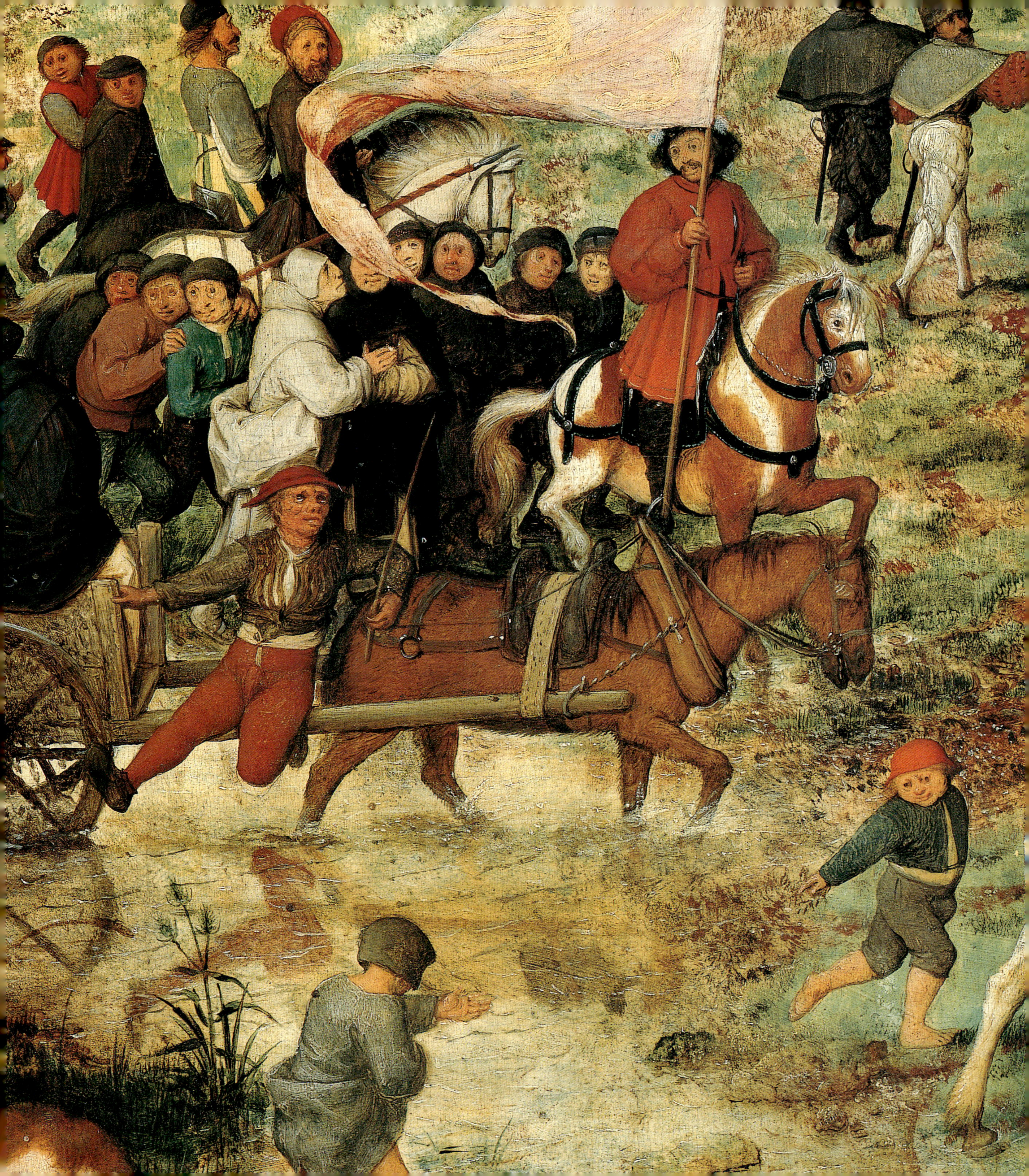

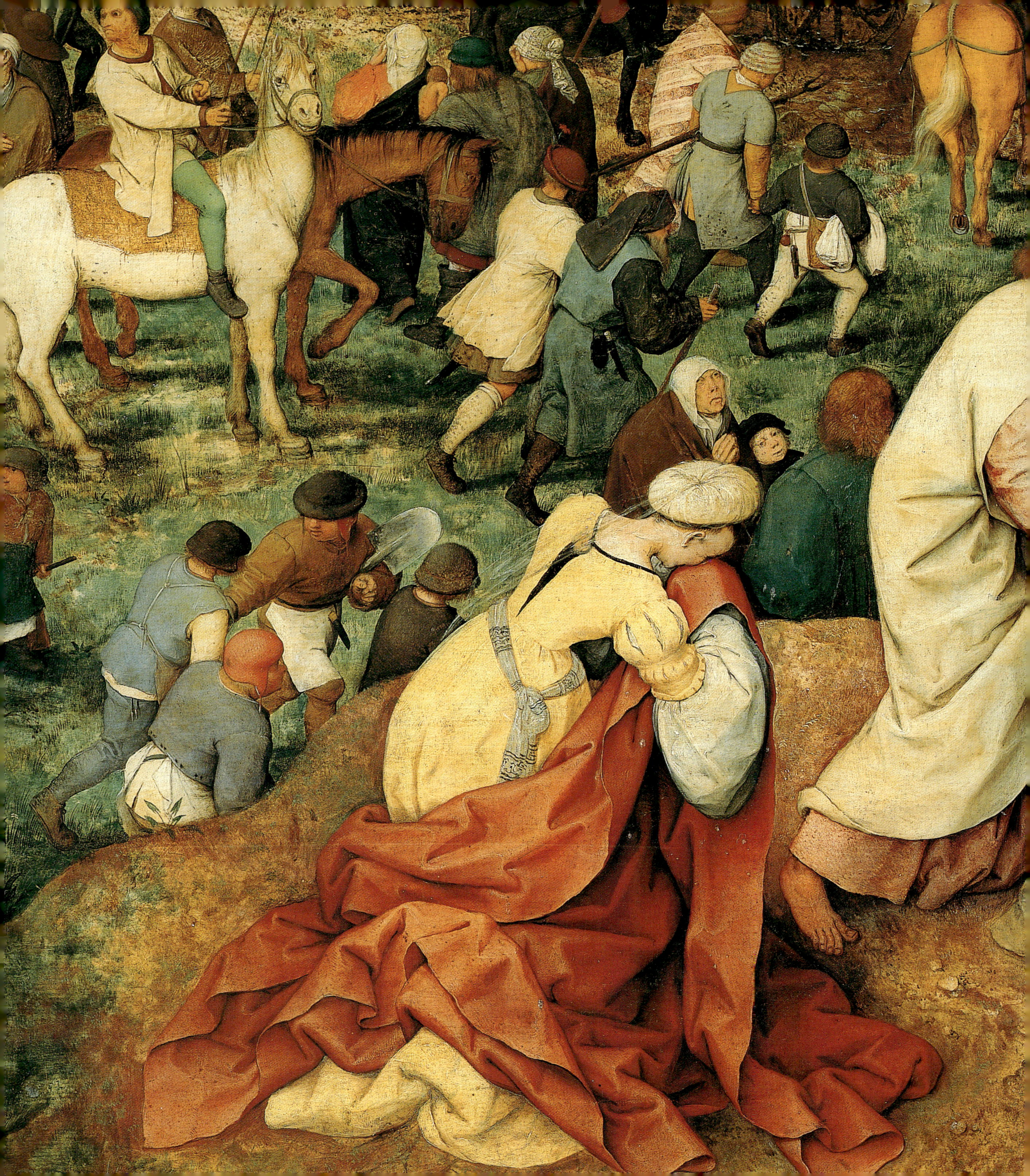

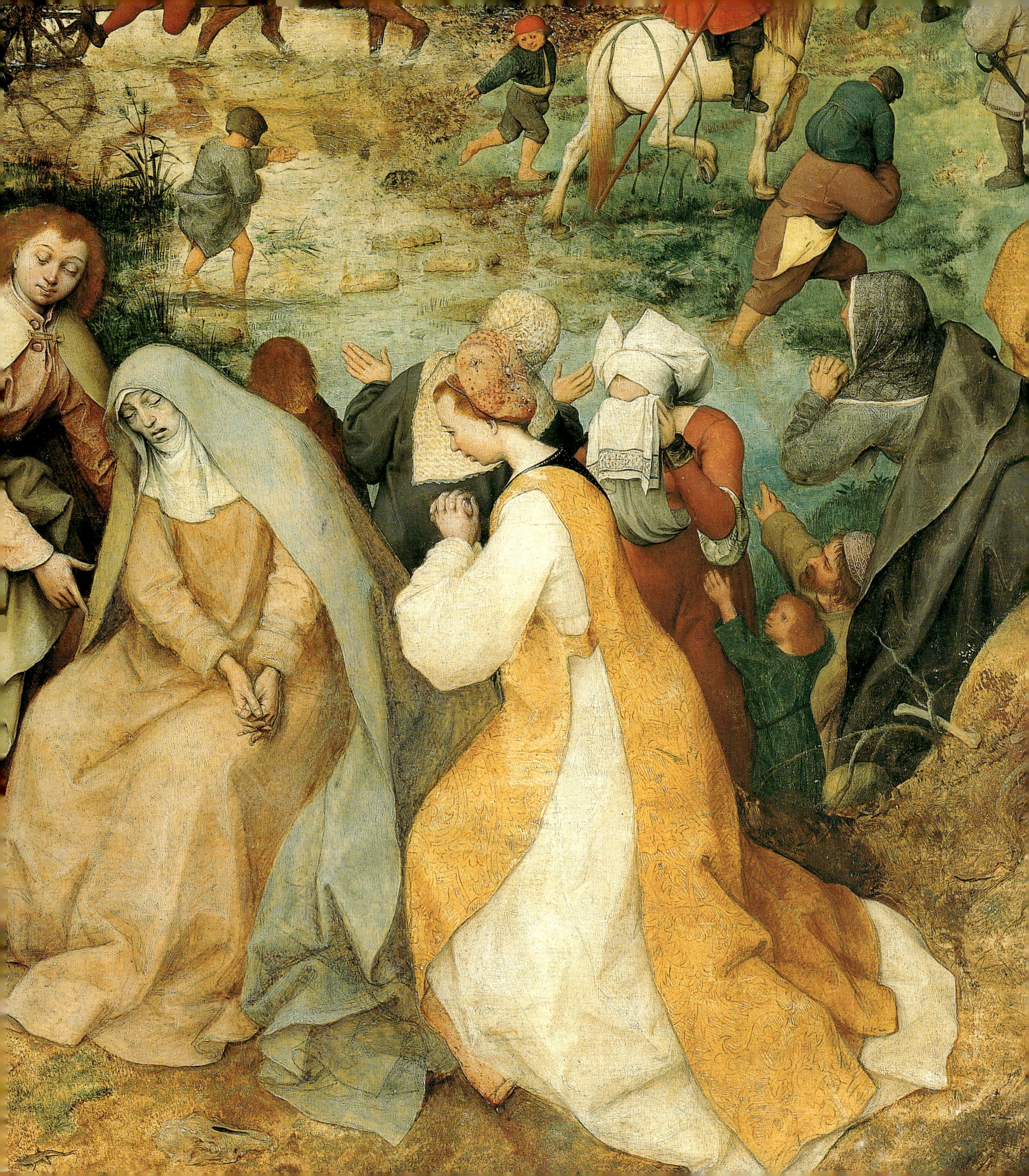

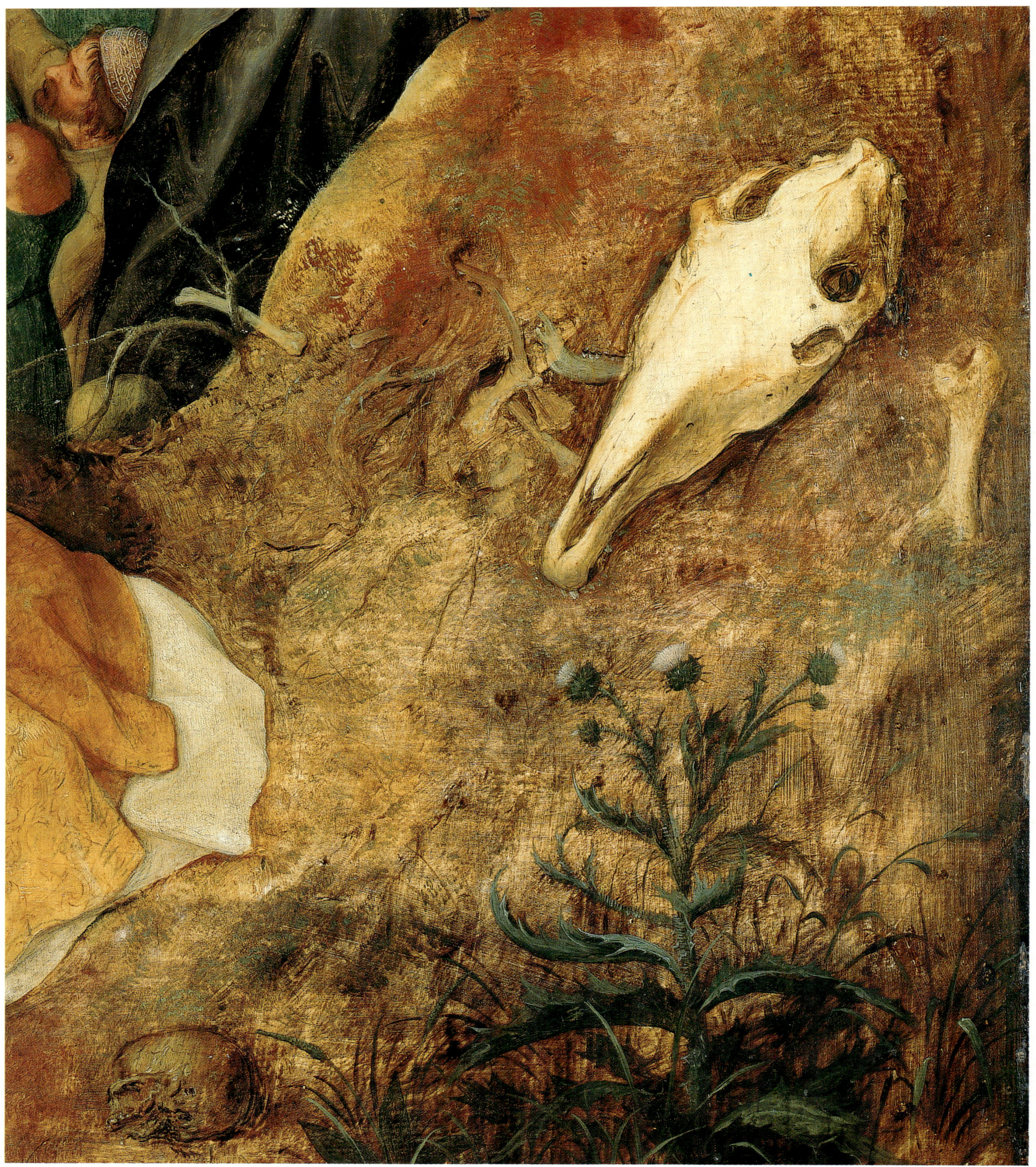

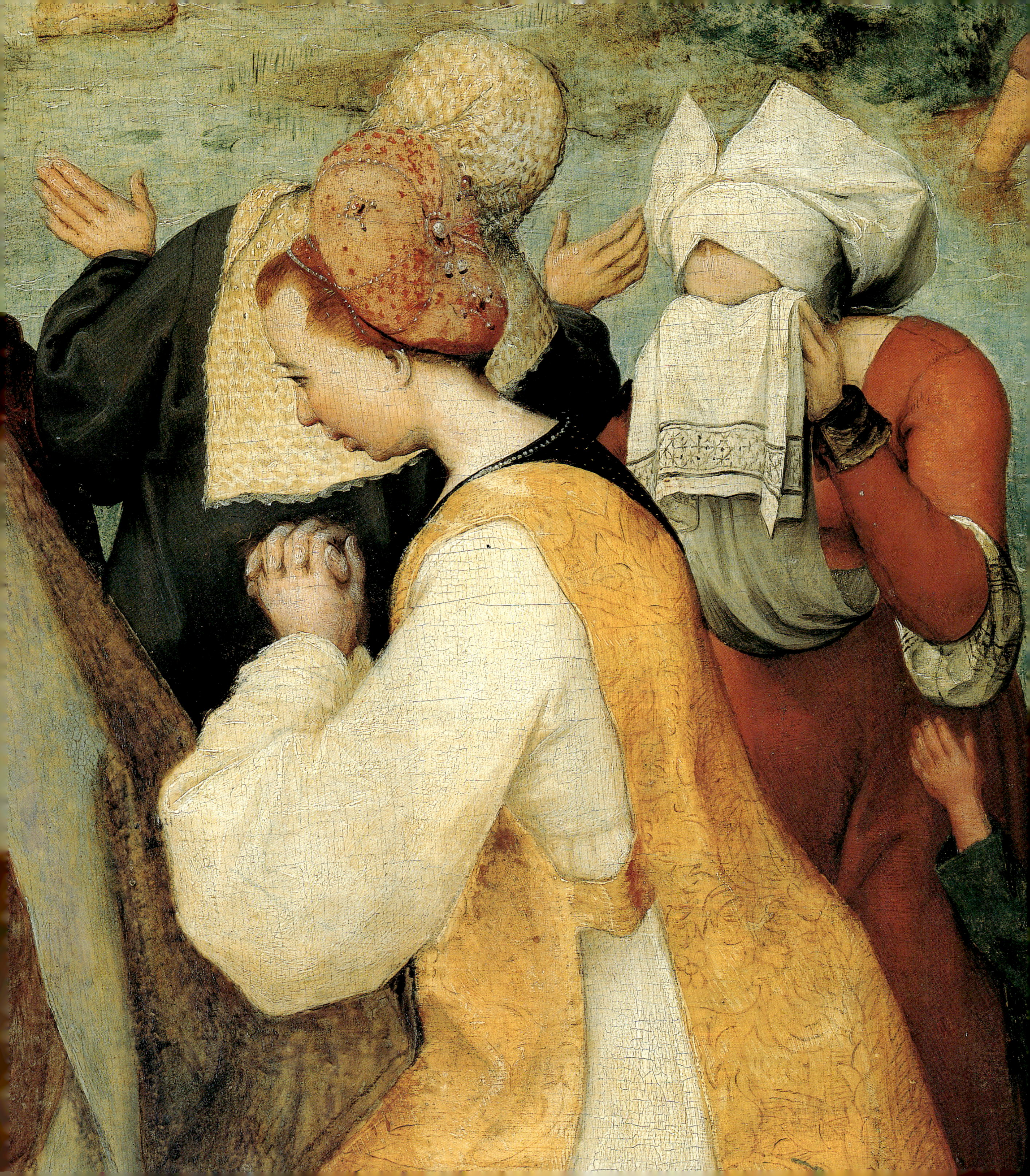

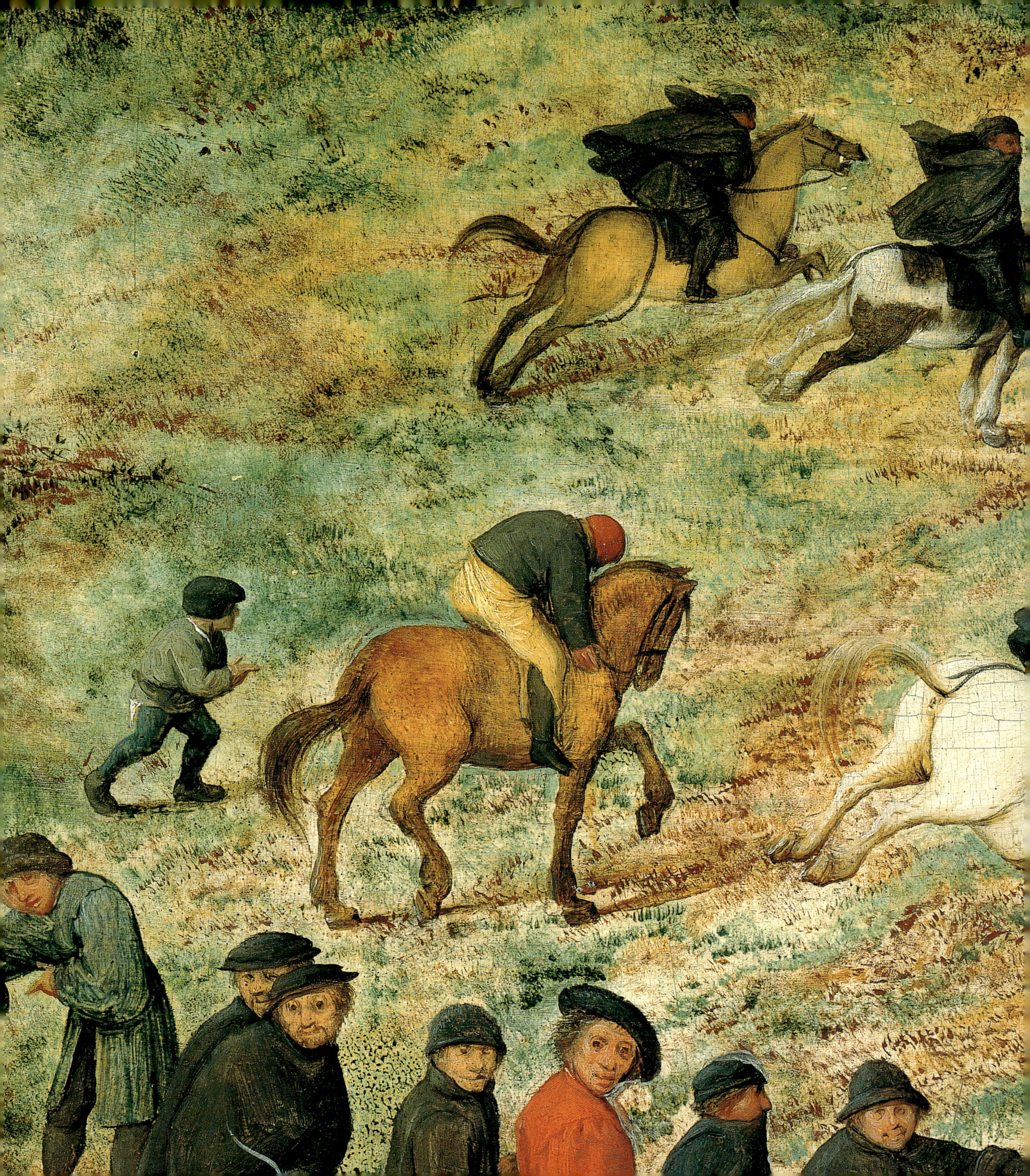

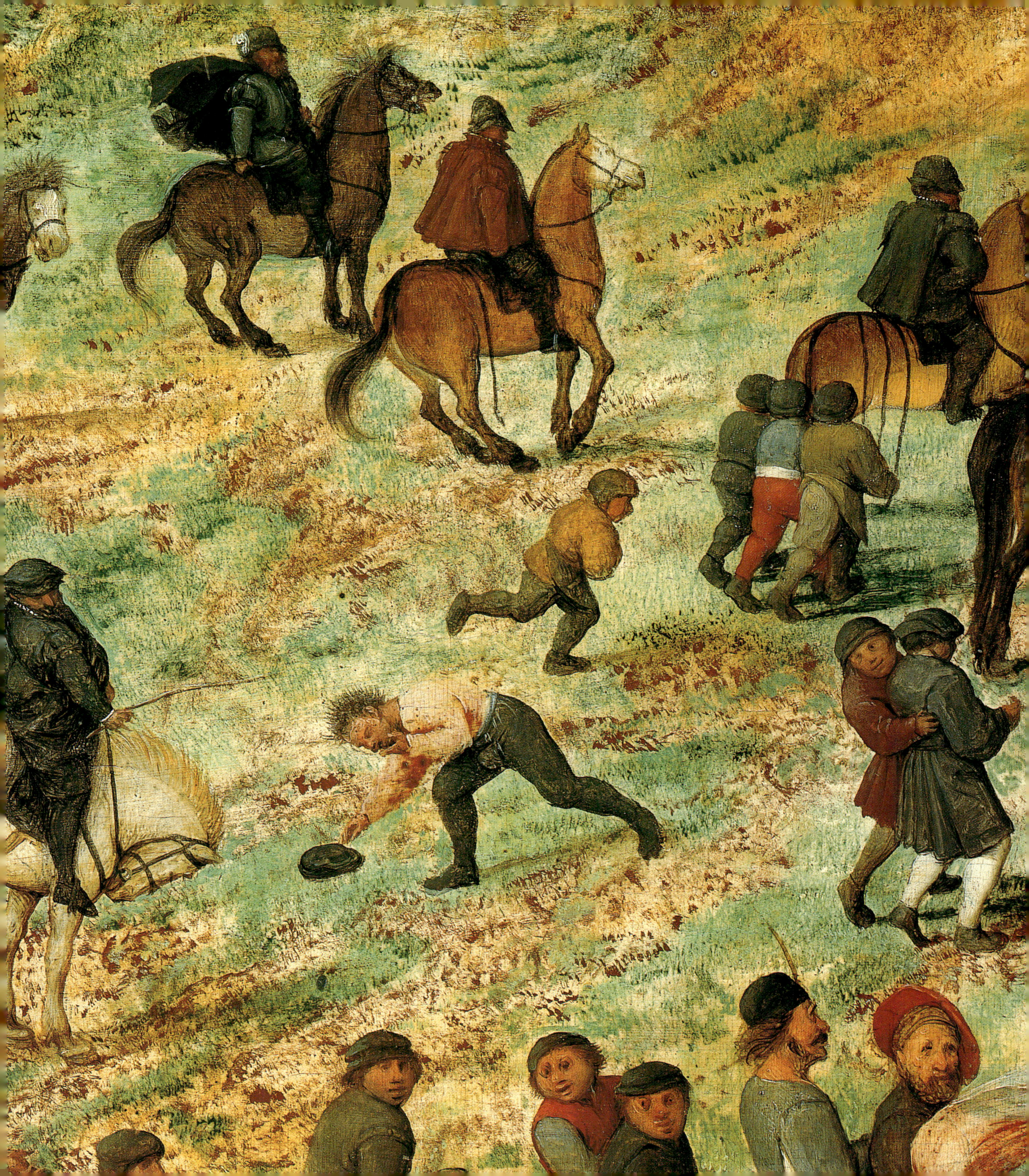

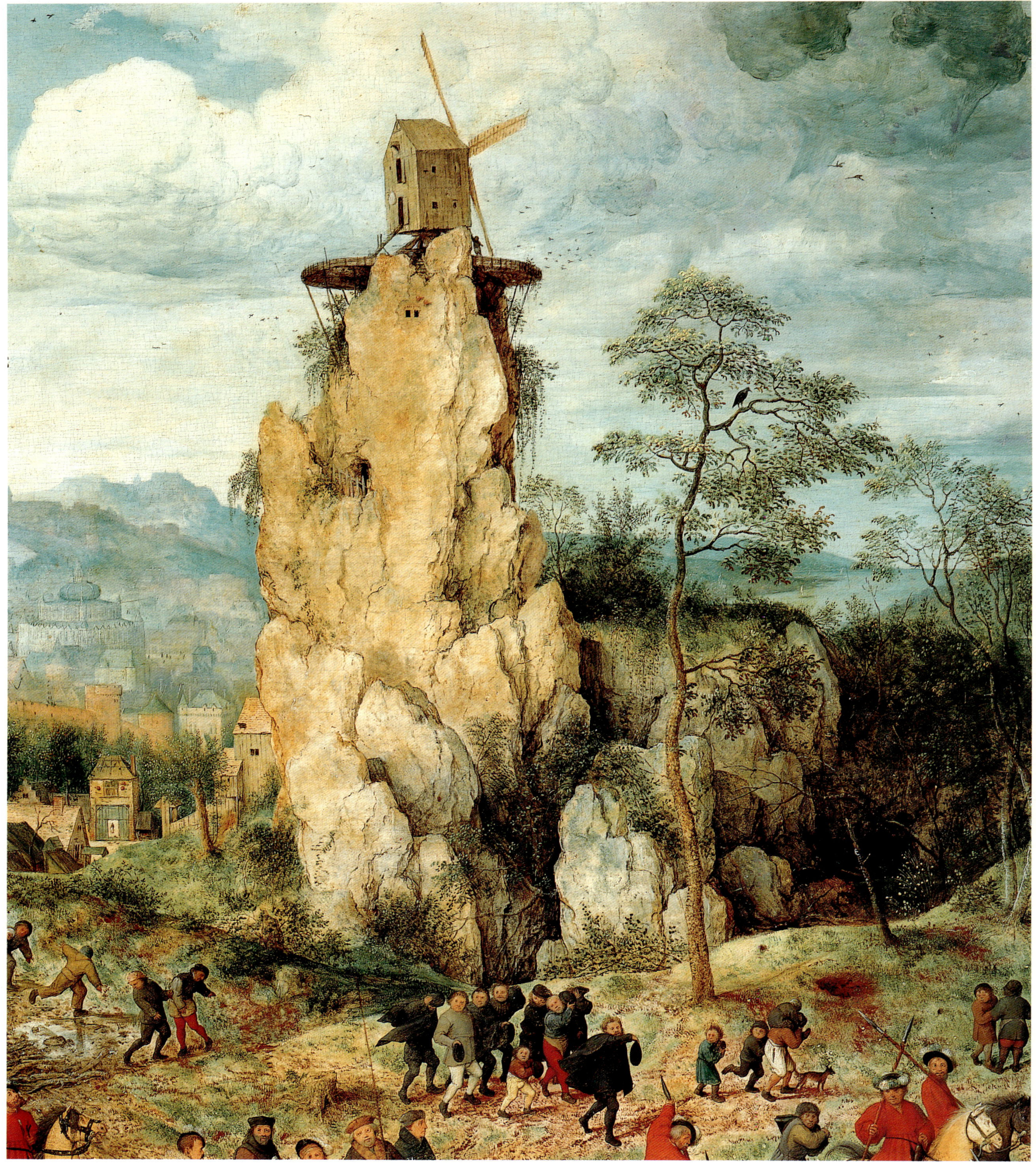

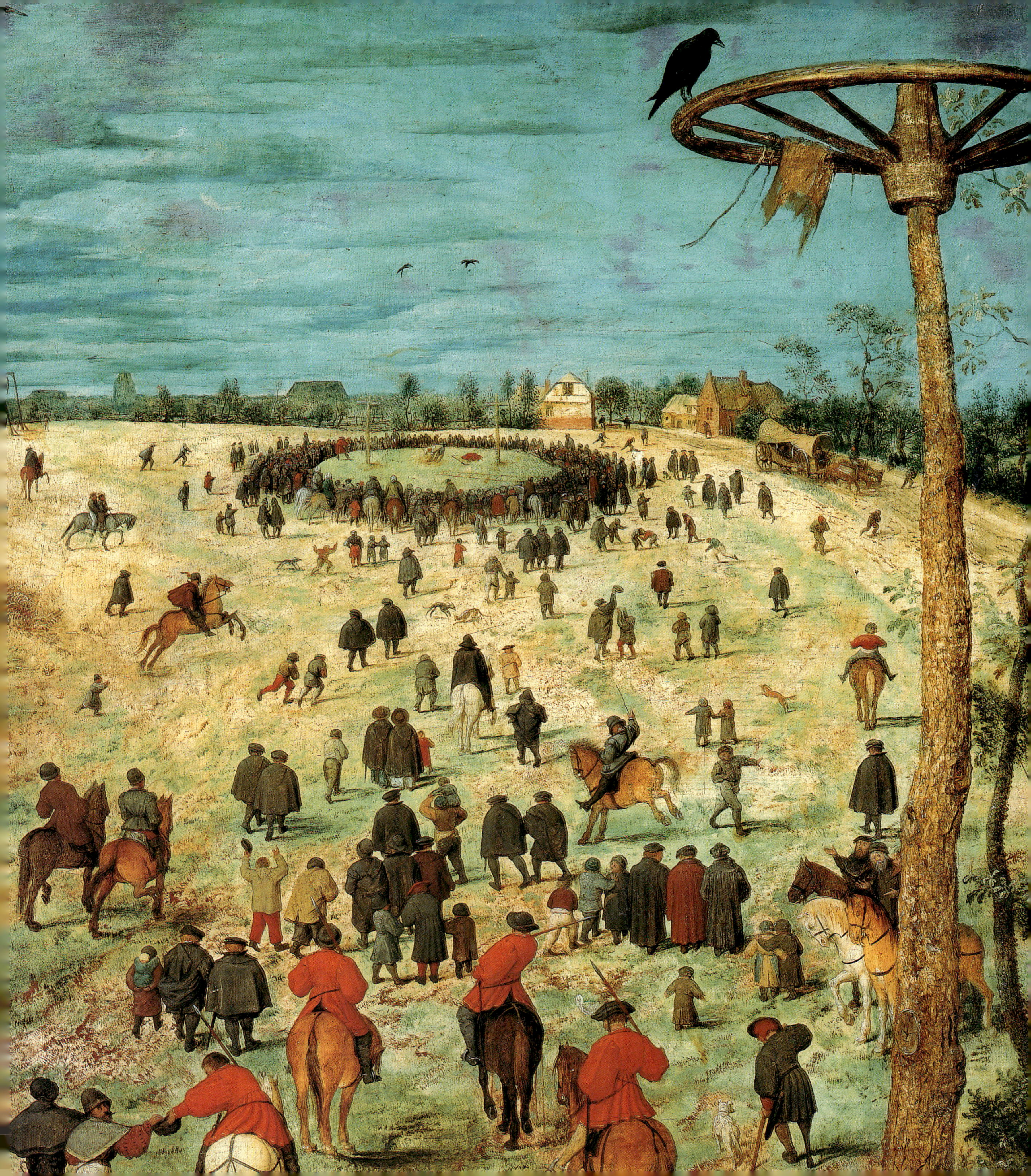

Seasons of the Year
1565

Gloomy Day (Early Spring)
1565

Below left: fragments of a signature and dating "(MDLX)V"
Oak, 118 × 163 cm
Nicolas Jongelinck; Gift of the City of Antwerp in 1594 to Archduke Ernst; Archduke Ernst's estate 1595
Inv. No. 1837

Return of the Herd (Autumn)
1565

Signed below left: "BRVEGEL MDLXV"
Oak, 117 × 159 cm
Nicolas Jongelinck; Gift of the City of Antwerp in 1594 to Archduke Ernst; Archduke Ernst's estate 1595
Inv. No. 1018

Hunters in the Snow (Winter)
1565

Signed below centre: "BRVEGEL. M.D.LXV"
Oak, 117 × 162 cm
Nicolas Jongelinck; Gift of the City of Antwerp in 1594 to Archduke Ernst; Archduke Ernst's estate 1595
Inv. No. 1838

Bruegel's most powerful work, the six-part cycle of the *Seasons* is the high point of his creative activity. When the city's guarantee of the Antwerp businessman Nicolas Jongelinck expired in 1594, the work was given to the governor, Archduke Ernst, and then to Emperor Rudolf II; finally it entered Archduke Leopold Wilhelm's collection, already minus one painting, and thence into the Vienna gallery. Napoleon's plundering subtracted another painting from the cycle (now in the New York Metropolitan Museum), and a third painting ended up by obscure means in Castle Raudnitz in Moravia (now in the Narodni Gallery, Prague). Information about the connection between the three remaining pictures in Vienna was lost and it was not until the 1920s that the five paintings were recognized as elements of a cycle. Before the compiling of the Gemäldegalerie catalogue in 1981, the link between these three paintings remained an unsolved mystery to scholars of Bruegel, known the world over.

As the old documents and inventories clearly show when read and correctly interpreted, the cycle originally consisted of six paintings. Its title varied. In Leopold Wilhelm's inventory of 1659, it is called the *Seasons of the Year*, and this, not "The Months", is the only objectively correct one. This requires an explanation.

Towards the close of the 16th century, after the calendar illustrations found in book illuminations, the cyclical theme of the portrayal of the months with the usual motifs of rural work and activities emerged in panel paintings. Usually it was a series of twelve pictures, as distinguished from the four-part representations of the seasons, which also had a familiar iconography. Even in Bruegel's time, however, a six-part variant was emerging, which referred to the division of the year into six seasons, just as common. This was a practical and natural sequence differentiating early spring, spring, early summer, high summer, autumn and winter for central and northern Europe. Both sequences, like the "Months", were based on the motifs of the seasonal activities, often the same ones. Neither had turned into a fixed canon. The study of paintings recognized as parts of a cycle started with the problem of their definition, designation and arrangement. Since the number is greater than four, only one sequence of months seemed possible (the idea that six-part seasonal sequences were also possible was overlooked). The question was therefore only whether the five pictures had been part of one of the familiar series of twelve, or whether, given the sum of characteristics in some works, a shorter sequence could be proposed, one consisting of six bimonthly periods. The field broke up into stanch camps over this, never to be united again. Since there was no canon of the characteristics of the months, and, as if that were not enough, Bruegel had followed his own, individual path, the identification of the months, or pairs of months, remained hopelessly controversial, like the debate over the size of the cycle.

In the meantime, a better understanding of the documents has settled the question of size. The "shorter" interpretation of the months ran aground for a variety of reasons, as did the "longer" theory. The insight, mounting to conviction, that we are not dealing with a monthly sequence at all, but a seasonal sequence offers a way out of the futile

dispute. Despite the tenacity with which the old error has been discussed until today, there are not "Months" by Bruegel. There are only the *Seasons*.
The next problem, which was practically impossible to solve for the hypothesis of the months, that of arranging the sequence, almost cleared up by itself following the seasonal approach. But which one starts and which finishes the sequence? Winter has usually been placed at the beginning, since the Gregorian year begins there. The 16th-century *stylus Bataviae*, however, kept the old March-February order, and that February 1565, in which Jongelinck's guarantee expired, was already that of the year 1566 in the Gregorian calendar. The official year, therefore, began in the early spring. Since the dating of the cycle's paintings is 1565, Bruegel must have worked on them between March 1565 and February 1566. *Early Spring* is the first (and earliest in the order of creation) of the *Seasons*, as the paintings themselves attest.
Bruegel probably designed the cycle for the salon in Jongelink's sumptuous residence in the Marggravelei. If we imagine the five surviving pictures (*Spring* proper has been lost) side by side and we notice that each one has a different dominant colour, the result is a "harmoniously balanced" colour composition between the poles of blackish-brown (early Spring) and white (Winter), beginning and end, with in between blue hypothetically (Spring), pale green (early Summer), yellow (high Summer), and gold ochre (Autumn). As we shall see, even as a formal composition, the paintings of the early spring and winter represent the beginning and end of the composition.
The most important thing, however, after these necessary preliminaries, remains the debate about the content of this masterpiece by Bruegel. If the cycle was intended to "show" something, and we can be certain that Bruegel always wanted to show something, it was not in the tradition of the calendar, nor, as was also thought, in the literary one of the *Georgics*, with the portrayal of the yearly cycle ever renewed in emulation of Virgil's description of the course of the agricultural year and rural activities. Bruegel's concept of a seasonal year is broader and more modern. He shows what only the painter can show when he advances from a simple task of describing realism to the "representation" of something difficult to express, something that can only be shown. He offers the whole not as a sum that can be broken down into elements, but as a consolidation into a unit; that is to say, he offers a visual concept of what each season in essence is, and how it shapes the world reality. Thus, his concern was not to display the year in its parts, illustrating the seasonal activities in a lively, pleasant way, which already in Virgil's time city-dwellers only found interesting from the point of view of aesthetics. Bruegel's *Seasons* are therefore not meant to be a "Flemish Georgics". He does not report what is familiar. Instead, he shows the little-known essence of nature, which as experience surpasses every concept, while in the course of the year it becomes the "world" in different ways. In other words, the whole experience that the year offers during its seasons to give an idea of what nature is as a whole. Bruegel's constant aim is completeness. The subject matter of this cycle provided him with the greatest of completenesses: nature and the life in it as a "world" with a fully

understood cycle. It has been declared that the paintings of this cycle were the first great, self-contained landscapes of Western art. This statement is surprising since, based on the rest of his oeuvre, Bruegel cannot be described as a landscape painter. Even more surprising, however, is the fact that here, embodied in painting, is introduced a concept of nature that probably already had parallels in the journeys of discovery and science (geography), but not in philosophy or even aesthetically, in art and literature. Bruegel's concept of nature stems from experience, but is at the same time an artistic "clear idea" of the universal idea of nature experientially perceived as "creative". On the strength of this idea, the phenomena subtly but effectively produce something that can be known. Something imminent, overriding everything, an infinite in a finite, seems to be present in his pictures, in the spaces filled in a temporal sense by the reality of the world expanded to the universe. The observer seems to be able to abandon himself to this something imminent, as in reality, obtaining in addition to a visual understanding of the concrete experience of reality a clear idea of how everything is connected in a single whole. This is more than a cosmic experience, it is almost specifically a Bruegelian experience. It was never to be equalled, let alone surpassed, again, not even in Bruegel's own work.

Six times a year, with the changing of the seasons, the world becomes a whole experienced differently. Bruegel's sensitive understanding stamps this three-dimensionally on the image of nature itself. Human existence, which pursues both the necessary and tradition in its simple pastoral activities, fits in perfectly with the universal law of nature. This is undoubtedly the keystone of all that Bruegel seeks to show. An immense scenic and graphic display, which can hardly be called didactic any more, serves as the vehicle for this simple wisdom.

Early Spring received its present-day alternative name of *The Gloomy Day* eighty years ago, when the picture was even darker than it is today because of aloe treatments. Originally, it certainly was much brighter. The alternative name was an unfortunate choice, however, as it does not take into account either the stormy horizons or the charged atmosphere that make this the most dynamic painting of the series.

The transition from the rigors of winter to the reawakening of nature in the spring is conceived as the thematic essence of this season. Powerful forces are astir, jolting the dark and lifeless world, shaking it right down to its core. This cosmic event and the surrender to an incomprehensible but all-powerful will is shown to be a terrible but beneficial necessity in order to have renewal. Nature had never been seen as violent as in this painting, and it must have deeply impressed the young Rubens. We step into the picture on a level with the ground and suddenly find ourselves high up anyway: the hill to the right is nudged up to the picture's edge like a balcony so that we may enjoy in the most natural way a vast view of the world from a high perspective. And what is it that the horizon pushed far out into the sea does not show! Like a huge initial C at the beginning of the composition, the mountains with their still snowy peaks, swept by gusts of föhn, stretch far into distance. On the horizon, at the point where the last foothills of the coast sink into the sea, the tiny spires of a church seem to gaze at us from afar, in correspondence to our own vantage point. The sky seems to be clearing slightly, leaving hope for improvement. The entire left half of the picture, with the village way below, and the churning river estuary, where the ships rock and founder on the wildly agitated waves, seems to have been already pushed back, behind and below us as in the preterit tense. The details describe a richly suggestive atmosphere. The view out into open spaces of the right half of the picture — the "later" half, as it develops — covers land flooded by burst dykes visible in the distance, where the sky is clearing. The essence of the season is brought to dramatic unity in its contrasts.

How peaceful is the life of man, as if protected under the vault of the event arching over it (the ships' distress and the water's anguish belong more to nature), his trivial activities completely trapped in the narrow confines of the space prescribed for him! Repairing the wall of the house, cutting and binding willow rods, the carnival group (with details borrowed from the 1559 picture) — all this gives a feeling of intimacy and domestic warmth to the life of resignation to the laws of nature. It is the world as it is and as it should be. And it begins in front of the town gates.

"Autumn", the penultimate picture of the cycle after the lost Spring, Early Summer (with *Haymaking*, Prague) and High Summer (the *Wheat Harvest*, New York), has boldly monumentally and impressively chosen as its title scene the "driving of cattle from alpine pastures" — a seasonal event unknown in the Netherlands, but very significant for the alpine countries (Bruegel had brought it back with him from Italy as a motif). (*The Return of the Herd*, not an old title, is not precise enough. A better suggestion, *Driving the Herds down the Valley*, has not been successful.) It coincides with the end of the fine weather, and we can already see how from the right (therefore running against the direction in which the composition is read and coming from the direction of the worsening weather), the darkening sky is drawing in over the mountains which appear gloomy and menacing. In the distance, under the mass of clouds, it has already begun to rain, as the rainbow there reveals. In the left half of the picture, there is still the other, earlier lovely weather of the autumn, the clarity, transparency and crispness lasting long after the leaves have fallen, with the brightness of the colours extending far into the spatial depth, as in the passing of the year, undisturbed by it. The (re)turning herd is also passing into the village protected by the mountains, once again, therefore, against the direction in which the composition evolves and moves. (The mounted "herdsman" or steward, the servants with their staffs keeping the magnificent animals, which have fattened during their time at pasture, on the narrow path.) Pasture time is at its end, the year is on the wane. The lone bird high up on the bare branch knows it. It has turned, as though complaining or chiding, towards the change in season darkly and menacingly approaching from "yonder". It is a vast, unforgettably expressive motif devised by Bruegel. The great poetry of the composition (which there is no need to verify) lies in the use of details and features as "motifs", and the way in which they combine to enhance the existential theme. We think we can hear in the overtones a symbolism of existence, a powerful "pastoral", so great is the extent to which each motif contributes to the harmonizing whole. The theme is even clearer here than in the other pictures of the cycle: the precarious, but harmoniously "resolvable" embrace of fleeting existence and living on earth with the immeasurable of all nature, no longer defined as opposite. What we see as joining in the precept and law of the season is an anxious search for protection, flight. The dark forces of the world expand, meeting no resistance. Thus, the whole picture, on the theme of the active-passive relationship of both its halves, which are united by the procession of people and animals as a parallel of the fate that catches up with it, moving in a direction opposite that of life, turns into a single, powerful metaphor of forces and existence. And, yet, it is nothing more than a view into nature, a "landscape".

Nothing needs to be said about its extraordinariness and beauty. It is the last stylized version, shaped by the "lofty" order of memories of a journey probably from the upper Rhine valley, which Bruegel had already sketched as a model for the engraving of his Emaus pilgrim. The intention was to localize the landscape, and even the vantage point. What is in any case certain is that Bruegel did not reproduce a topographical view in any of his paintings, and only in a few drawings, which are the exception. His subject was not a given corner of the earth, but the "world". Only his complete conquest of nature, leaving the clumsiness of the older "universal landscape" far behind makes it possible to forget that he was no realist, but a poet. Even the title of the winter picture, *The Hunters in the Snow*, is modern, and not a happy choice, because it slips into the anecdotal, making one forget that this is a representation of a season, of winter as such. One must realize that it is not just the first, but also the most important picture of winter in European painting. Since reference has already been made to the hunters, something must be said about them.

Their entry into the picture has been classified as an *introitus*, proof that the picture is at the start of the cycle. The problem takes on a different light, however, if there are twelve months (the portrayal of which this was long thought to be), beginning with the winter ones, or if the seasons, whether four or six, are counted in their natural sequence. Winter then comes last. And it was also last in the Dutch year, even when calculating by months, because the year began on 1 March. In both cases, therefore, Bruegel had to put the winter picture at the end. But how, if the return of the hunters is actually seen as a "return home", and entry into the wintry silence and numbness of all life at the end of the year? It is not an *introitus*, then, but an *exodus* of the *dramatis personae* from the stage, the artist taking his leave here at the end of the cycle. In fact, the movement of the hunters descending into the distance is so "definitive", with the triple contour of the hills accompanying it, and the row of trees in perspective delineated like a specified path, emphasizing the fact that this, together with the hunters and the doleful dogs (Bruegel the honest humorist naturally identifies with them) trudging back home after the most wretched luck, can only be considered a retreat, a modest and humble leavetaking from the viewer. (The fact that the inn, before which a slaughtered pig is being roasted, is called "Dit is in den Hert", "The Hart", according to the sign representing St Hubert, only heightens the impression of the pantomime moving discordantly, with the retreat in contrast with the hunters' pitiful lack of success.)

Thus, the winter picture is the last in the six-part sequence of seasons, and compositionally it is also a "final statement". Above all, it is striking that the composition, with the motif of the hill jutting out like a balcony onto which the viewer steps to enjoy a "natural" panorama, with the other half of the picture beginning far below, stretching out into the distant plain of the sea, and, lastly, the wall of high mountains forming a boundary to the whole piece, framing the composition even here at the end, it is striking that all this is the exact axially symmetrical counterpart to *Early Spring*, which marks the beginning of both the cycle and the journey through the year. Bruegel therefore must have pondered the organically cadenced rhythm of the composition and carefully related beginning and end to one another as "outer movements" (even the "retreating" hunters moving off into the distance have their counterparts in the carnival group emerging from the visual space in *Early Spring*: entry and exit are in "complementary" equilibrium, like the little figures in a revolving weather house.)

The fact that whoever is viewing the picture can no longer advance, but just look corresponds with the theme of the "final note". The seething activity below, comically and harmlessly scattered into the furthest depths, underlines the season's denial in its lack of purpose. The tiny figures with their gnat-like agility do not appear to be conscious of the oppressive bleakness under the overcast sky, the boundless, still uniformity of the snow-covered world. It is a balance consisting of both laughter and seriousness, uniquely blending solace and sorrow, a balance that holds the viewer spellbound in dreamy reflection and does not let him go. One senses that the work presents a clear formula of the entire relationship between nature and man, world and existence, eternal diversity and harmoniously possible whole. But it has the physiognomy of a melancholic enigma. Nature, in the pathos of the mountain peak maintaining the sole supremacy of cosmic law in the freezing denial of winter, remains the inevitable fate of existence. This is most easily tolerated unconsciously and submissively, because it remains impenetrable to even the most intimate experience.

It is a strange conclusion, however one wishes to explain Bruegel's paintings. The subject matter of the *Seasons* embodies and relates to the whole of the relationship between nature and man. The artist's power of stylization can formulate the inexpressible, unsayable, but also what he is deeply familiar with. We understand, as we accept, what is silently shown. The statement issued in these pictures has not found equals. We need Bruegel's pictures in order to understand something about the enigma of the world, to which he alone, by rendering it visible, has found the answer.

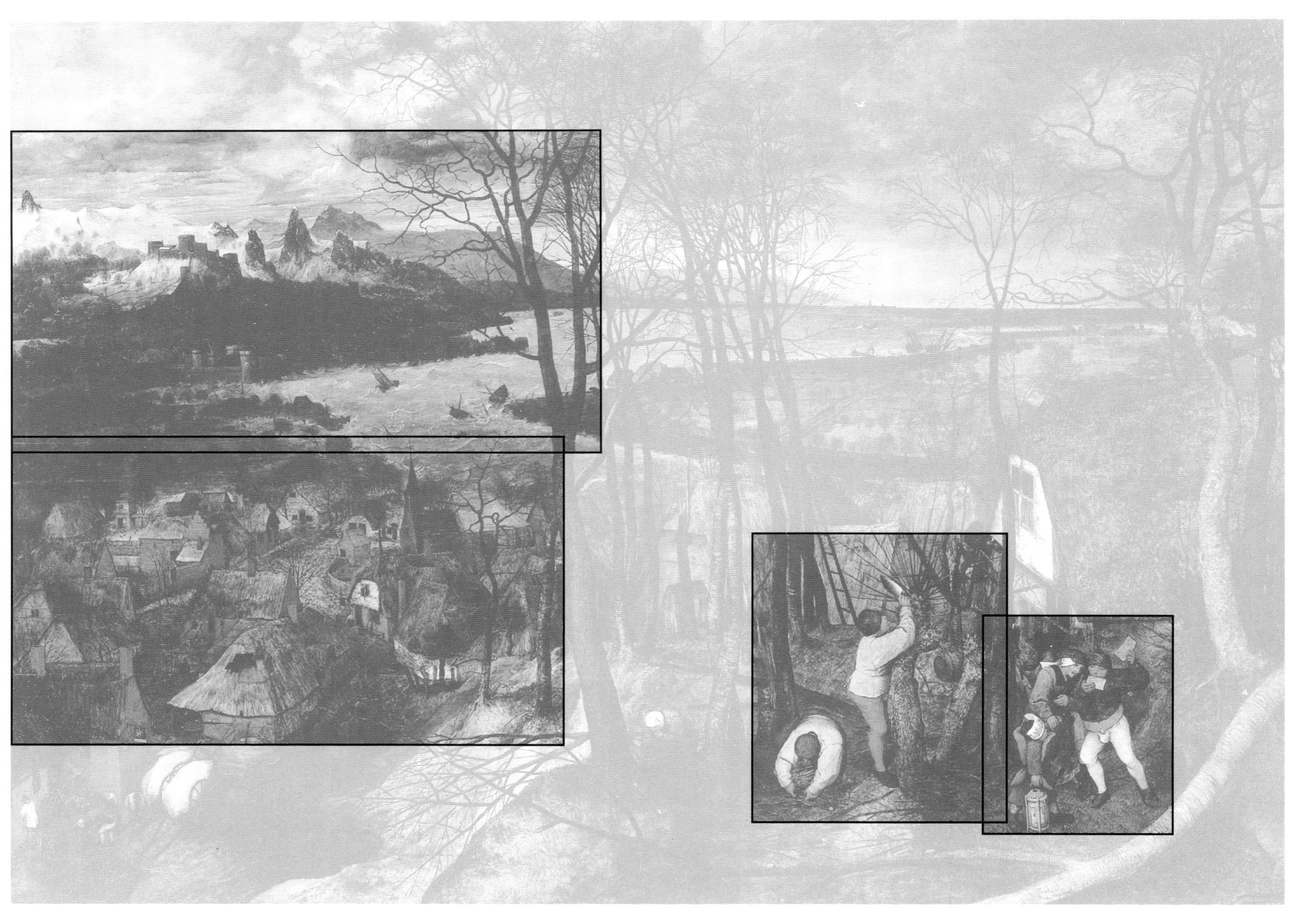

Gloomy Day (Early Spring)

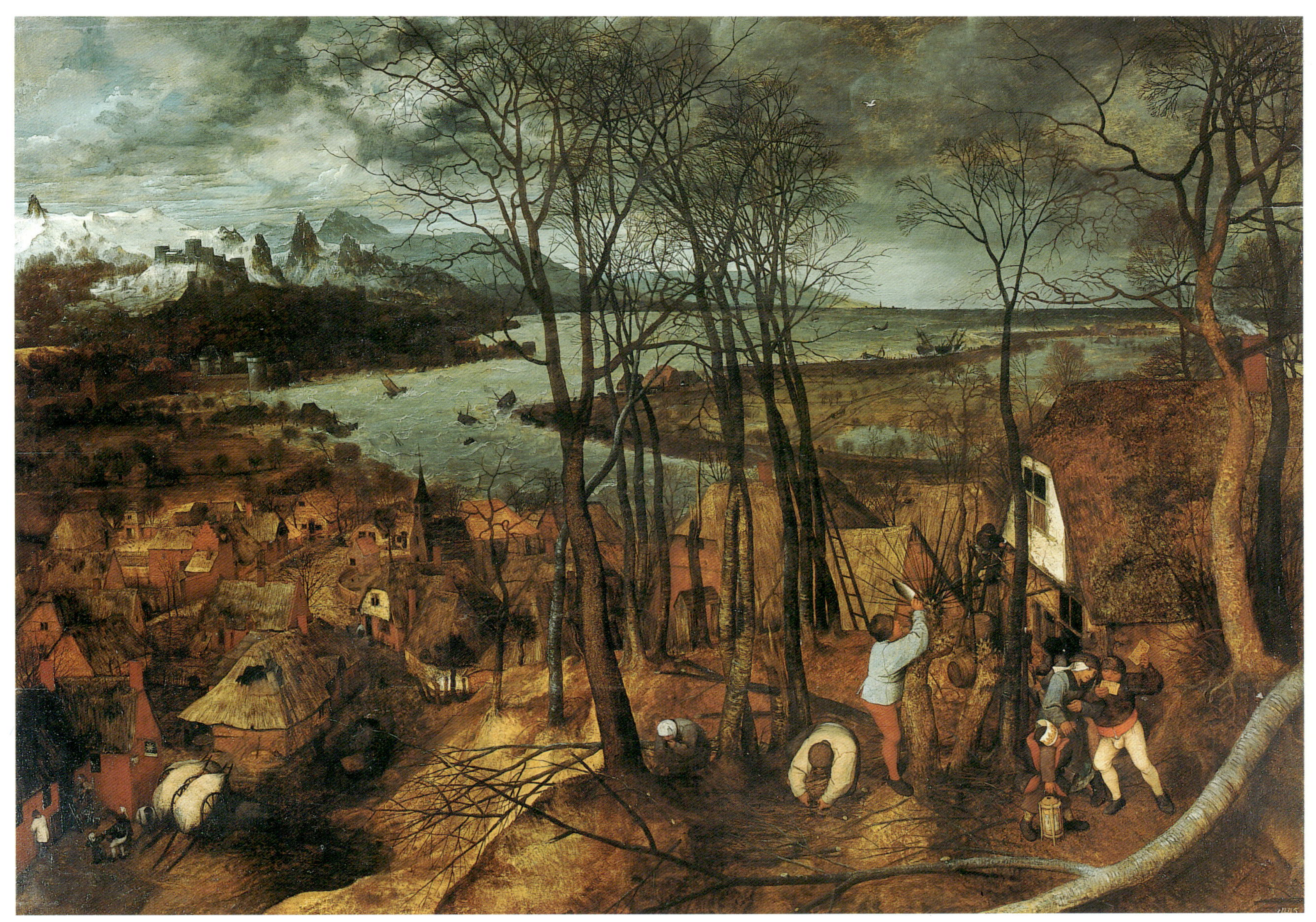

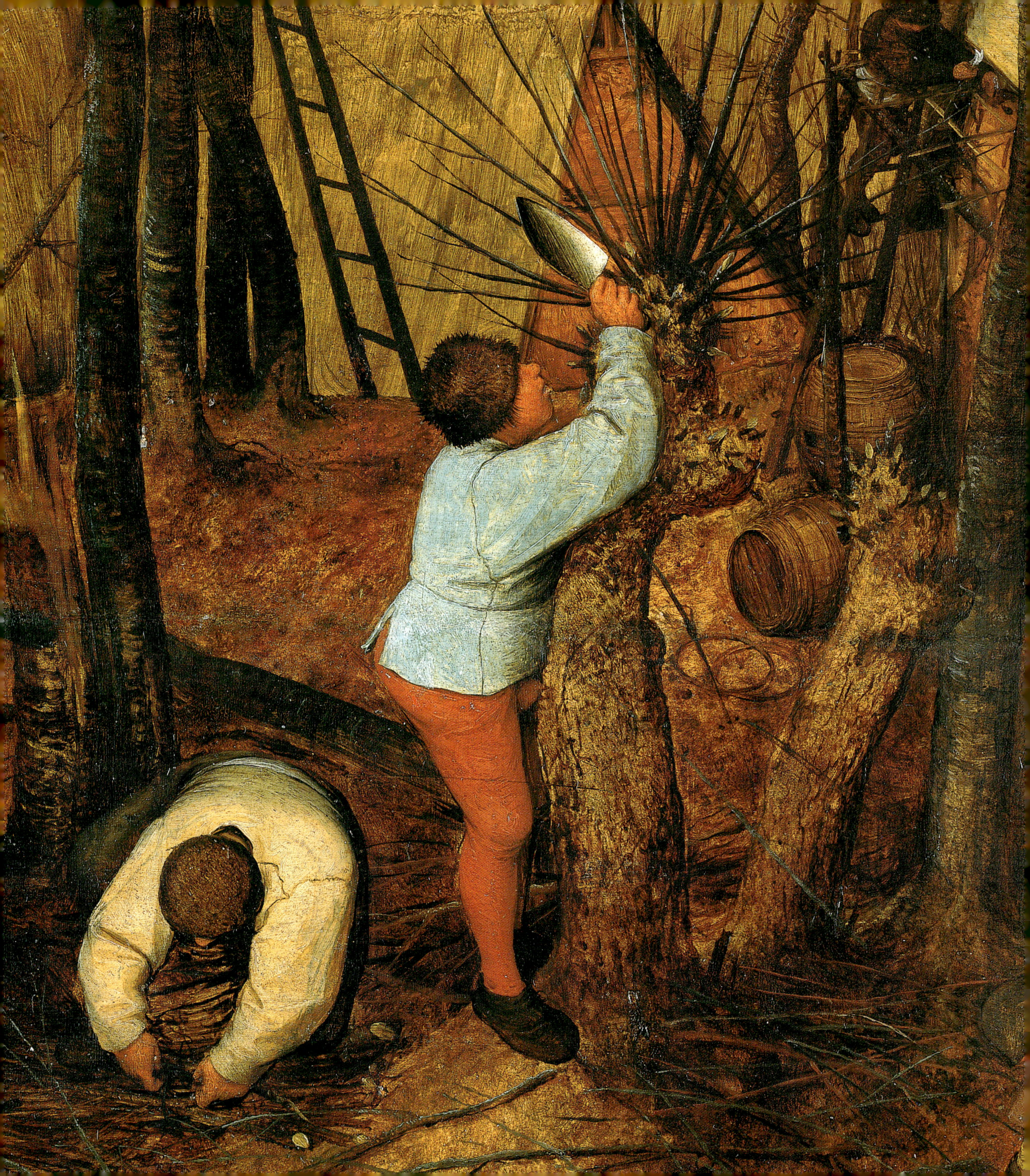

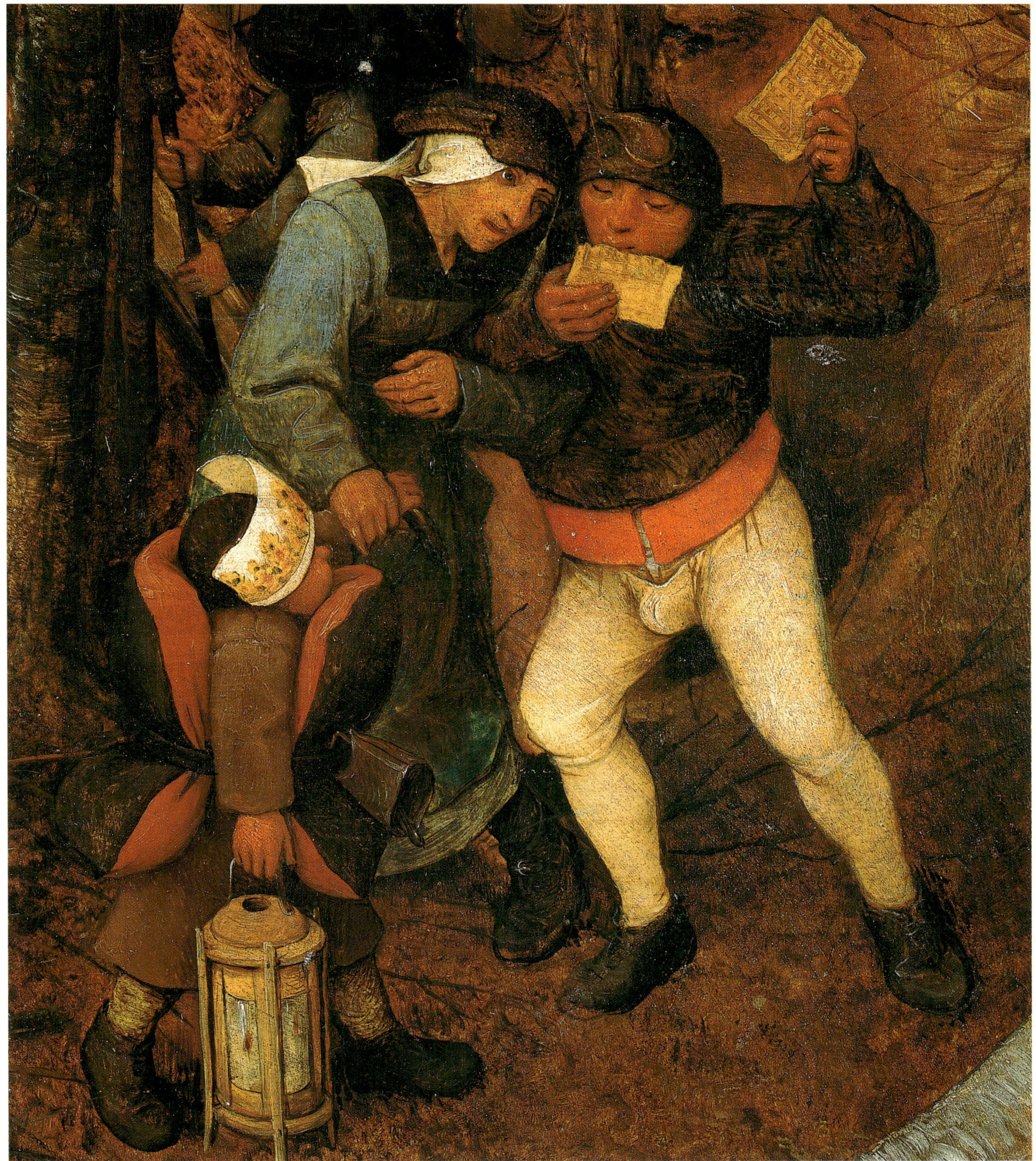

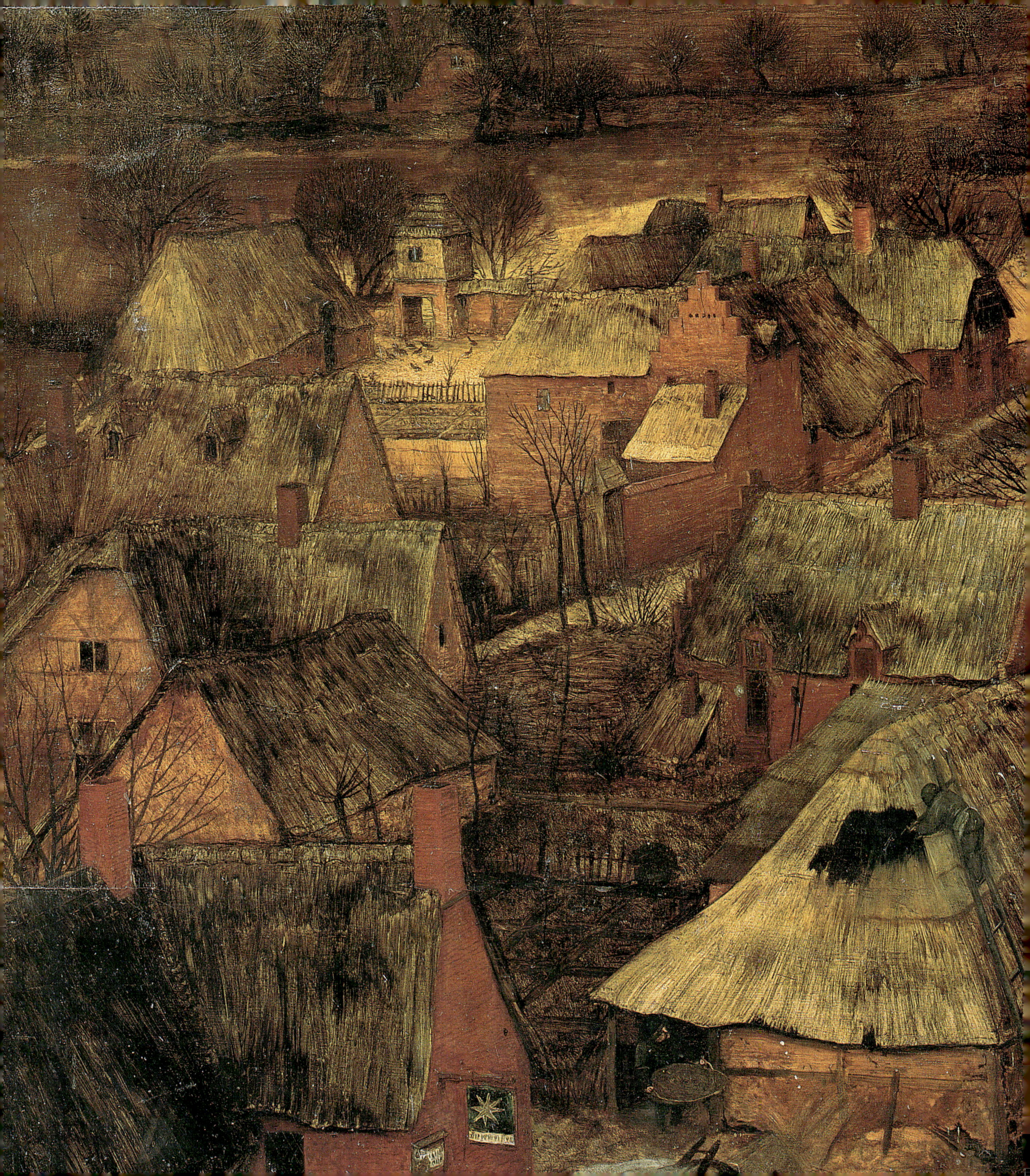

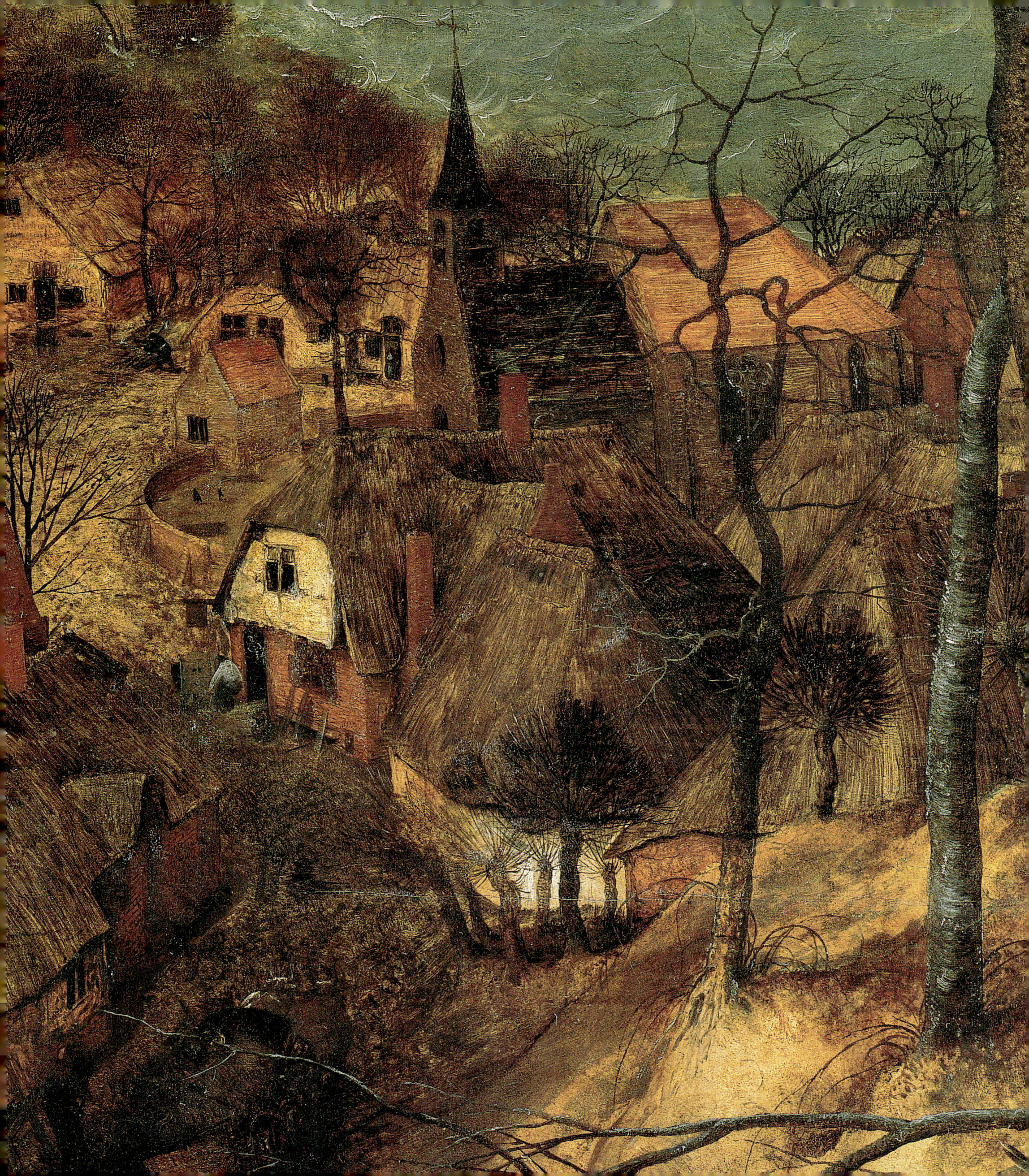

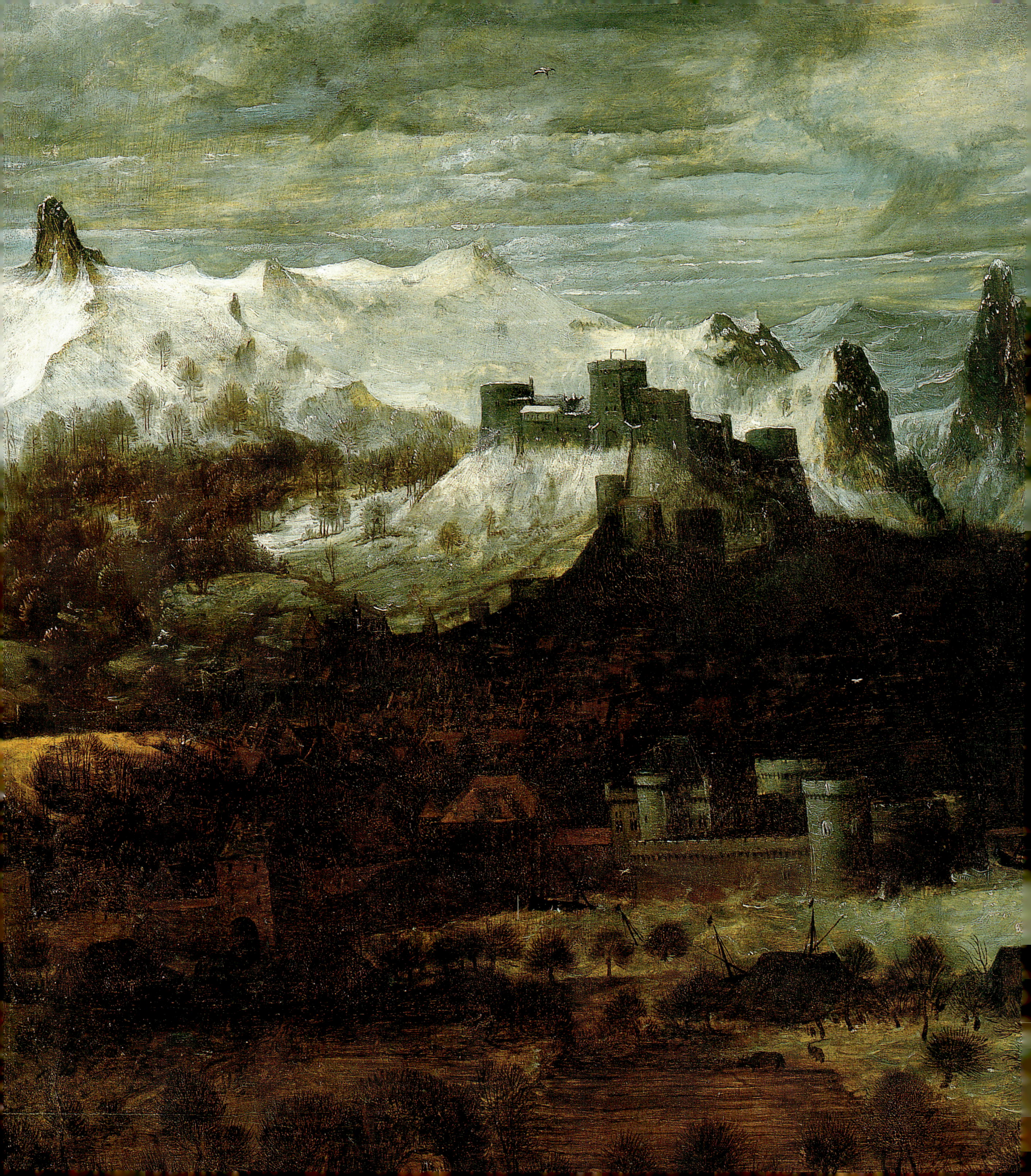

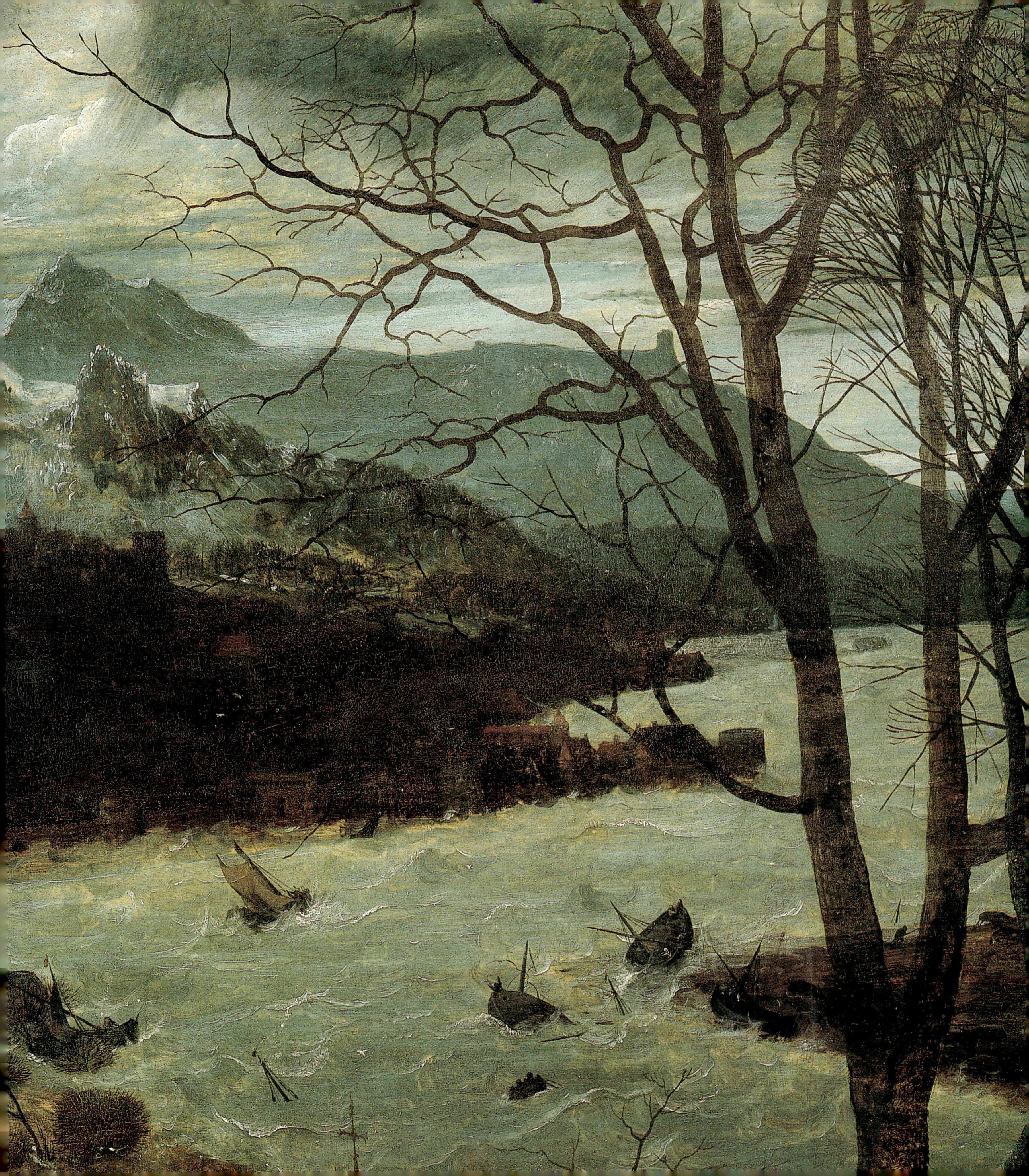

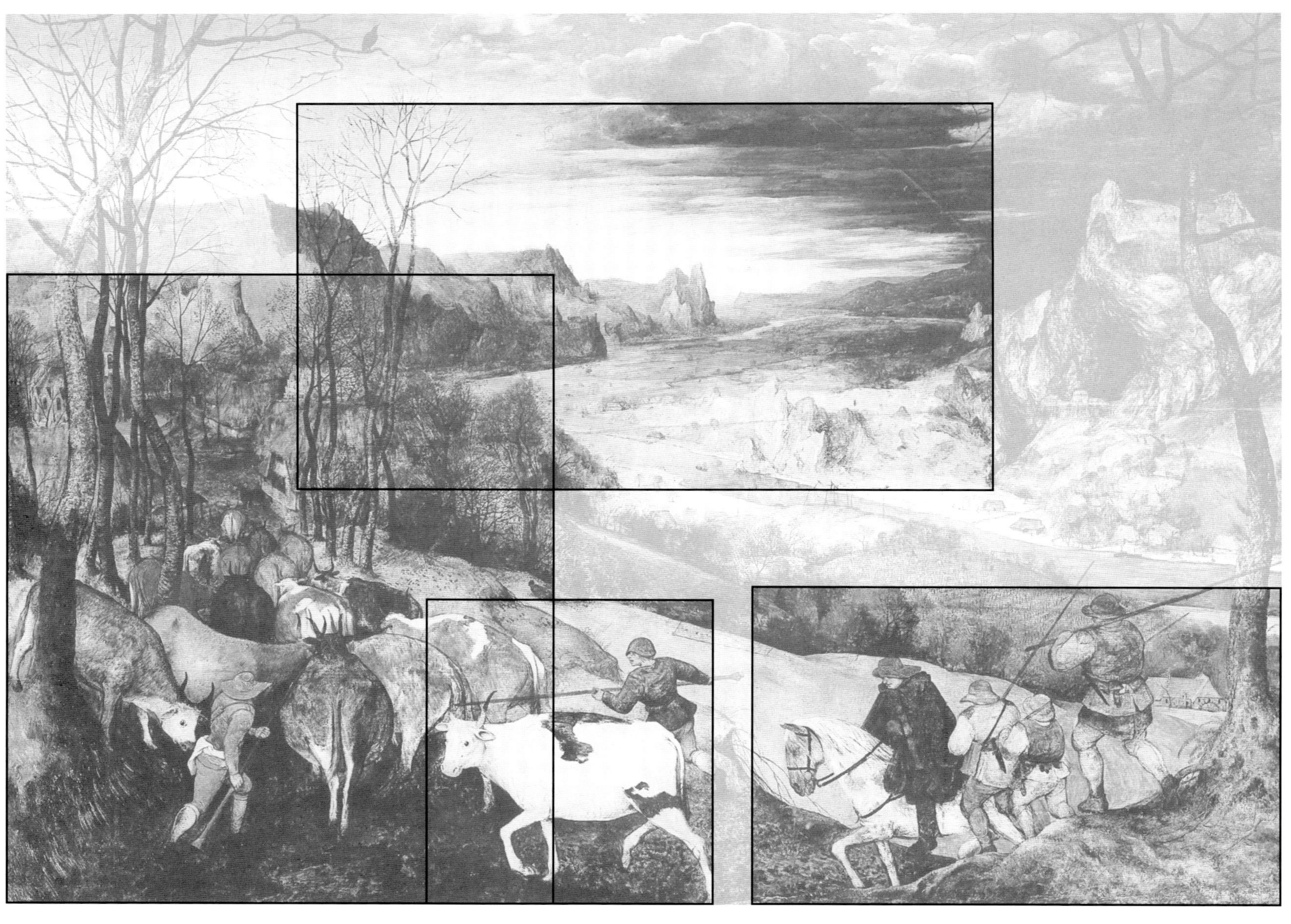

Return of the Herd (Autumn)

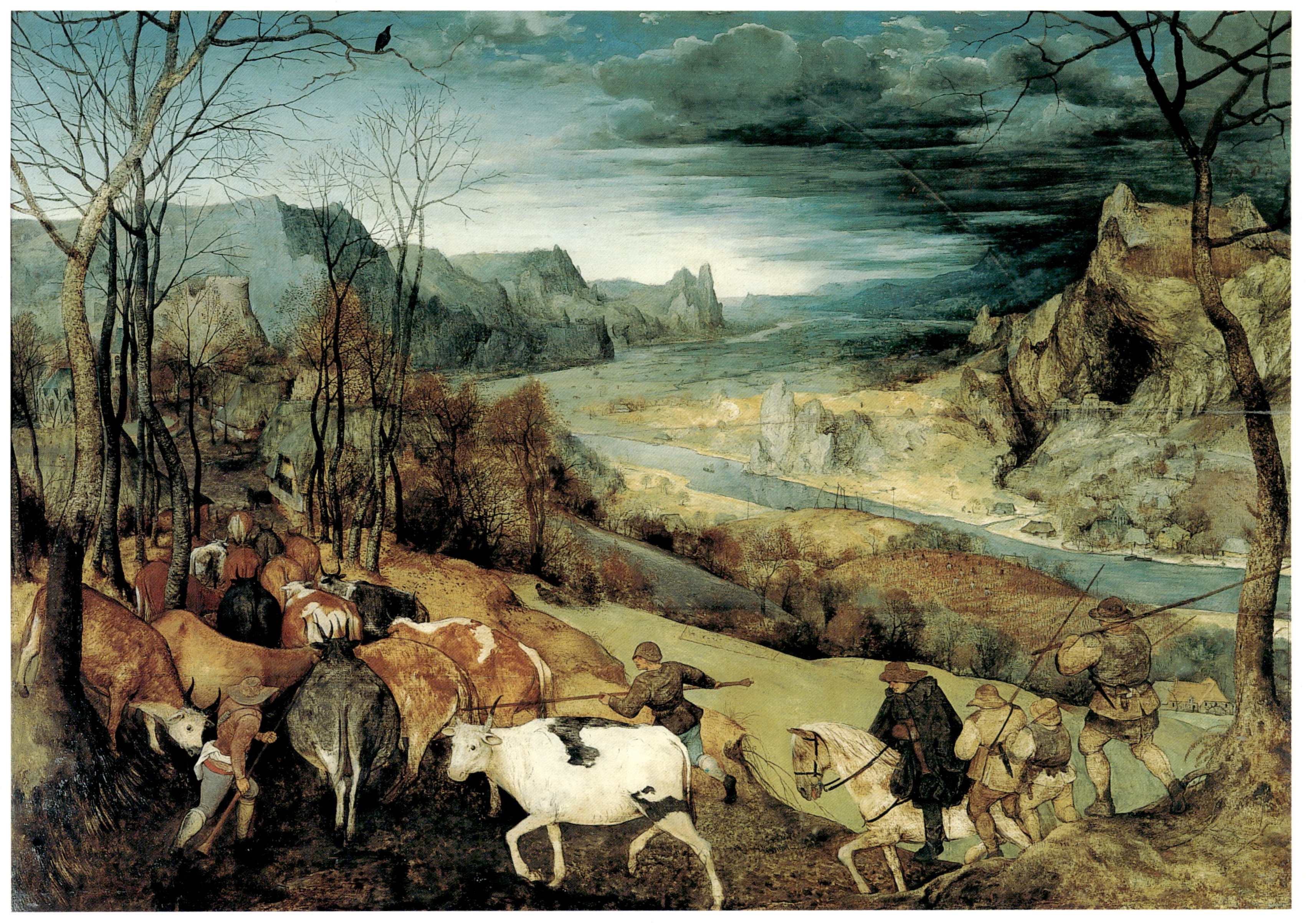

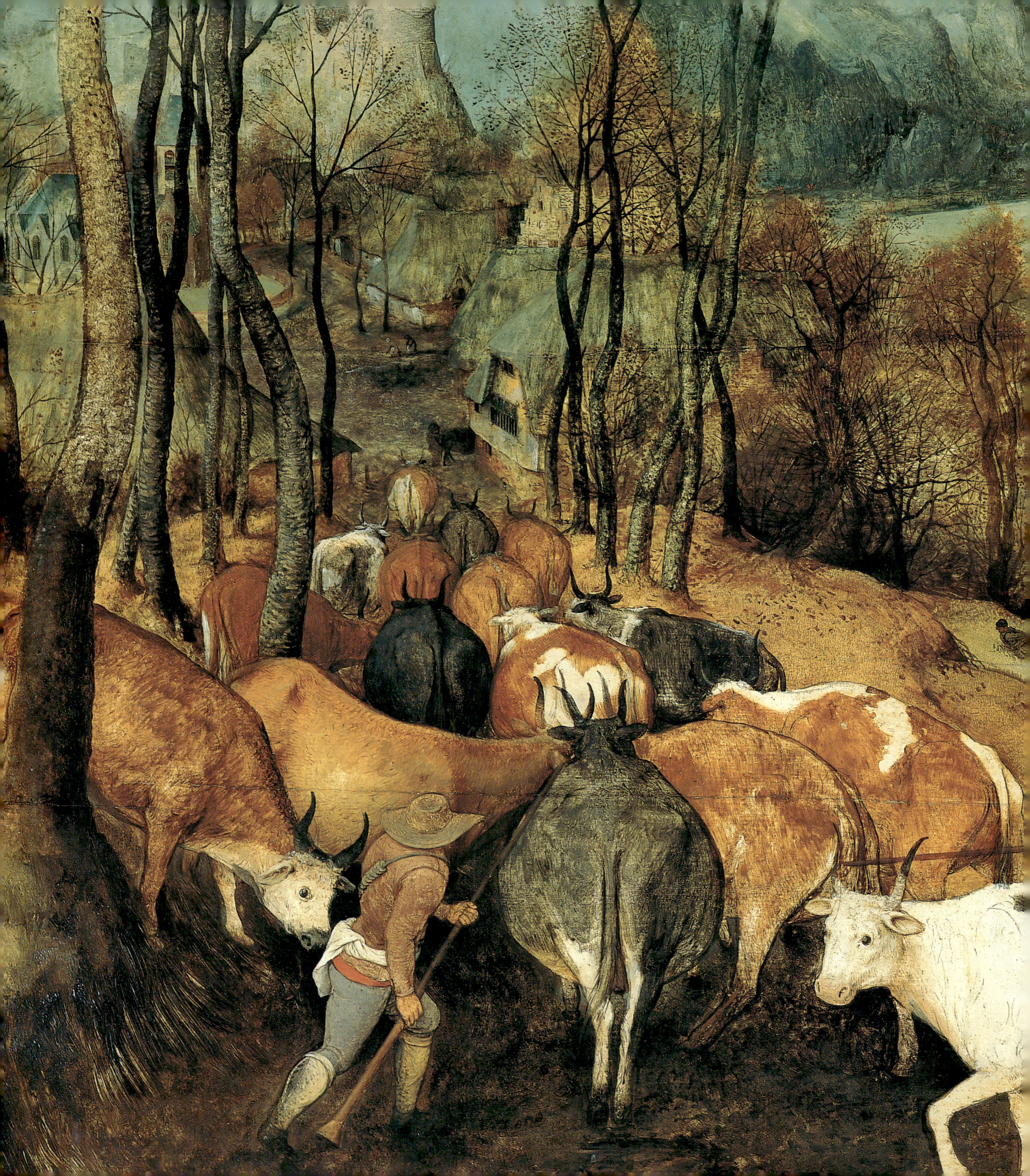

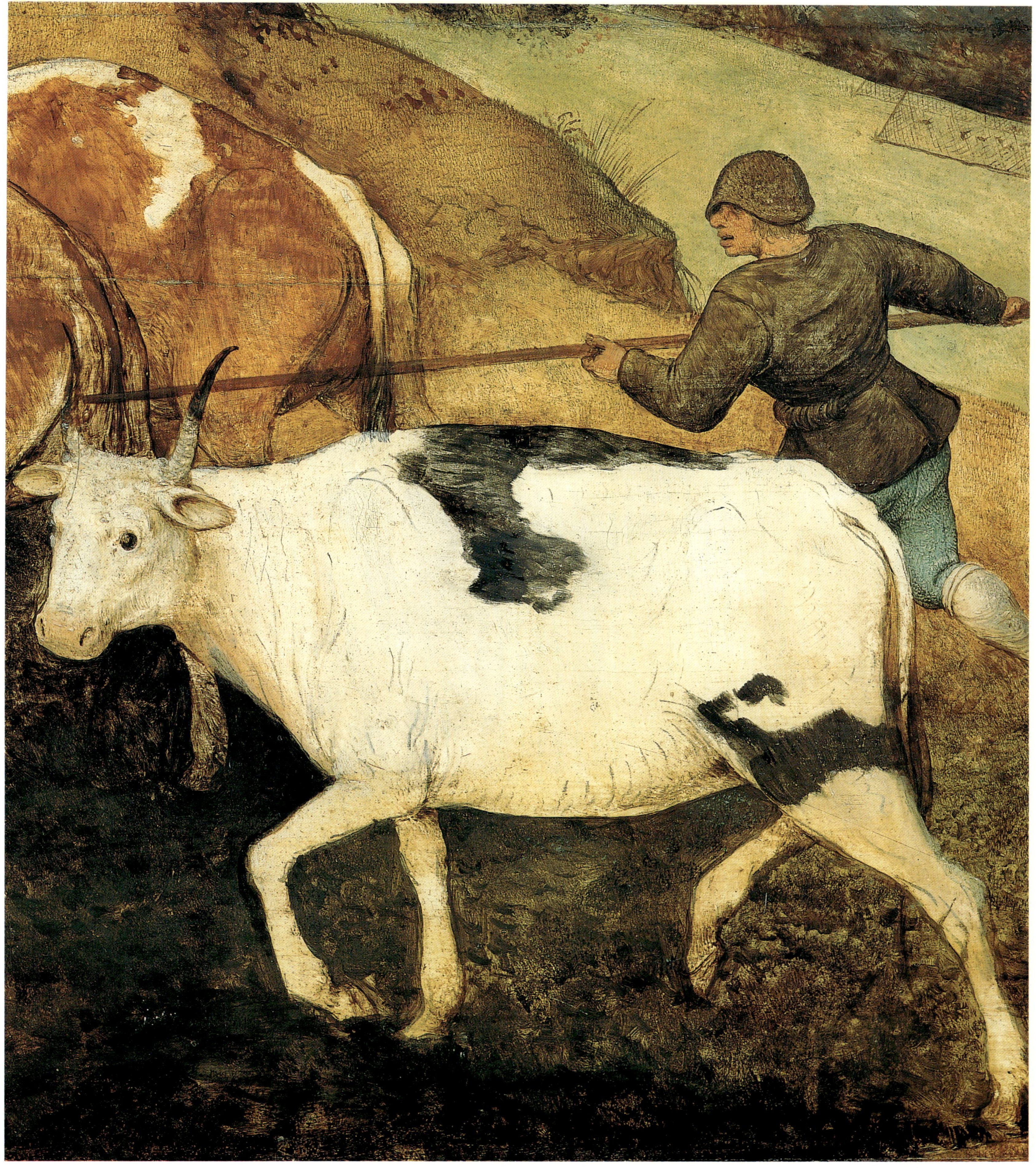

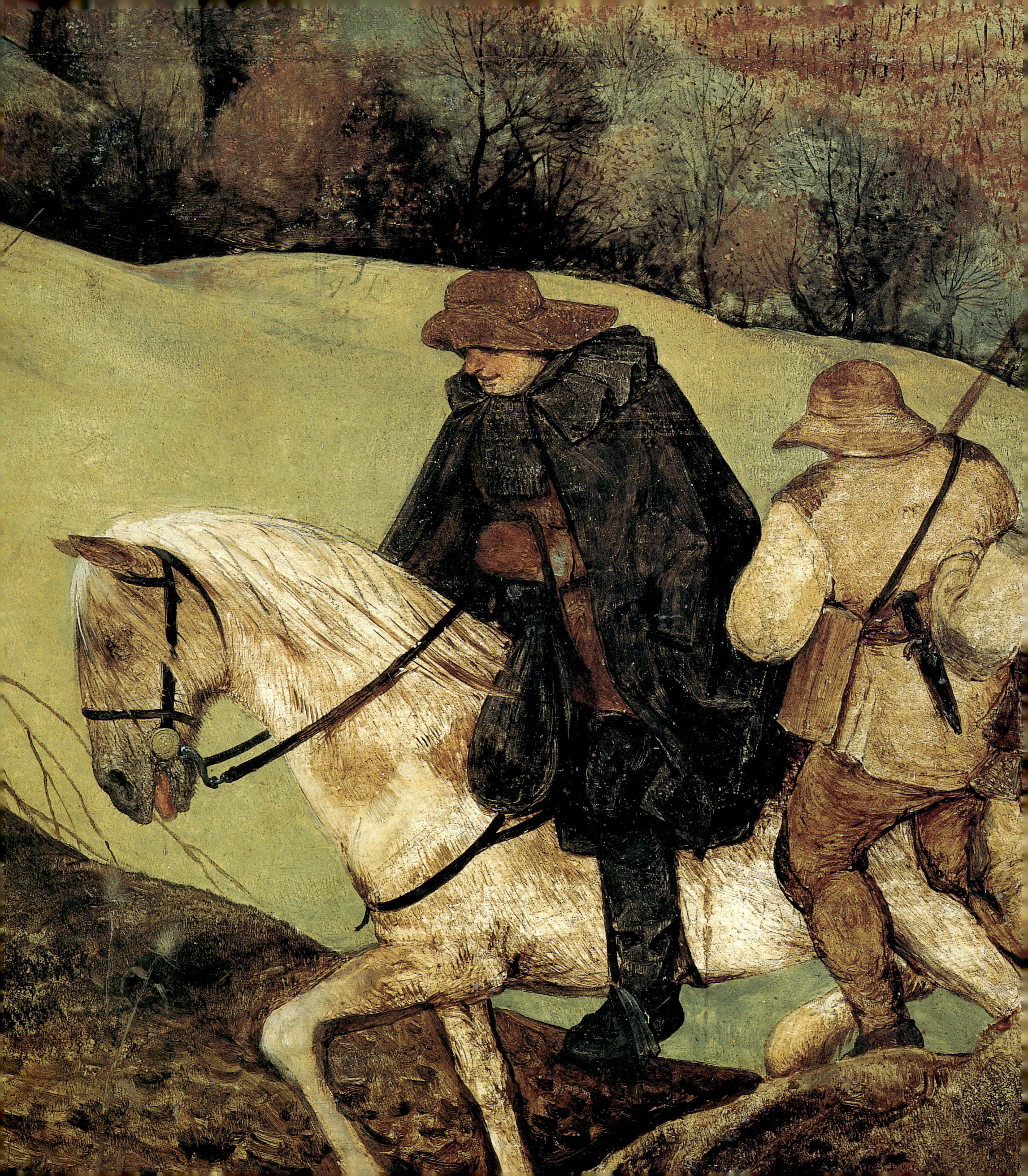

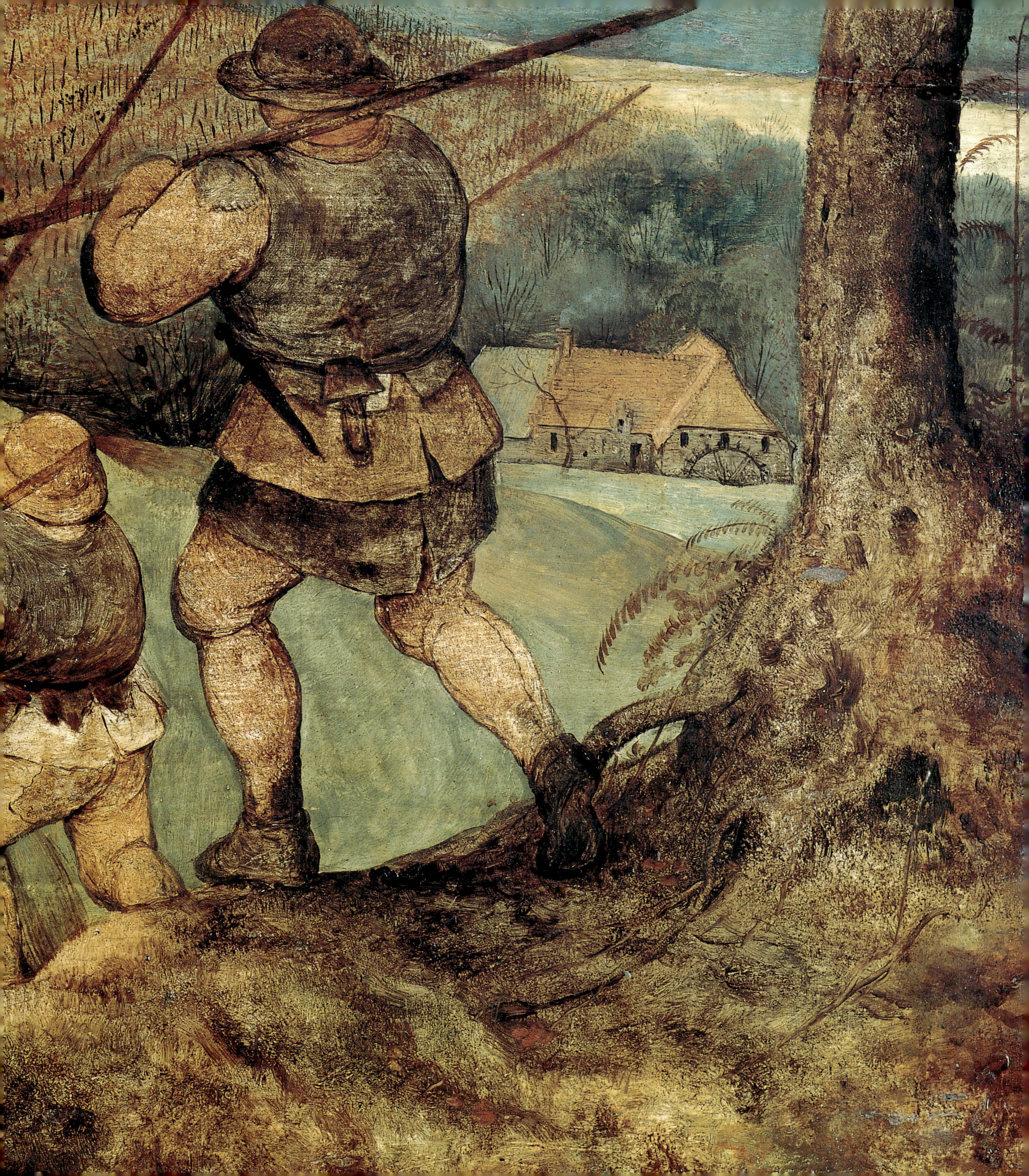

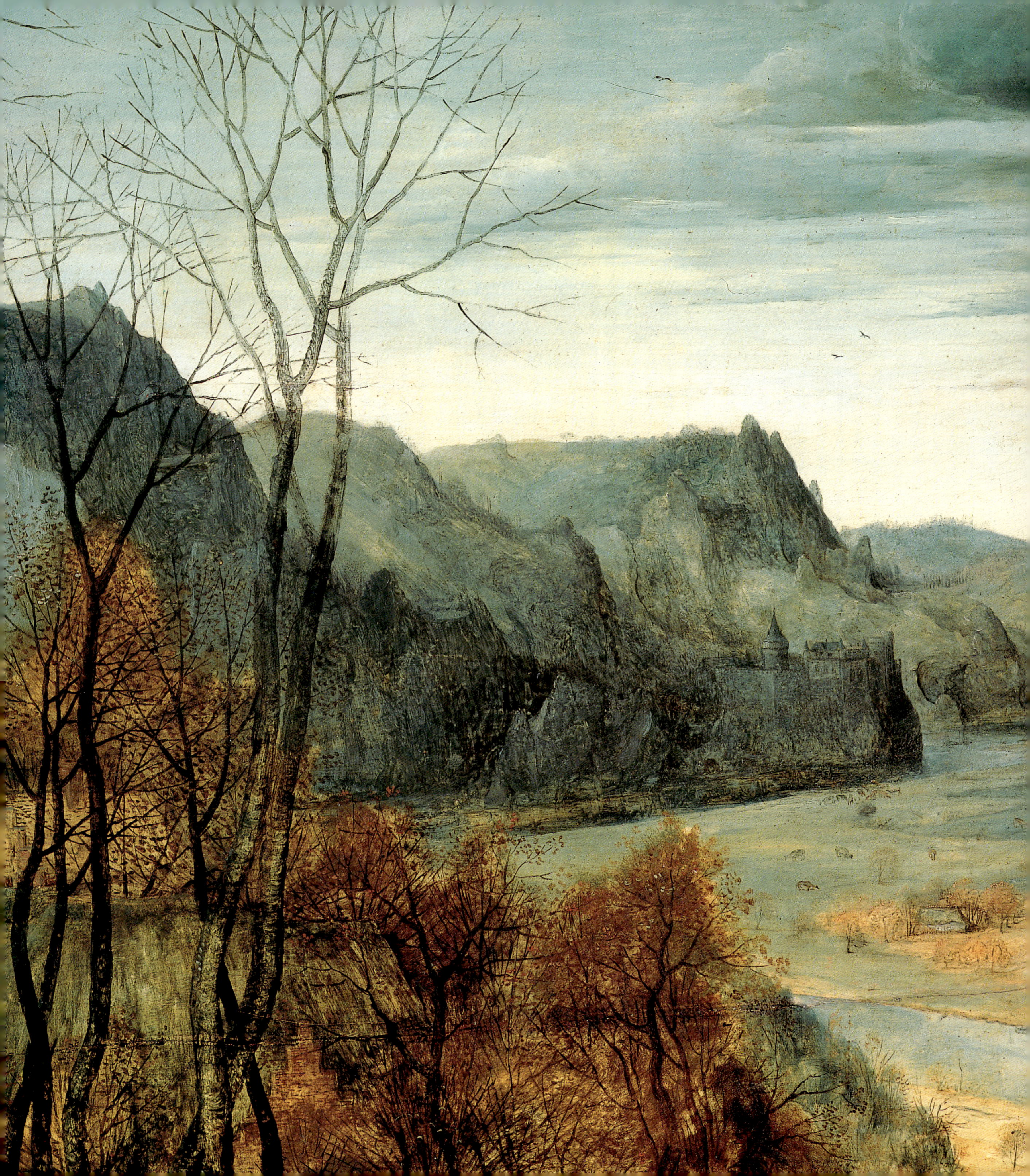

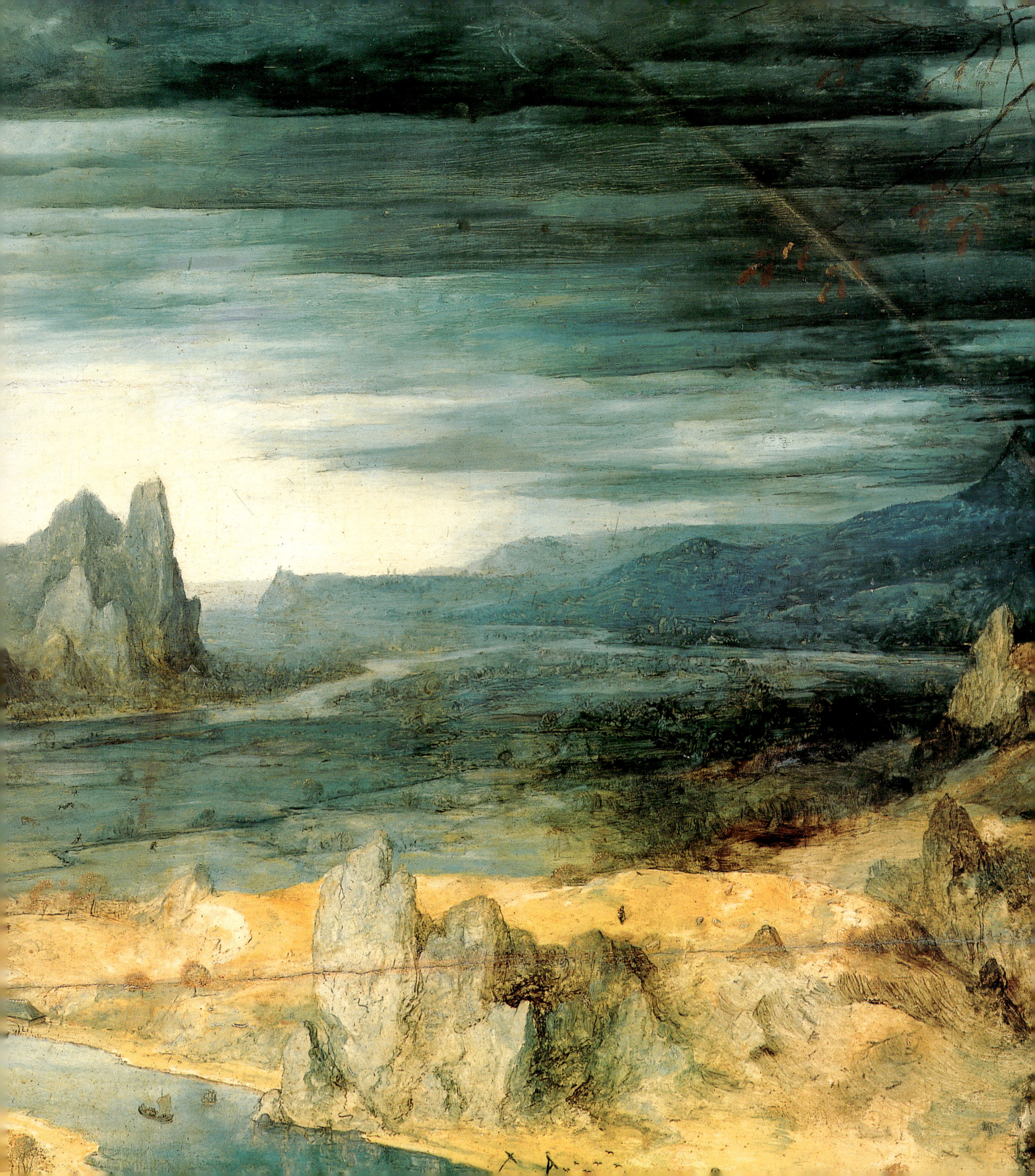

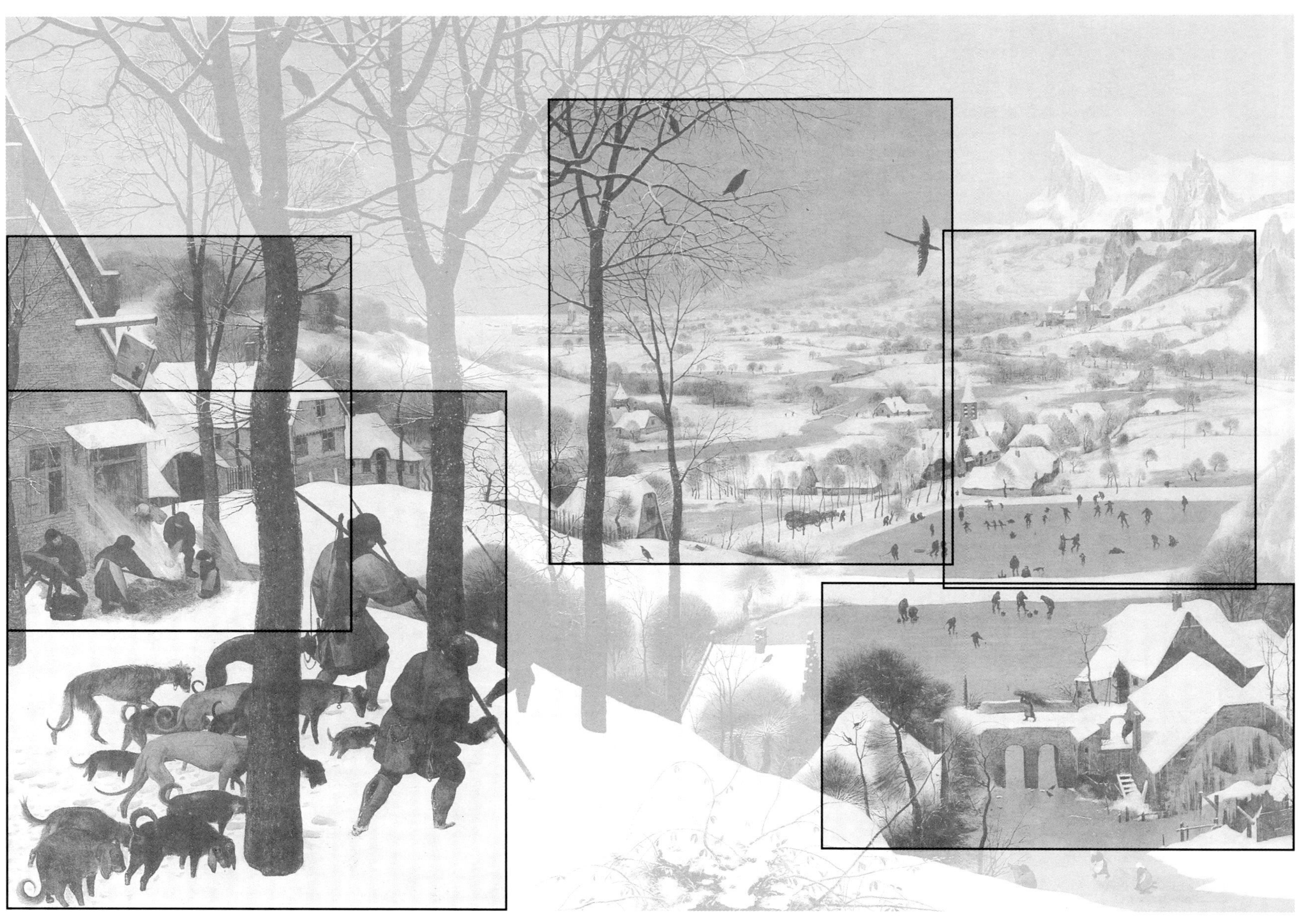

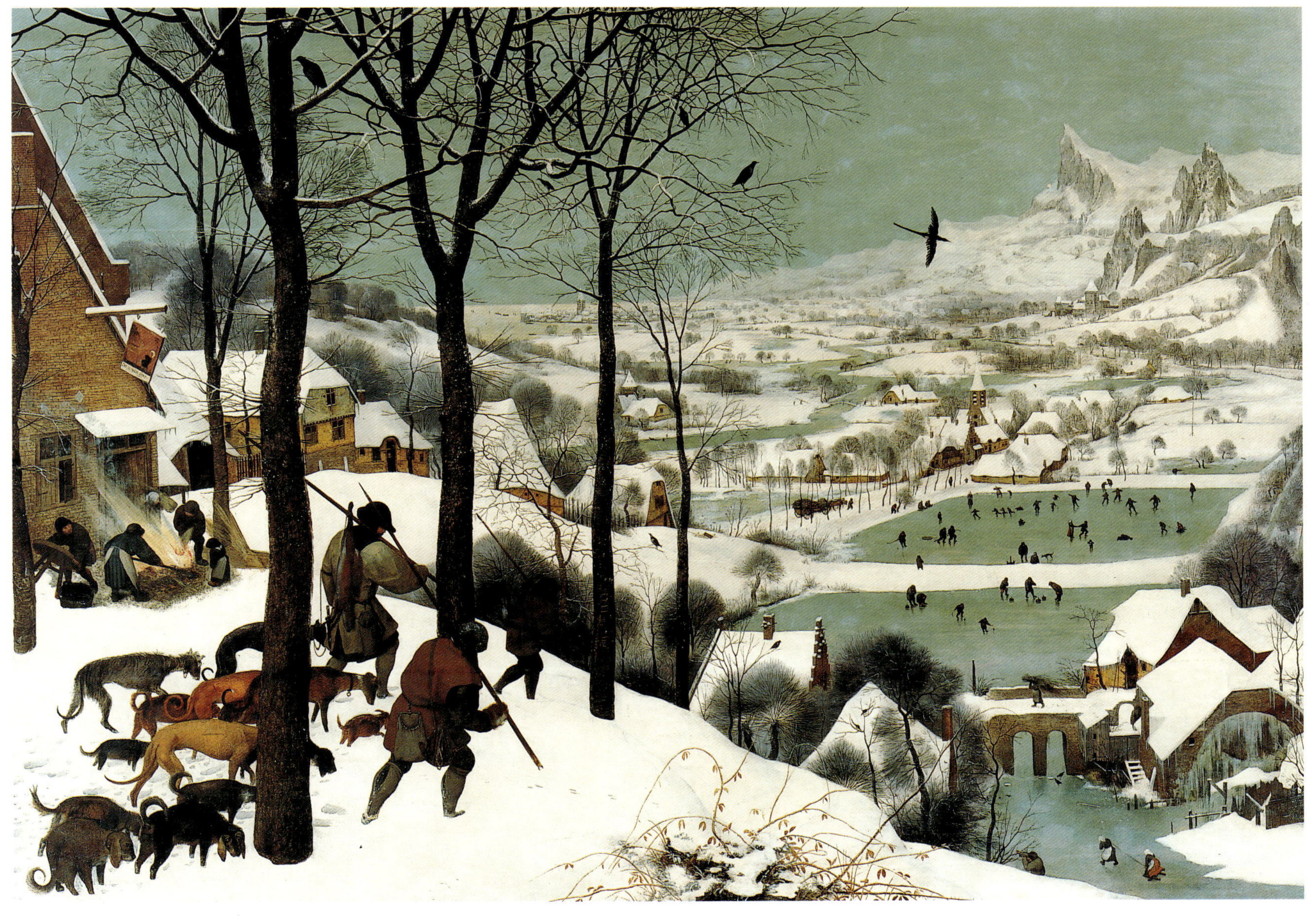

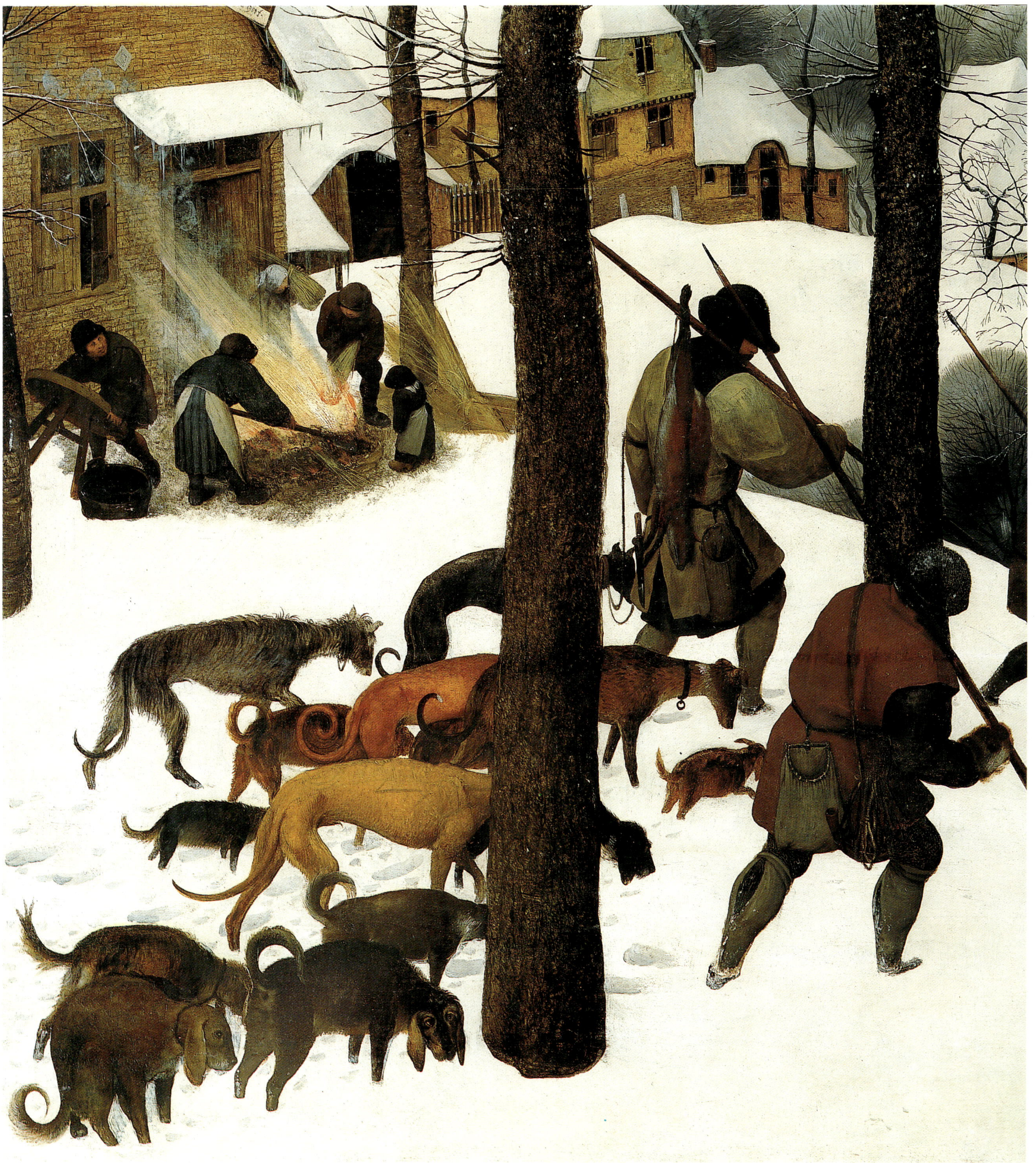

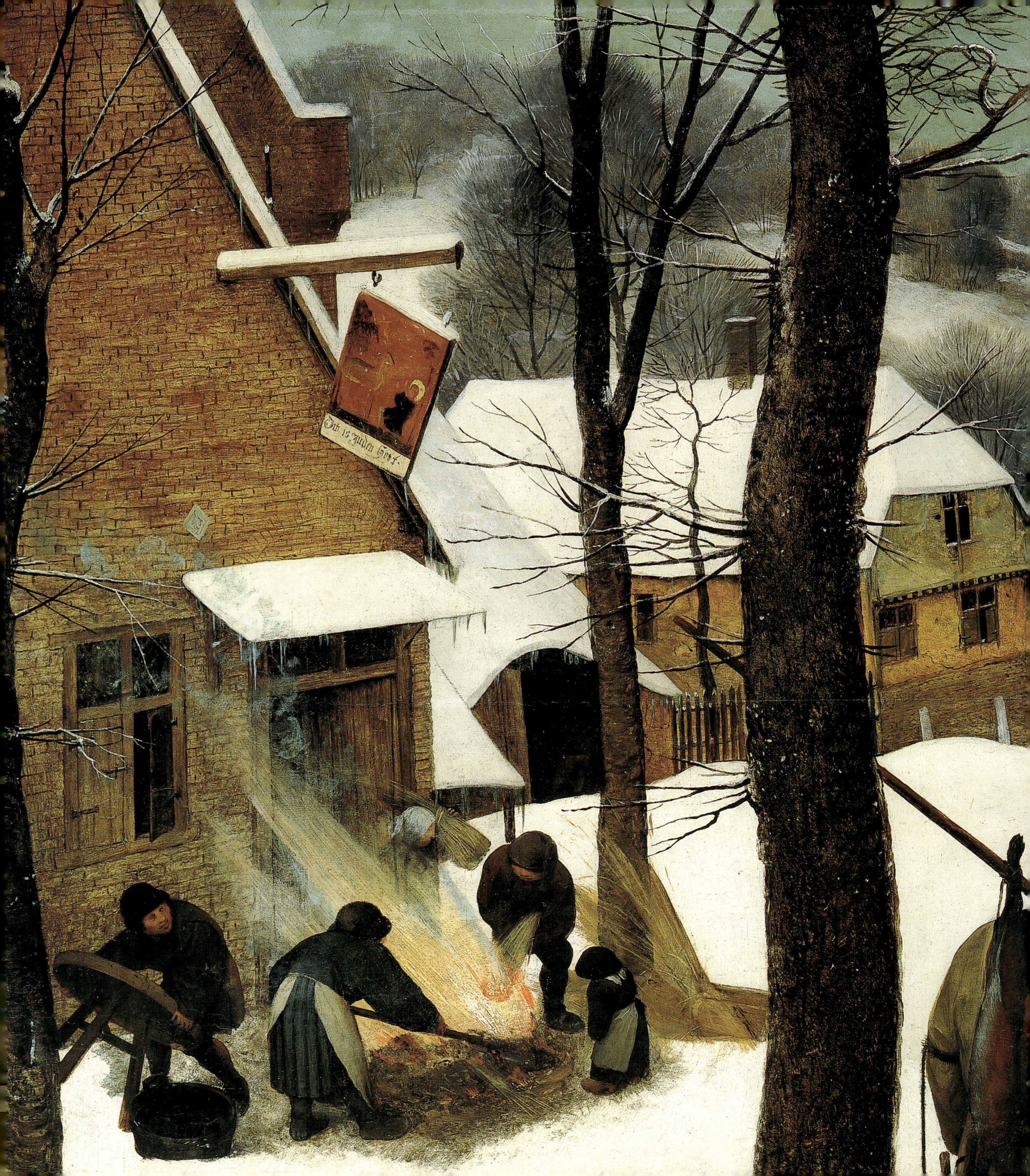
Dit is inden Hert.

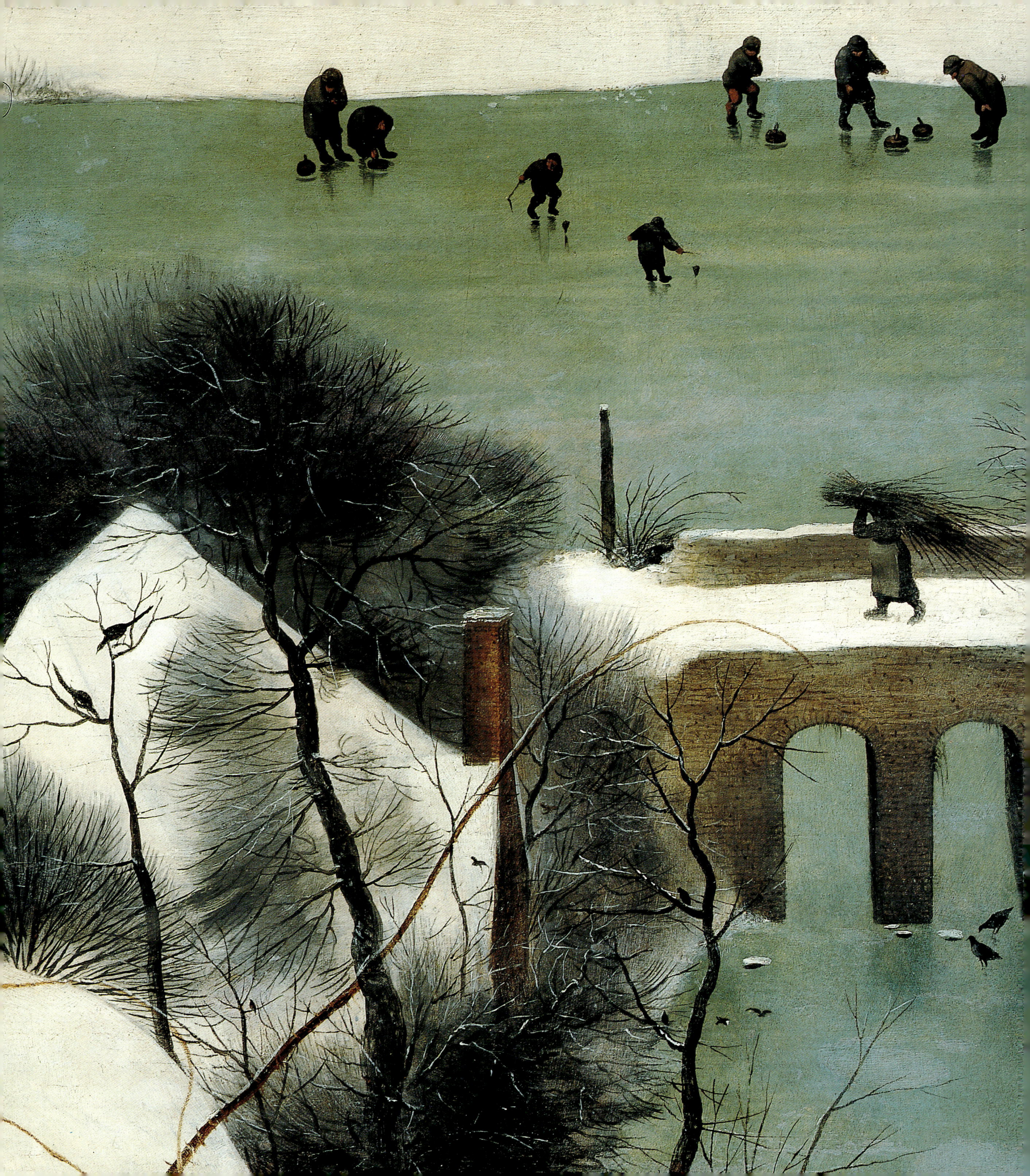

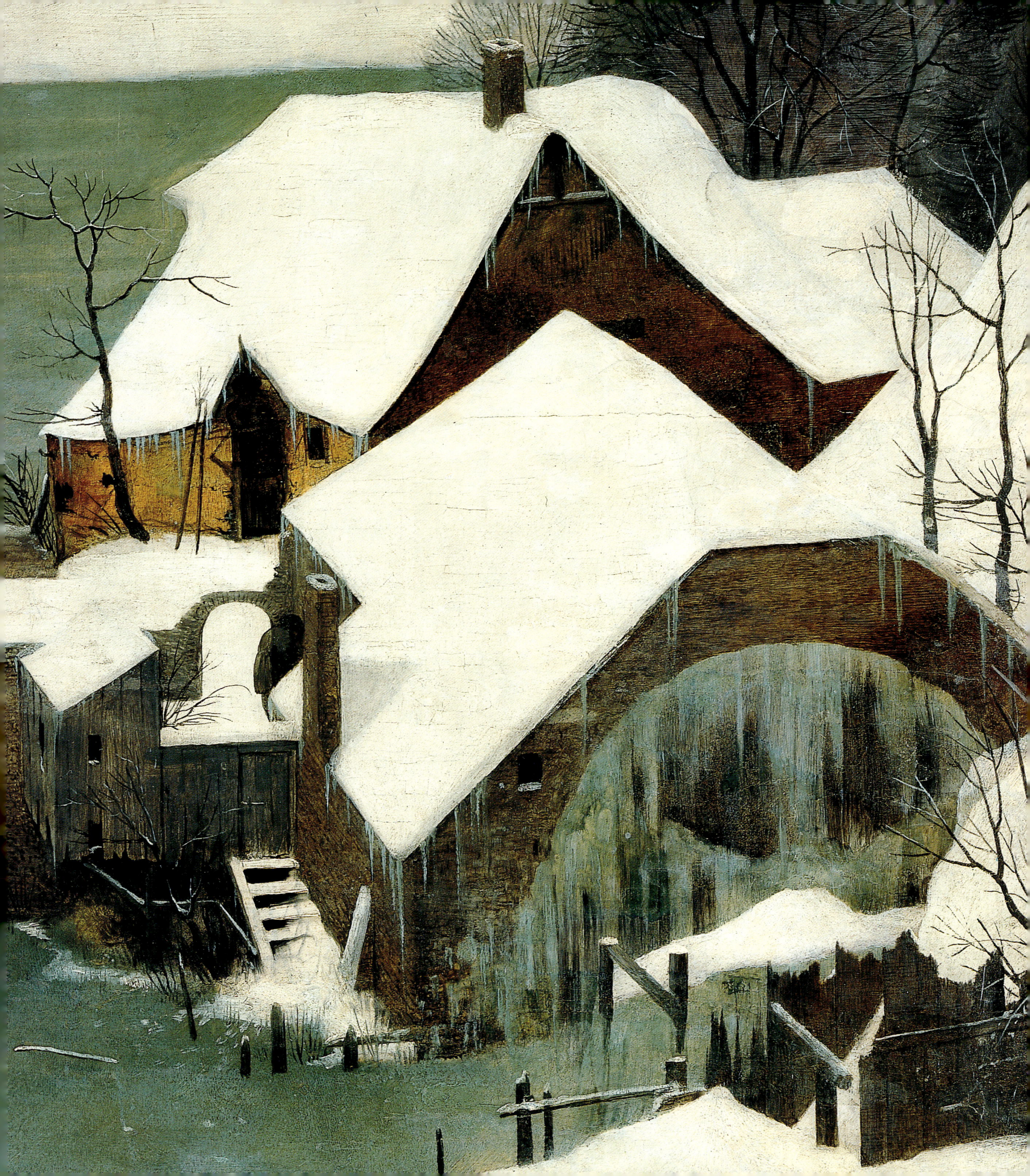

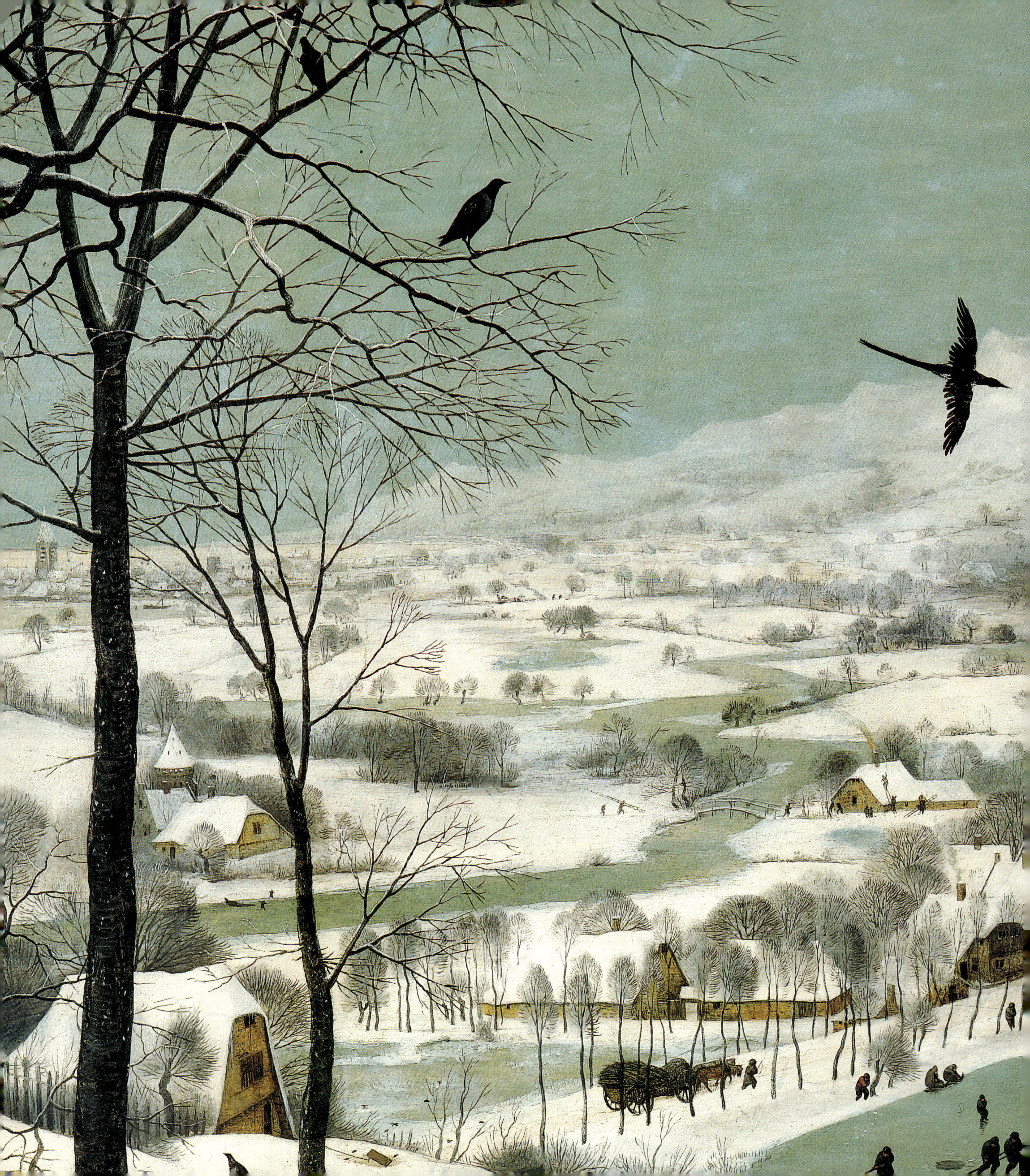

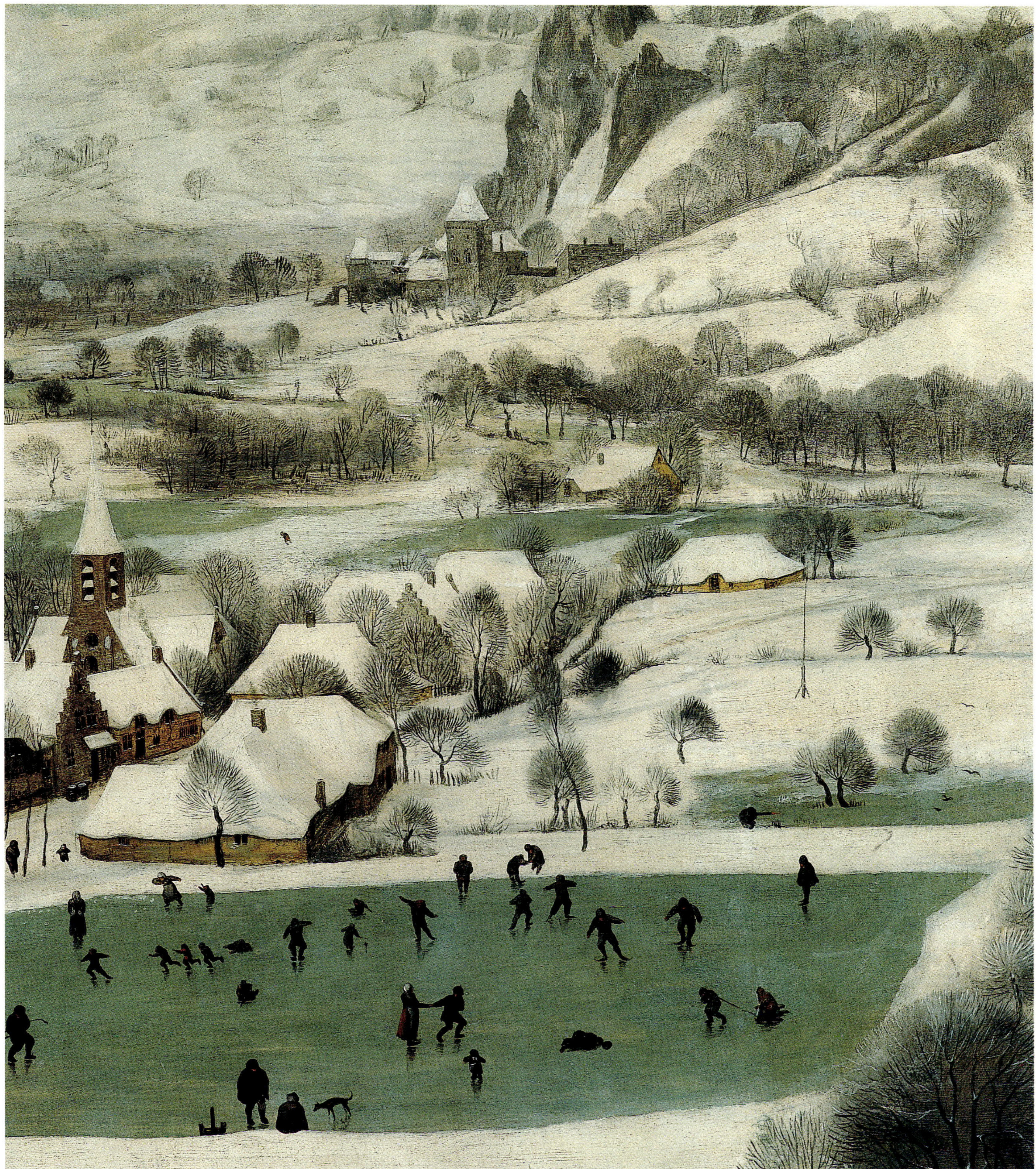

Conversion of Paul
1567

Signed below right on the rock: "BRVEGEL. M.D.LXVII"
Oak, 108 × 156 cm
1594 acquired by Archduke Ernst in Brussels; Inv. No. 3690

This painting is one of Bruegel's religious historical pictures only to the same small degree as the *Tower of Babel*, although objectively, of course, it is one. Rather, it is one of the artist's didactic dramas, almost a complement to the "lesson" shown in the *Tower*. Strangely, this has not yet been recognized, probably because Bruegel the humorist was presumed not to be interested in this subject. However, in this case, he once again gave into his didactic instincts, which drove him to portray a pressing truth about humanity that was close to his heart. (Let us leave the man to one side for the moment and consider the picture first.)
Again the scene is one of Bruegel's vast landscape compositions, this time the high mountains (which so captivated him on his journey back from Italy through Switzerland). Here there are "very fine rocks" reaching up to the sky, as his countryman and biographer said, a terribly steep mountain pass that rises up from the plain below, and a mountain pass or via mala that from a plateau where a small wood of splendid larches grows, as if in a fairy tale, narrows further into a higher, more distant point touching the clouds. It is not the kind of terrain for which the army, ascending it in disconnected groups with scattered armoured camp followers, seems equipped and prepared. (Some soldiers seem to have lost their way and wander uncertainly on the mountain, climbing rocks along the unprotected paths on the crest.) In the middle ground, where Bruegel often quietly reveals what is most important, a crowd has gathered round a horse lying down and a man in blue who evidently was unsaddled. He gazes upwards, to where a pencil of light, just barely visible, singles him out from above left. It is Saul, at the very moment of his conversion into the Apostle Paul. Why, one asks, has Bruegel relocated the "Damascus episode" to the high mountains? The Acts of the Apostles do not mention the mountains. Did Ortelius, the geographer and Bruegel's friend, tell him about Mount Hermon? But the route from Jerusalem to Damascus did not pass over it. Is it therefore merely an imaginative enrichment of the story? Scholars of Bruegel have settled for this answer, though some have come up with another idea over and above this one: that Bruegel was alluding to the Duke of Alba's troops' procession over the Savoy Alps (in 1567, the year the picture was painted!), piously hoping that he would not turn out to be "Saul", persecutor of the Christians in the Netherlands. Preposterous! The picture continued to be silent. The title, however, speaks out loud and clear! With a little irony, admittedly. What does "conversio Pauli" mean exactly? Conversion, turning back, turning away from the wrong path. And suddenly the picture becomes a demonstration of the impossibility of this intricate and obviously

improvised undertaking of an army crossing the mountains, a powerful metaphor of pride going before a fall. There is no alternative but to turn back. Conversion equals turning back. What is taking place inside is illustrated by what is happening outside! For how else could that be credibly portrayed? But to what extent is "turning back" outwardly represented? Indeed, has Bruegel not done his utmost to make the mountains unfriendly and insurmountable? Is there even the slightest hope for the distant and tiny head of the army as it forges on in the increasingly terrible via mala? No horizon is shown; there is no end in sight to the mountains. It is all rock and walls. And if nothing else can convince us, do not the clouds state clearly enough, just as in *Tower of Babel*, that there is nowhere further to go here? Paul, rising up as a new man, will not continue the path that he began as Saul. (This has nothing to do with his actual path to Damascus, when he did not turn back. As in the mountains, we are removed from the flat, revisable reality and placed in an allegorical situation: in the "inner" area already close to Heaven.) It is made difficult for Paul to rebel, and he experiences the total correction of his wrong ways. He turns back. Just as puny men can do little to subdue nature, that of the high mountains in its most sublime form, rebellion against God cannot really be sustained. The painting is therefore — and this alone explains the choice of the Alpine setting — the symbolic illustration of humanity losing its way, of mankind getting stuck in the impossible and meaningless. It is a metaphor of crisis and peripeteia: the *conversio*, or turning back.

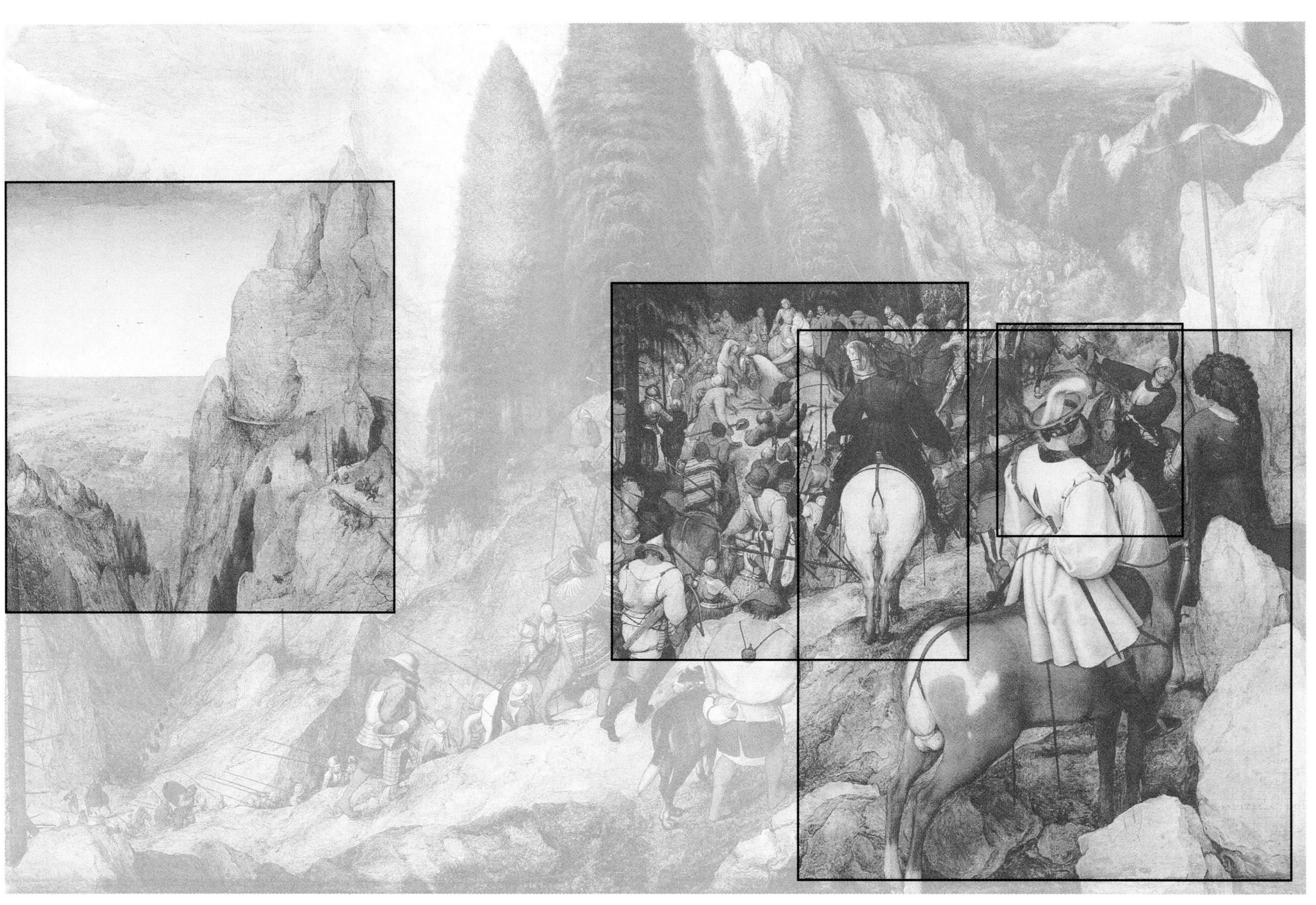

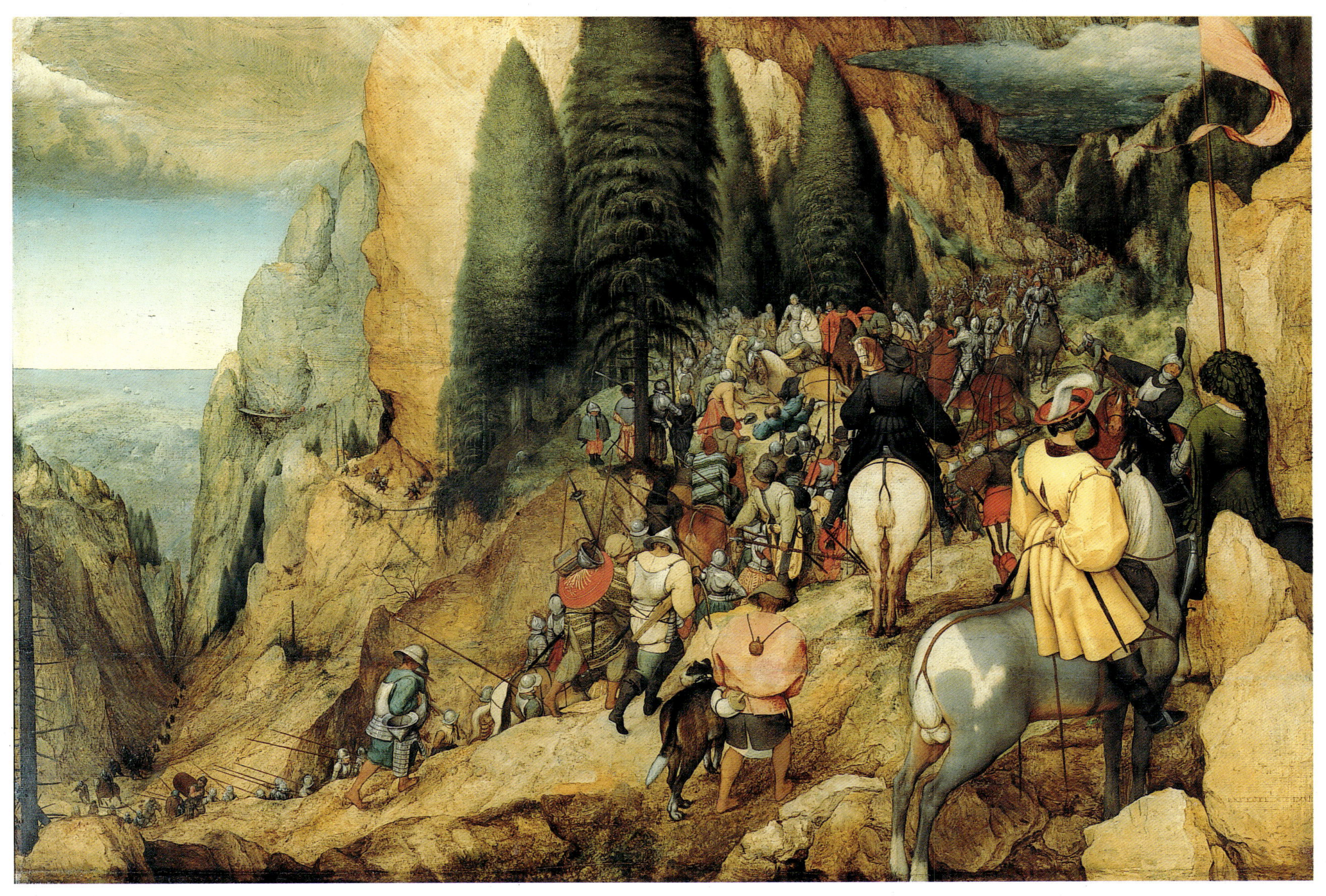

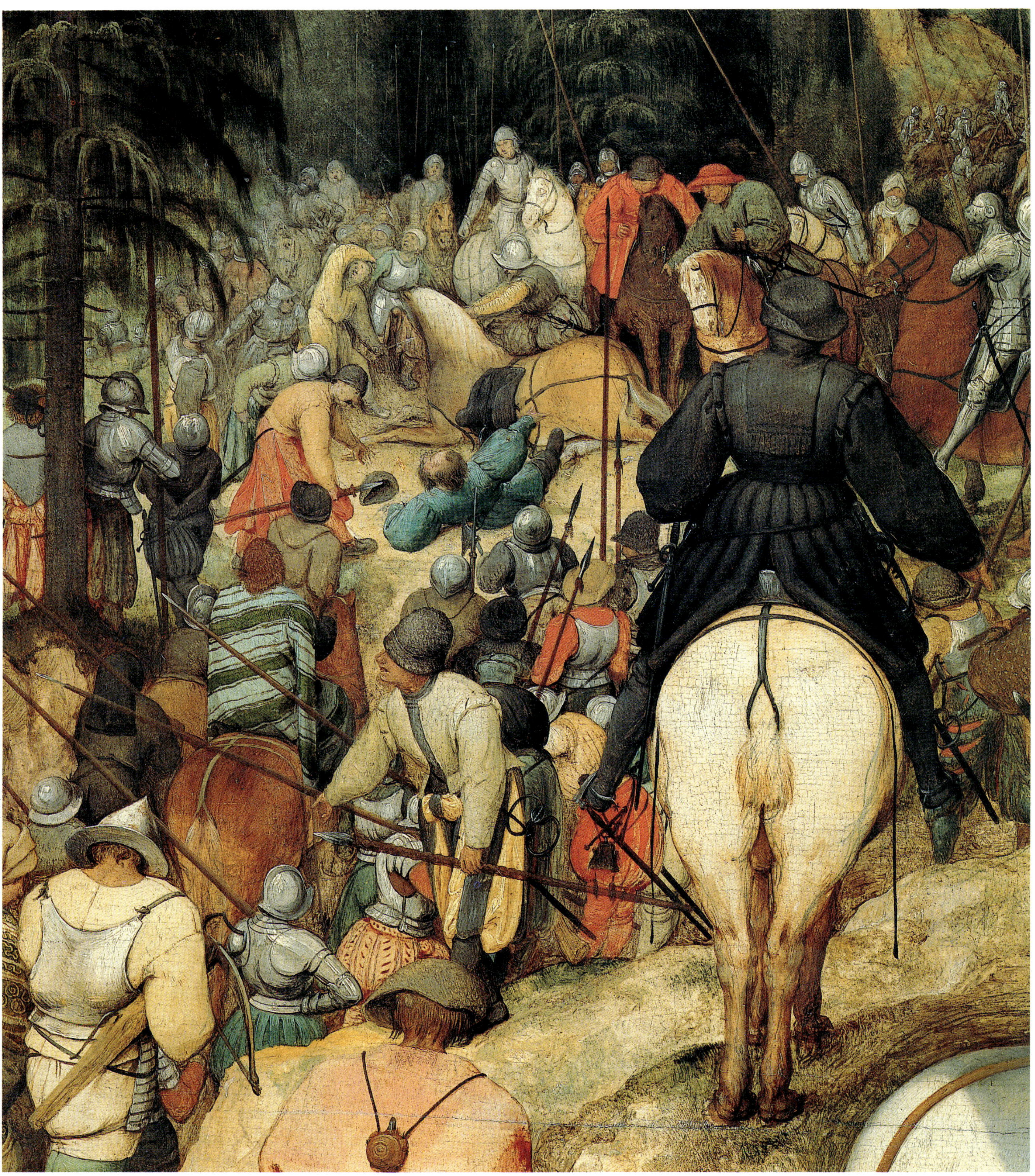

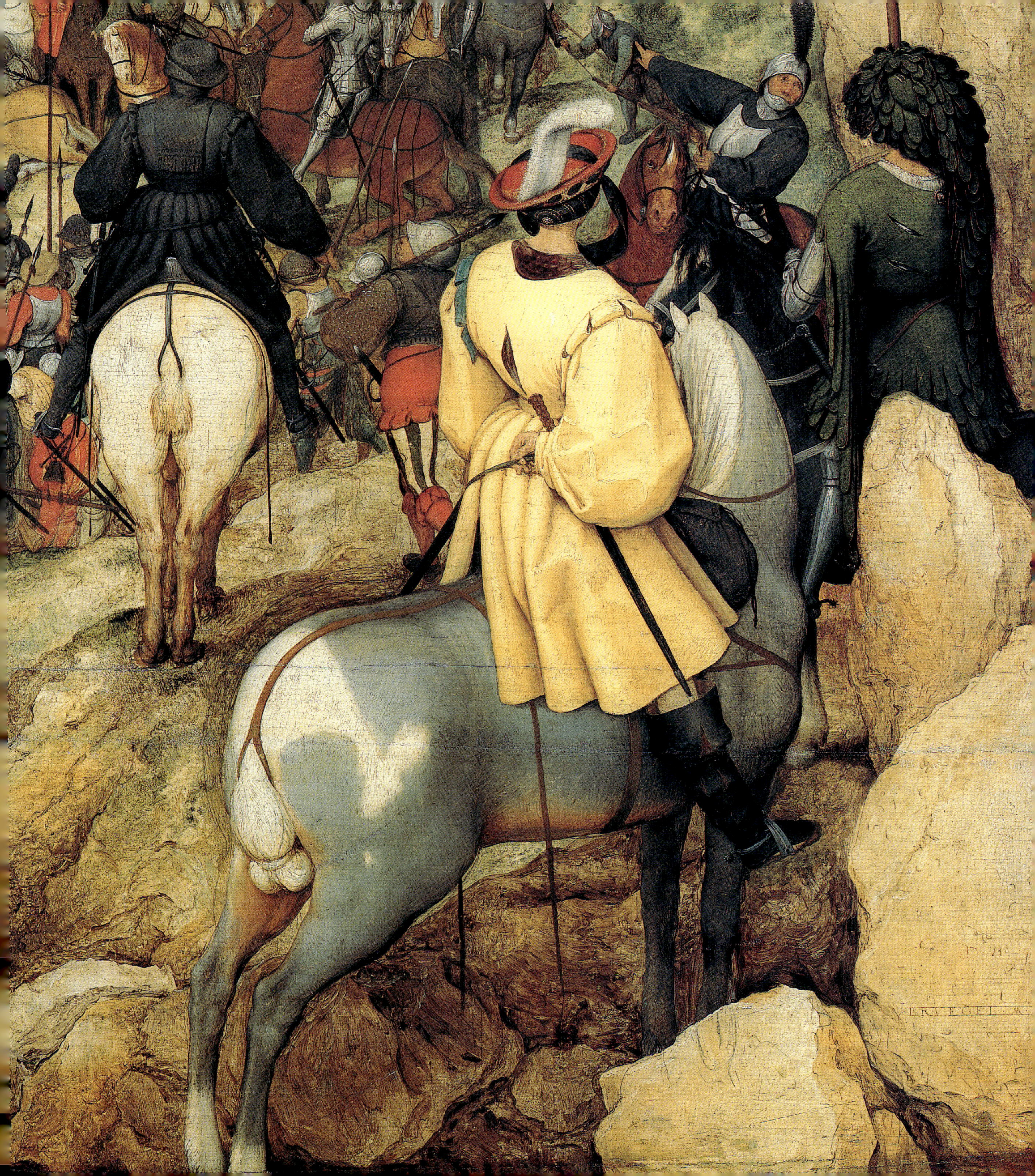
BRVEGEL M

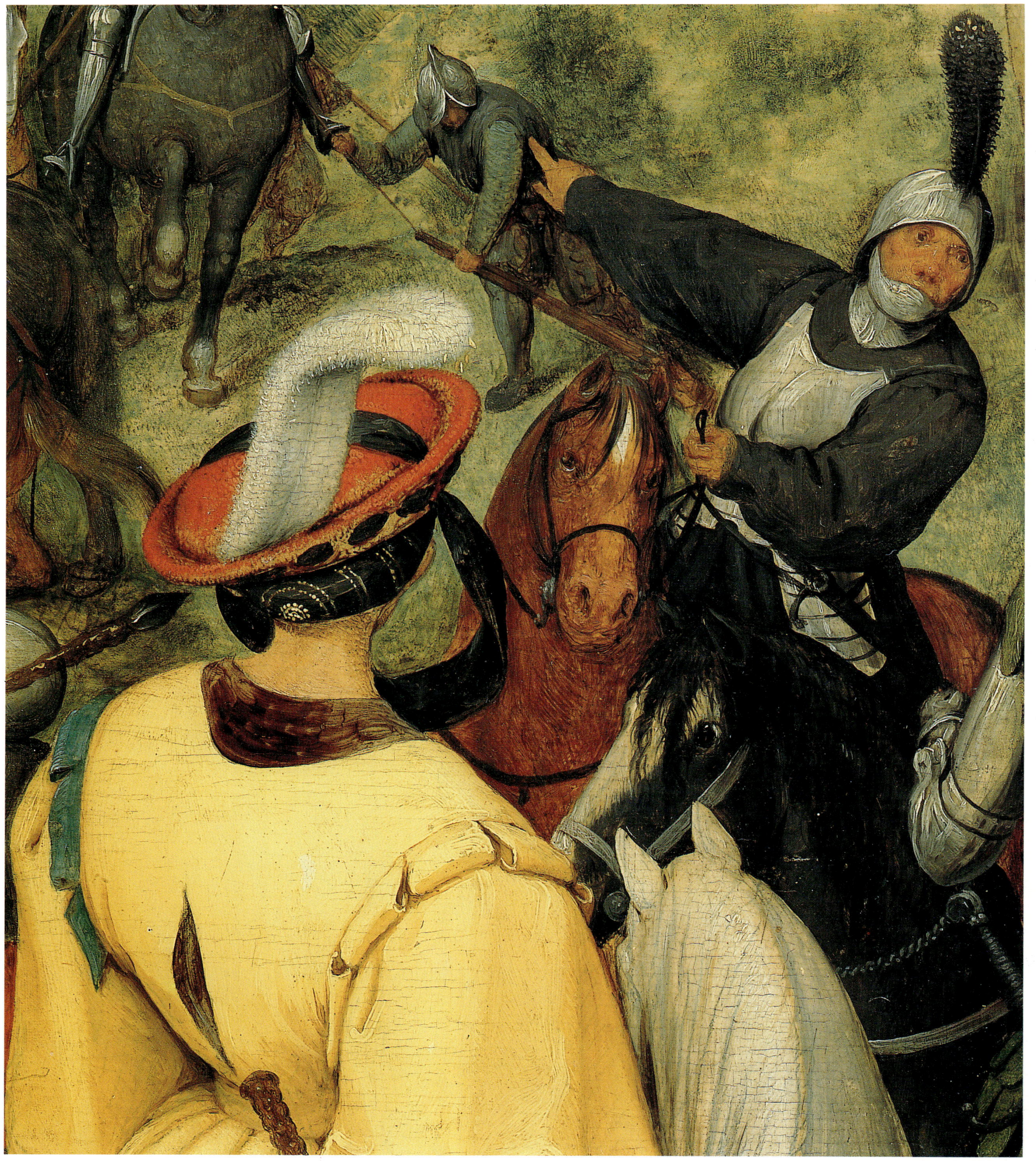

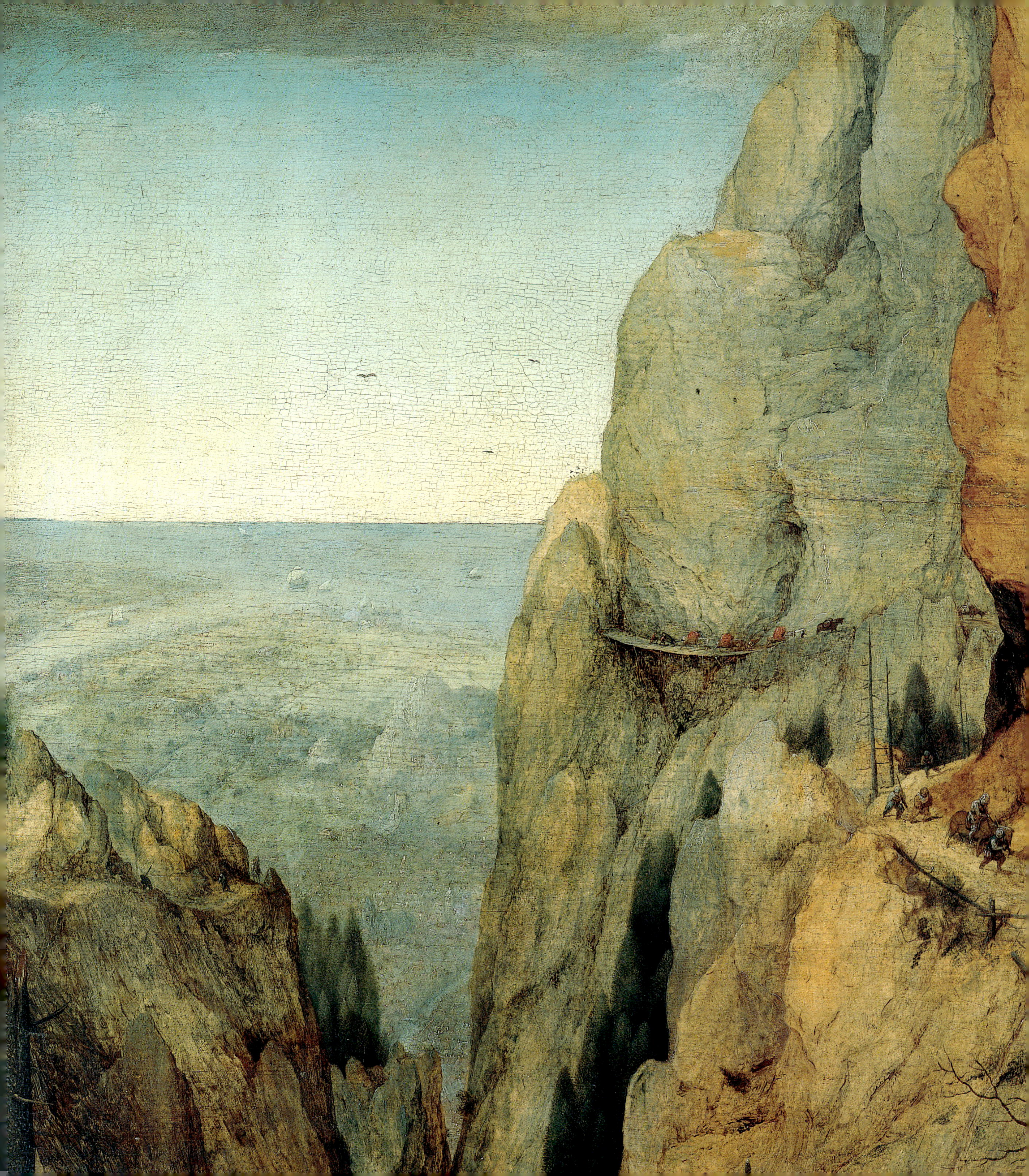

Peasant and the Nest Robber
1568

Signed below left (in gold): "BRVEGEL. MD.LXVIII"
Oak, 59.3 × 68.3; trimmed on the right and below
In Leopold Wilhelm's inventory 1659; Inv. No. 1020

Bruegel was always devising new forms for his didactic aims in order to express the "truth" to be illustrated by the whole picture in the form of an idea. Throughout his work there are unique pictorial ideas such as these, for example, in the *Tower of Babel,* in the way it inherently demonstrates the impossibility of finishing it because of a fundamentally wrong architectonic concept, or in the *Conversion of Paul* where, by playing with the lexical meaning of "conversio", it erects an entire mountain range in order to have an army stranded on it. In both cases, the relationship between man and nature proves to be absurd, out of line, stubbornly offending reason, scale and common sense. The *Seasons*, the meaning of which is not easy to fathom, show concretely how this relationship should be (even though this is a secondary effect of the whole idea). Even the *Suicide of Saul* shows both orders that make up the world, nature and human existence, once again in an inharmonious relationship when seen in historical perspective, but which in the individual case in question is presented as "normal". The early "encyclopaedic" pictures show no common sense at all (interpreters exploring in this direction are still incorrigible), but they still use humour to heighten awareness about what everybody knows and has experienced: this applies to the *Proverbs* painting (Berlin), to be ranked together with *Carnival and Lent* and *Children's Games* for the nature of the form which swings between metaphor and literalness, typical of Bruegel's obsession with reality, but often taken as such for the theme. This picture of the *Peasant and the Nest Robber* is a late phase of this truly Bruegelian form of humour and didacticism, which turns words into images and takes the meaning visually from the words.
With certain of Bruegel's works, it is not easy to find the key to the idea (*Tower of Babel* and *Conversion of Paul* show how imperative this key is to an understanding of the theme); here, it is still missing. We cannot make up for its absence or replace it with our own interpretation. Each detail has almost literally been turned over and many elements found at which Bruegel himself would very probably have laughed out loud. But the simple, overall meaning of the "literal" action, probably related to a proverb or saying is still starkly missing.
The picture shows a very beautifully painted landscape, farmland with meadows, a farmstead, horses being led into the barn, a trunk of a willow tree, a tree-lined stream (the painting has been trimmed on the right, but we know how it continues there) and a row of oaks. A peasant is walking toward the viewer, and with his next step he will go right into the stream, which he has reached without noticing, so obviously captivated is he by what he wants to point out to us. His foolishly smiling face (unfortunately it is impossible to decide whether it intends to express superiority, spiteful glee, self-righteousness or simply cunning), accompanies his pointing gesture. There is a boy in the tree, stealing birds or robbing the nest; his cap is falling off his head, probably into the stream. It is impossible to say whether he will fall down after it himself, or whether this little mishap is, to the contrary, intended to emphasize his audacity. His small bundle, which already seems to be full of spoils, lies in the grass.
On the basis of a fragment inscribed on a drawing by Bruegel with this detail of the boy, a proverb has been deduced, the best version of which reads as follows: "Die t'voghelken weet/die t'vanght/die hevet" "he who knows where the nest is has the knowledge; he who robs it has it". (This same idea is expressed more ribaldly in the merry folk ditty where the daring lover steals the bride from the shy suitor.) Thus, the boy "has" and the peasant simply "knows". But why will the latter fall straight into the water? Is this based on the biblical parable of the self-righteous Pharisee who tends to the splinter in his brother's eye while ignoring the beam in his own? This does not quite seem to fit the way Bruegel distributes his emphases. Or is it about the peasant who not only is without blame, but also

comes to harm in a world that allows the wicked to get away with their wrongdoing, and moreover remains the victim of the "craftier", who derides him to boot? This feels even less like Bruegel. We sense that the right "word" that would solve all these problems immediately has not yet been found in any of the many proverbs that have been proposed. The picture has not yet disclosed its humour and message to us. Surely the artist has alluded to something that was on everybody's lips, setting it in relief through his sense of humour and intelligence for even the most demanding audience. But the talk on everybody's lips (the 16th century was an era of figurative language, a century of proverbs) has been lost. We are not persuaded that it is there to be found in one of those voluminous collections chock-full of wit. And so the picture remains silent; it can no longer, and perhaps never again, be read as Bruegel intended. This does not prevent the viewer from finding sufficient material to examine in the details, though we are unable to determine the attitude of the protagonist, the peasant standing in front of his world. In any case, this world is quite positive in its realism, and it is shown to us in such a peaceful, even beautiful, light that there must be a reason for it. We have entered here into the subject matter of Bruegel's last two works, which, after the *Seasons*, again deal with rural life, but in a substantive, even monumentalized form that marks the artist's highest achievement in terms of style.

Postscript 1997: None of us reads the Bible enough, as much as it was heard and told in the time of the Reformation, and still in Goethe's time. In the Gospel of St John, III, 29 ff., John the Baptist, standing near the river Jordan, points out Jesus (and Bruegel's *Sermon of St John the Baptist* in Budapest comes to mind, where we are shown a meeting of Baptists prohibited by the authorities — *Doopsgezind* — and oddly enough Christ is shown nearby): "He that hath the bride is the bridegroom: but the friend of the bridegroom, which standeth and heareth him, rejoiceth greatly because of the bridegroom's voice: this my joy therefore is fulfilled. He must increase, but I must decrease". From the bird's nest proverb with its bridegroom metaphor to the peasant shown about to step into the "river Jordan", does it not all fit neatly into this reading of the "scene on the river"? The painter, like the Delphic divinity, "does not speak out and does not hide, but gives a sign (makes himself understood)". Bruegel's illustrative art often resorts in any case to a literal quotation. If this interpretation is correct, Bruegel's suspected relationship with the Baptist assembly finds further confirmation here, and the painting rises from the lowly level of the ordinary proverb — the level at which it has to now been viewed without comprehension — to acquire an evangelical significance. As with the ageing Michelangelo, from whom Bruegel, as it has often been remarked, got the inspiration for the main figure, this art of demonstrating and convincing in the final work serves as an (un)veiled confession of religious faith. "Dije den nest weet* — Johannis am III." Sapienti sat.

*"Dije den nest weet": He who knows about the nest [Ed. note].

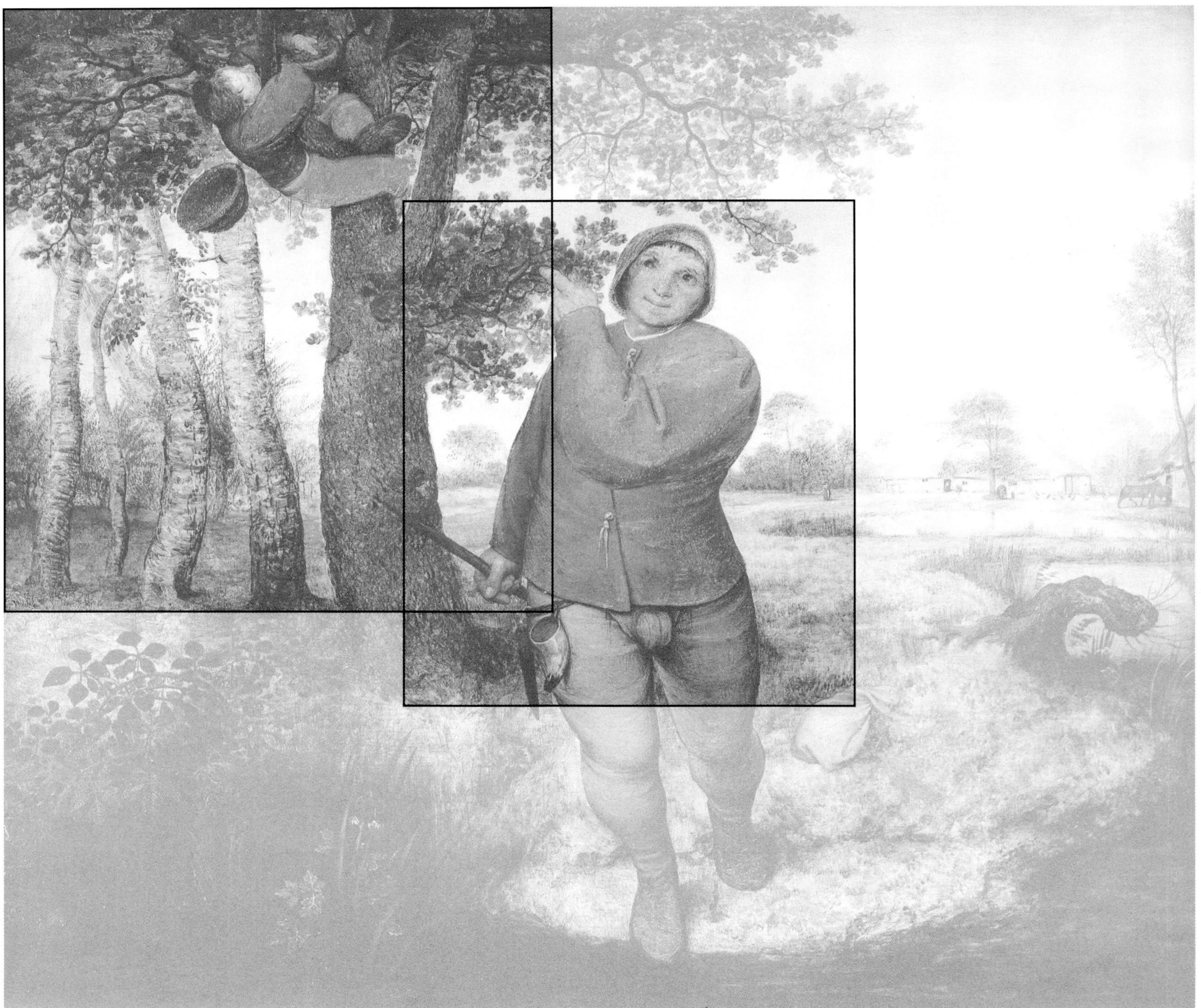

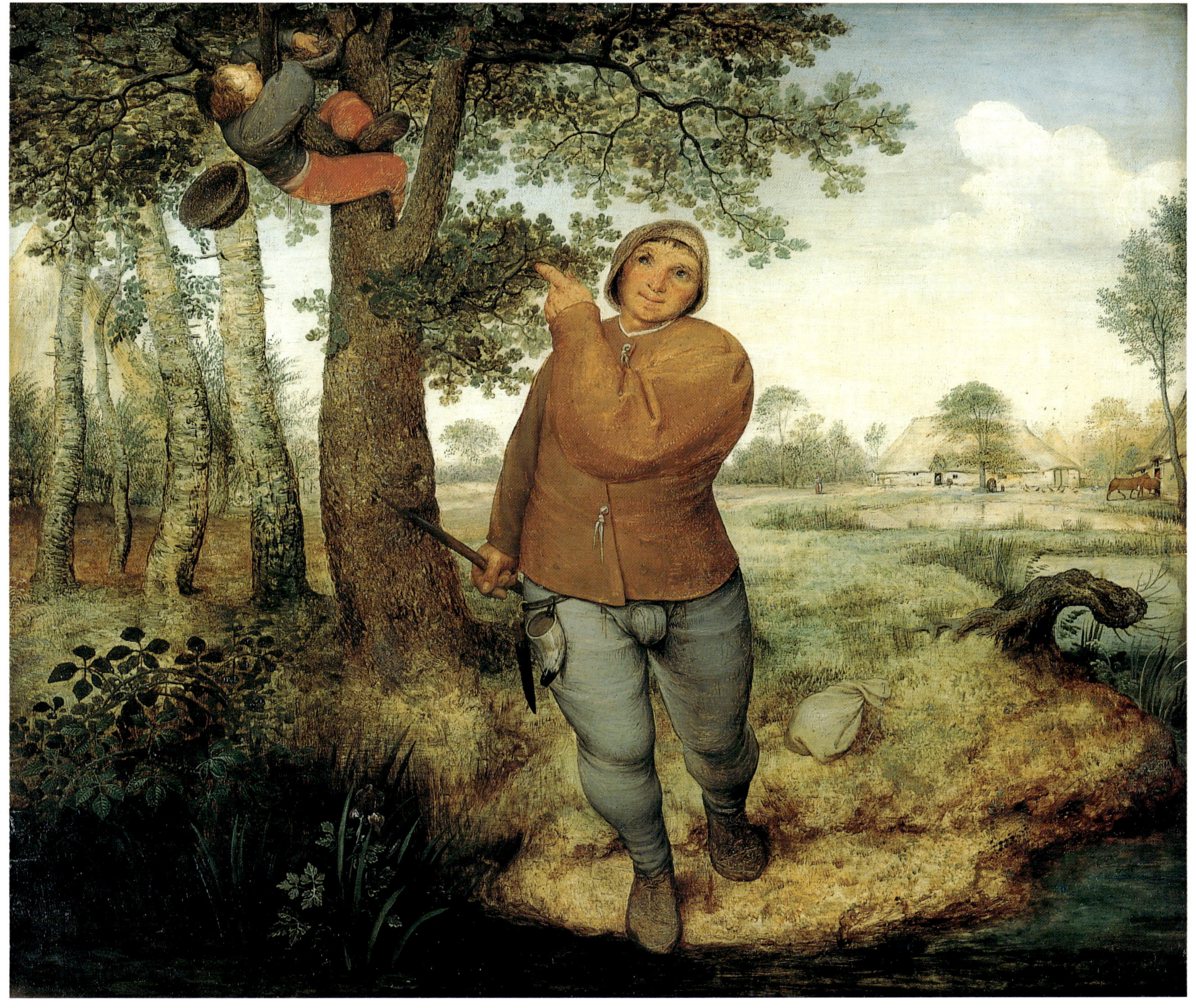

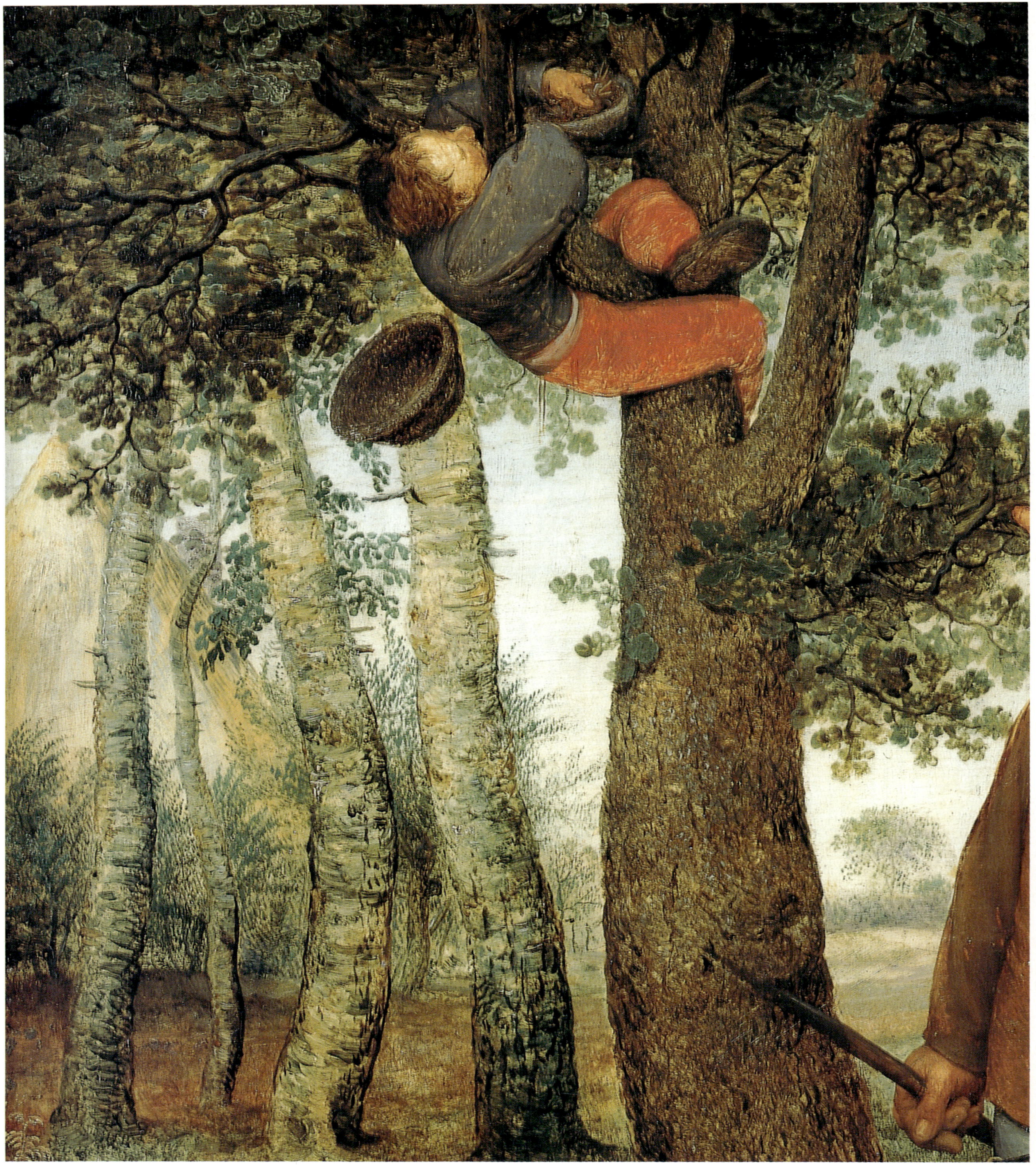

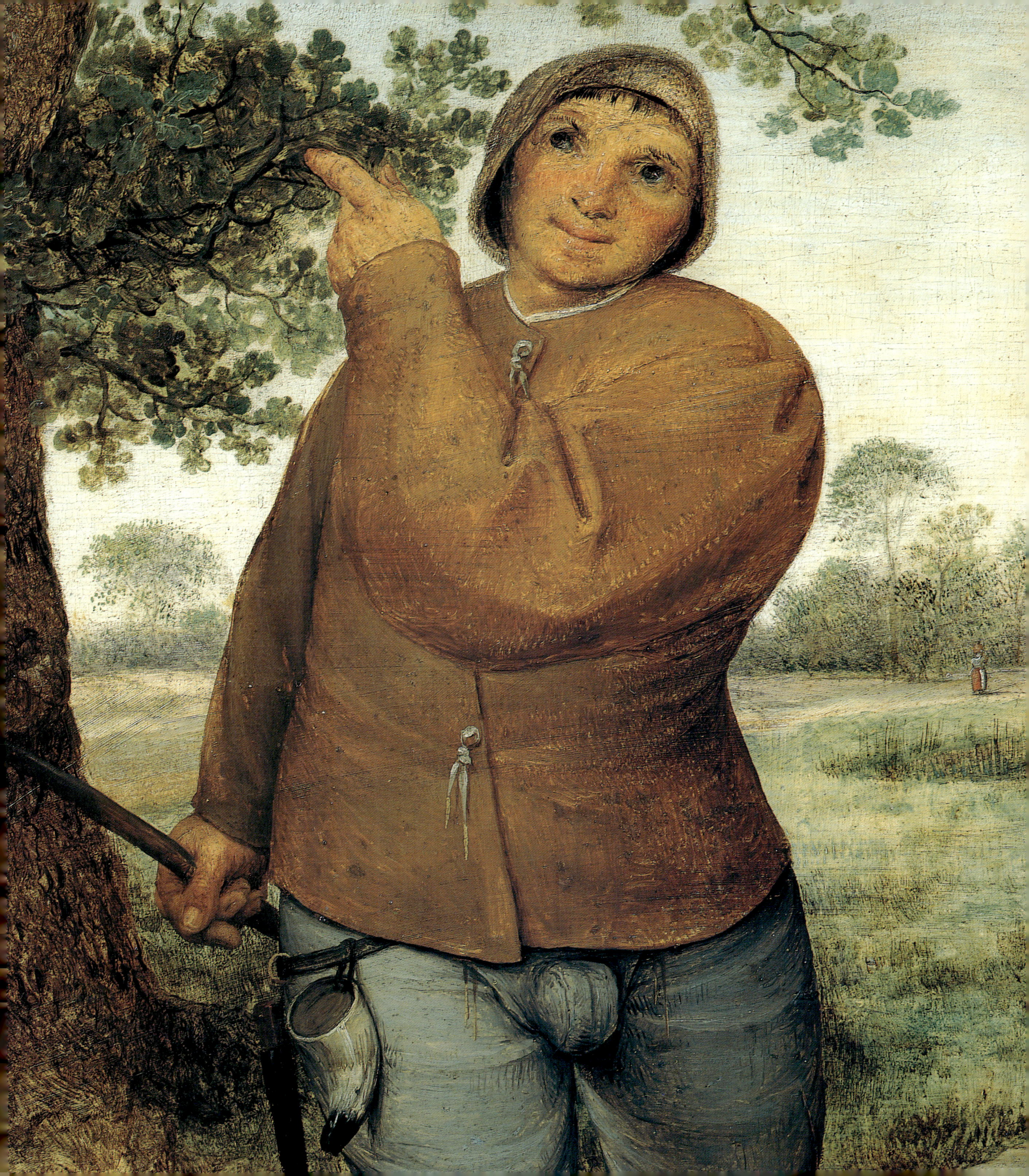

Peasant Wedding
Around 1568

Oak, 114 × 164 cm; trimmed, a later piece 5.5 cm wide added at lower edge
Purchased by Archduke Ernst in Brussels in 1594; Inv. No. 1027

The two large-format, large-figured peasant pictures in Vienna, though closely related in subject matter and style, probably did not form a pair of companion pieces. Both have, with good reason, contributed much to Bruegel's fame, and, indeed, the names he has been given in both German and French — "Bauernbruegel" and "Bruegel le Drôle" — are derived from them, like his fame as an illustrator and singer of Flemish and peasant customs. These are the pictures that come to mind whenever the name Bruegel occurs. Popularity such as this is never unfounded for works of art. But at the same time, it encourages wrong ideas and somehow obstructs the view of the work, drowning out its message. Modern criticism, which aims to deliver us from error and subjectivity, has rushed to our aid with interpretations of the two works, but these have become the cliché the world over, and are on the wrong track. Listen to this: presumably, Bruegel, under the influence of the Freudian school, has in both pictures taken as his subject the animal excess of the catalogue of all the mortal sins. Here, in the name of all city-dwellers, he presents with a contemptuous and morally indignant sneer, the ridiculous and repugnant crudeness of the peasant, regarded in the 16th century by men of culture as little more than an animal. Drunkenness, gluttony, lust, arrogance, anger, irreligious behaviour and yet other sins are there to be seen by whoever is able to interpret them, shown with realism or by allegory with skilfully encoded direct and indirect allusions. A more scrupulous and unfounded interpretation could not have been formulated under the Inquisition. (Another, less radical iconological position holds that the element of the ridiculous, the comic in the peasant world — which, of course, it does not question — is morally indifferent.) A third voice chimes in with its interpretation of the work as an example of political comment of the times — Bruegel as a resistance fighter during the Spanish occupation. The differences between the various voices do not matter and just one thing is against the rules: to leave the work of art to the eye, which in Bruegel more than any other artist may be presumed to be the central organ that mediates reason.
However, there is nothing in the least that supports the fact that both pictures are different from, and something much more than, other compositions showing rural life, however well-crafted. (For a very long time even Homer, to say nothing of the Bible, was understood according to the "multiple literary meaning"; he was meant to be interpreted, because it seemed too easy to have the poet simply "narrate".) Naturally and justifiably so, we hesitate to describe it as a "genre". This type of picture was just emerging then, and without reference to Bruegel. But Bruegel had first of all to scale it down, to reduce it to a level that would satisfy the curiosity for the coarse, ridiculous and foolishly comical, the level on which genre painting was based. The human world is portrayed in the peasant pictures just as it is in *Carnival and Lent* and in *Children's Games*, and had the latter substituted their encyclopaedic narrative method with the new realistic one, they would have been "genre" works. However, this term is not appropriate for Bruegel; it is impossible to apply to him, because of the high perspective from which he paints. Bruegel's style is epic, his representations are of a greatness and simplicity that is Homeric, his focus of interest is unwaveringly on the object. However, and this should be born in mind from the outset, in Dutch painting there are no masterpieces that are purer in form after Hugo van der Goes and Bosch. Bruegel portrayed the concreteness of a rich peasant wedding feast exactly according to the decorum of custom.
The wedding table is set up in the barn. There are two sheaves fastened to the straw wall with a rake; these are raised as a sign of blessing and used here with exactly that symbolism. As they suggest, the preferred time for weddings was after the harvest. A paper crown is fastened to a drape hung on the wall behind the bride who, as tradition requires, is alone, wearing a small wreath on her loose hair, and

has eyes cast down and hands folded; she is not allowed to speak or eat, and sits at the middle of the table. In a high-backed chair sits the notary who is needed to draw up the marriage contract; he is wearing a beret and a fur-trimmed cloak. The Franciscan at his side is deep in conversation with the aristocratic owner of the dog. The bridegroom was once assumed to be the man who, like the master of the banquet at the wedding in Cana, is pouring the beer into mugs. But according to the custom, the bridegroom could not join the bride until the evening of the wedding (unless custom required that he run off with her beforehand). The finer clothing and the physiognomy are not those of a peasant and suggest that he is a servant of the gentleman, who has provided the wedding beer. Thus, as is the custom, the bridegroom is not to be found at the wedding. (This tradition is known to scholars of folklore, but the iconologists — wrongly — thought they smelt a rat.) Two bowls of creamy porridge are being served up, one coloured with saffron, these, too, are loaded with symbolism in reference to the harvest and traditionally served at the wedding meal. Two bagpipers, the man giving out the bread at the end of the table and the servants or the curious crowding the entrance complete the assemblage. Let us not leave out the child sitting on the floor in the foreground licking out of the bowl, wearing a hat with a festive peacock feather. Not a single one of these lifelike and individually characterized types is a caricature of the comical, coarse or plain ugly, and everything happens in unembellished but orderly realism. We can almost speak of Bruegel's Homeric poetics.
A spontaneity, which does not suggest an epic style of representation, accompanies every detail of the event. Definitive proof may be found in Bruegel's composition *The Visit to the Tenant Farm*, dating from about the same time, but in a small format (a version by Jan Bruegel the Elder is in the Vienna Gallery.) In this composition, which is given the guise of a genre painting, details from both large peasant pictures have been recycled. It is not easy to discover the underlying *genus humile*, as the borrowed details share an allegorical nature representing the mortal sins or a mockery of the peasants.
Let us spend a further word on the classical nature of the composition. It follows an older, animated, highly effective formal scheme (based so unobtrusively on reality that one perceives the form as natural), with the table set diagonally in the space (just as the scenes of the wedding at Cana, and the Last Supper, or Belshazzar's Feast are constructed). The "corner solution" is produced with artistic skill. The food bearers carrying the door covered with bowls and their link to the table provided by the person sitting arms outstretched like a hinge (there is not one foot too many!) are Bruegel's great, unforgettable formal inventions. The entire piece is exemplary for its clarity and legibility, at the same time maintaining a lively interest and peerless intelligence.

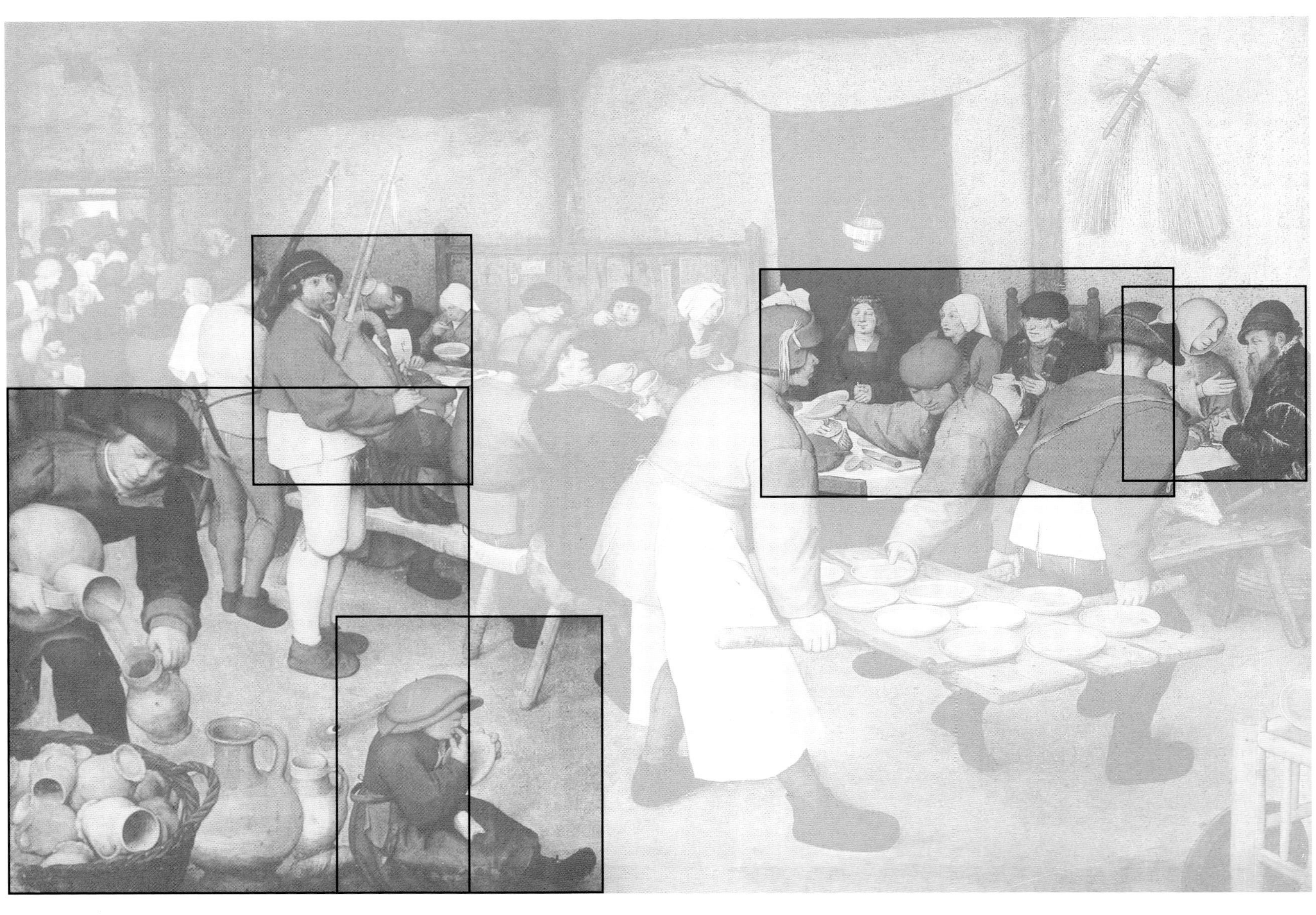

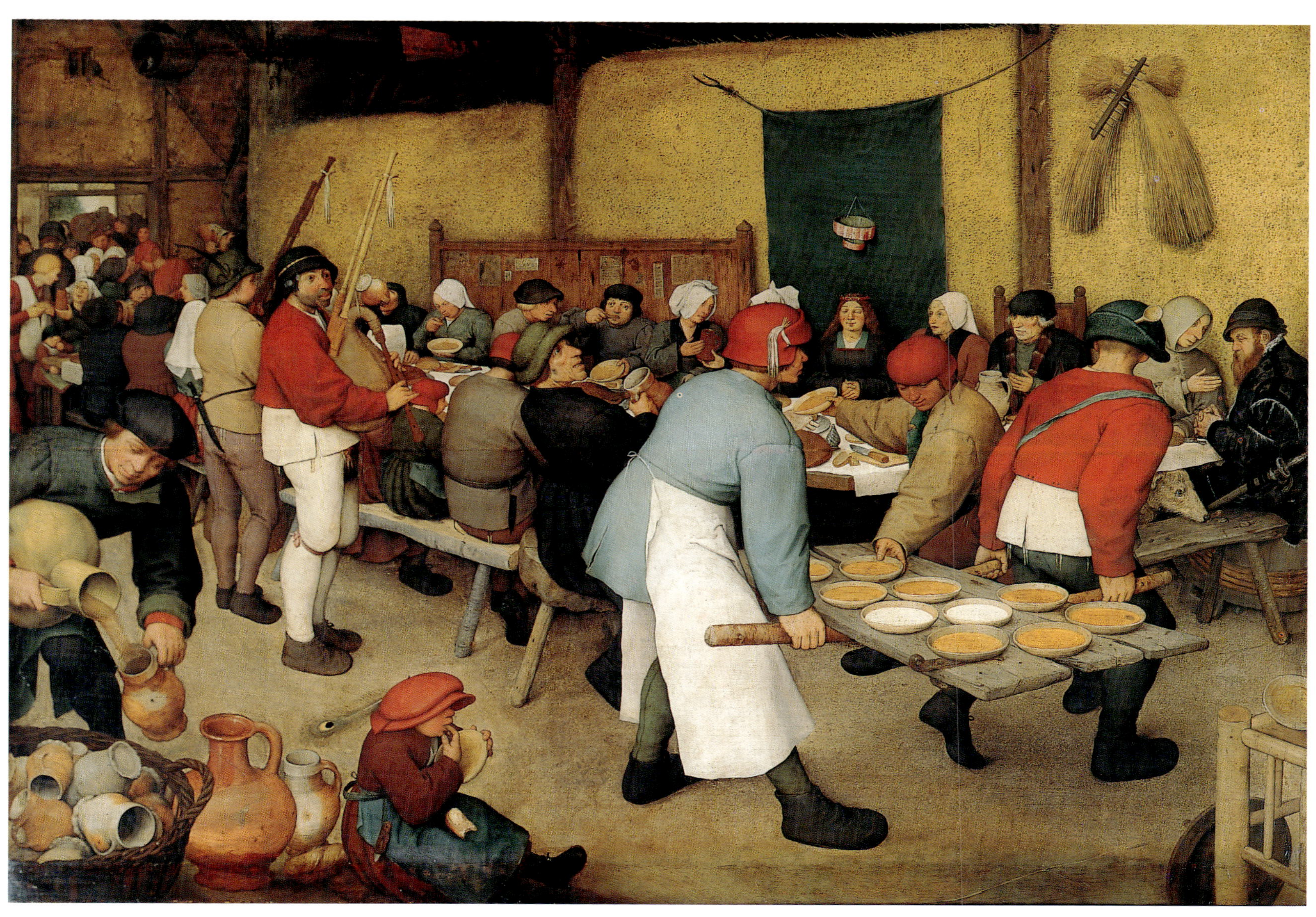

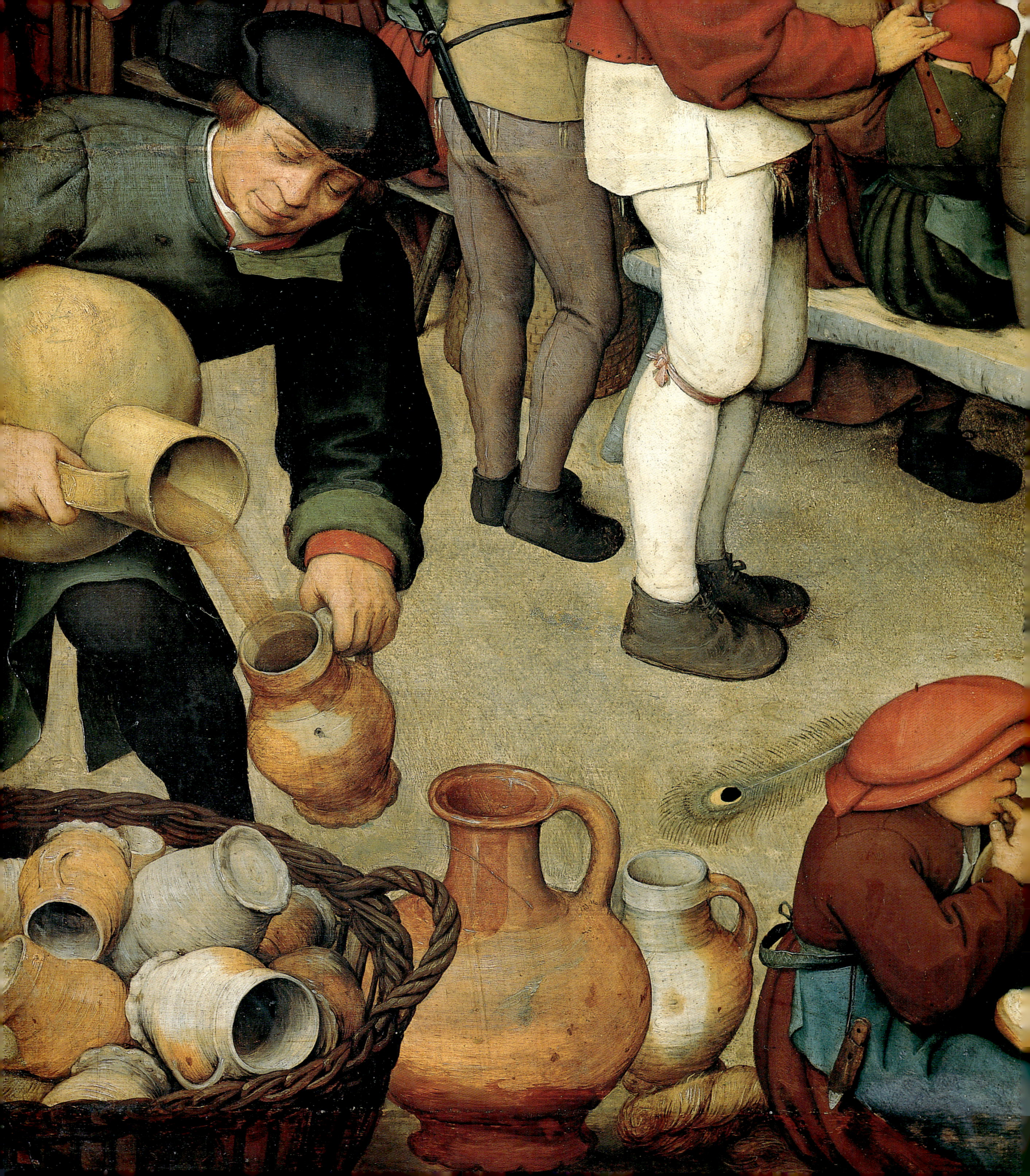

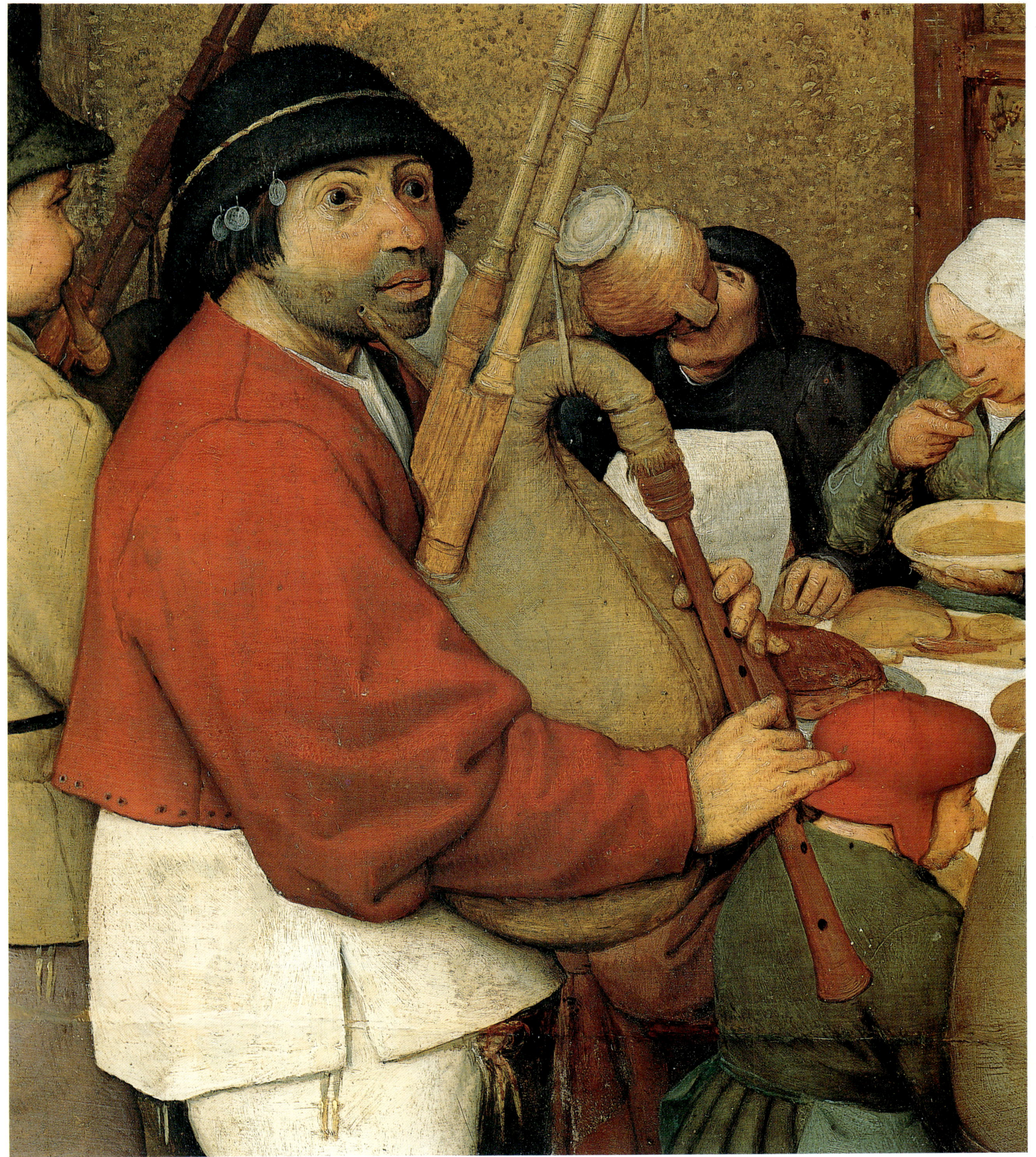

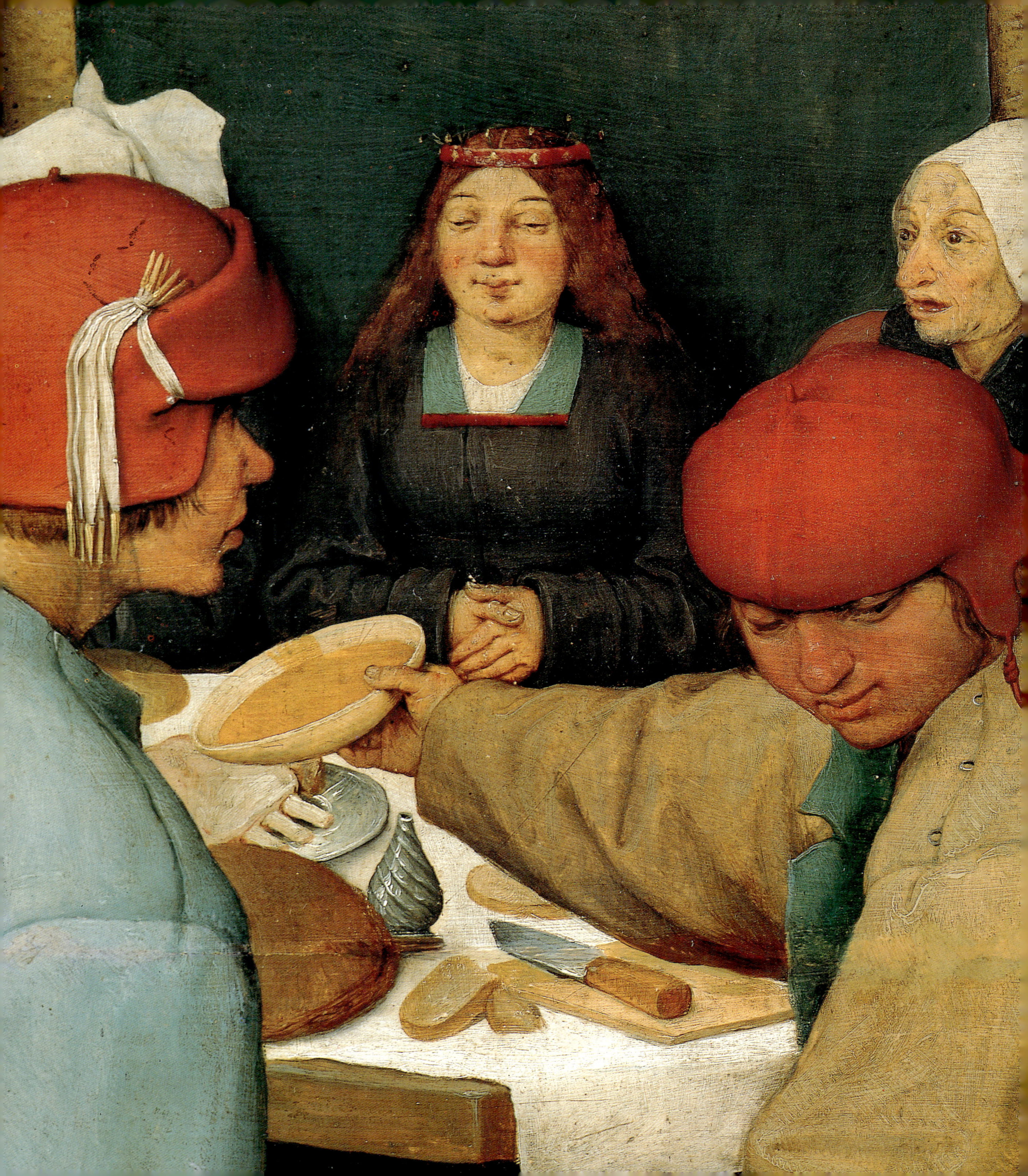

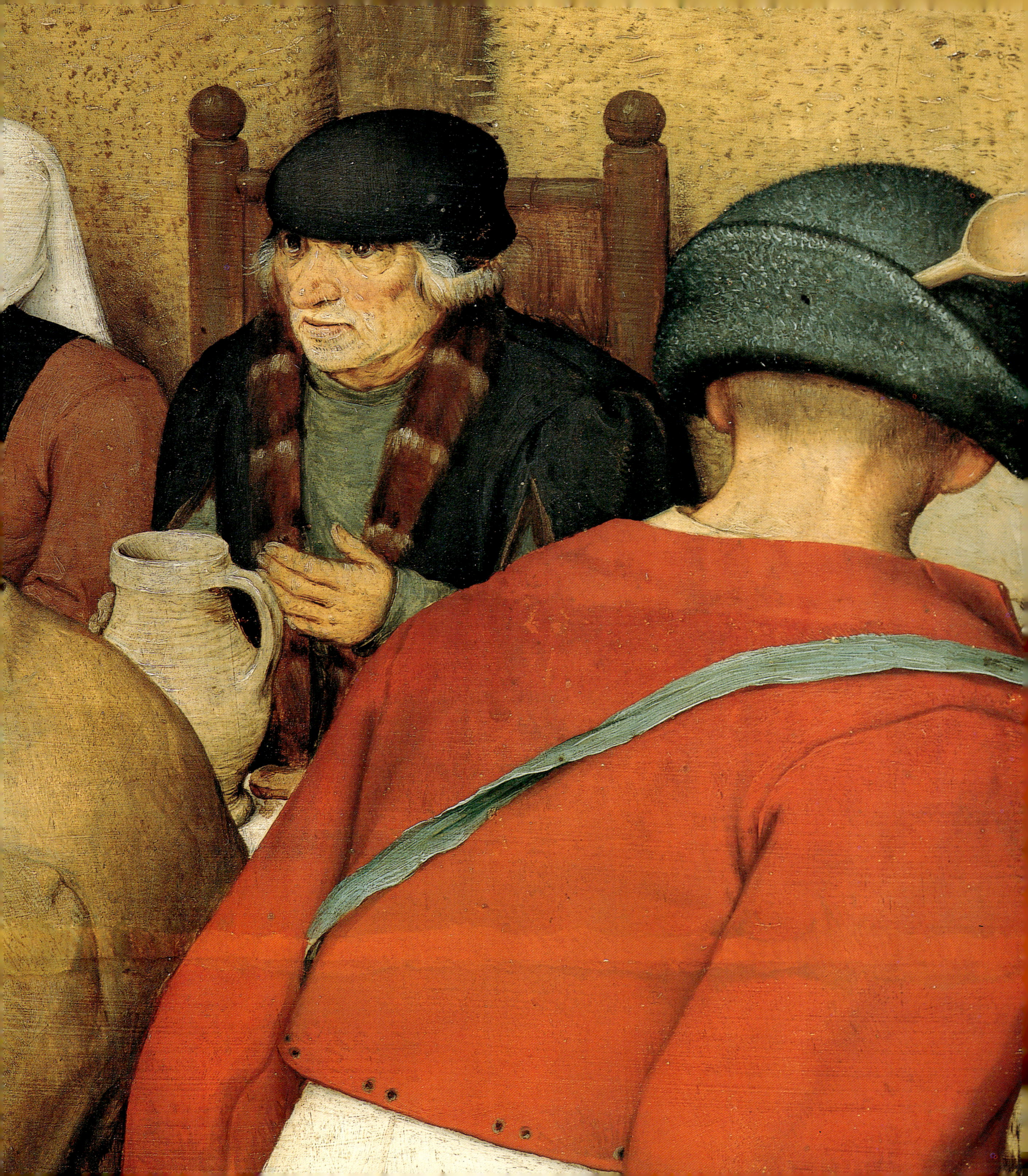

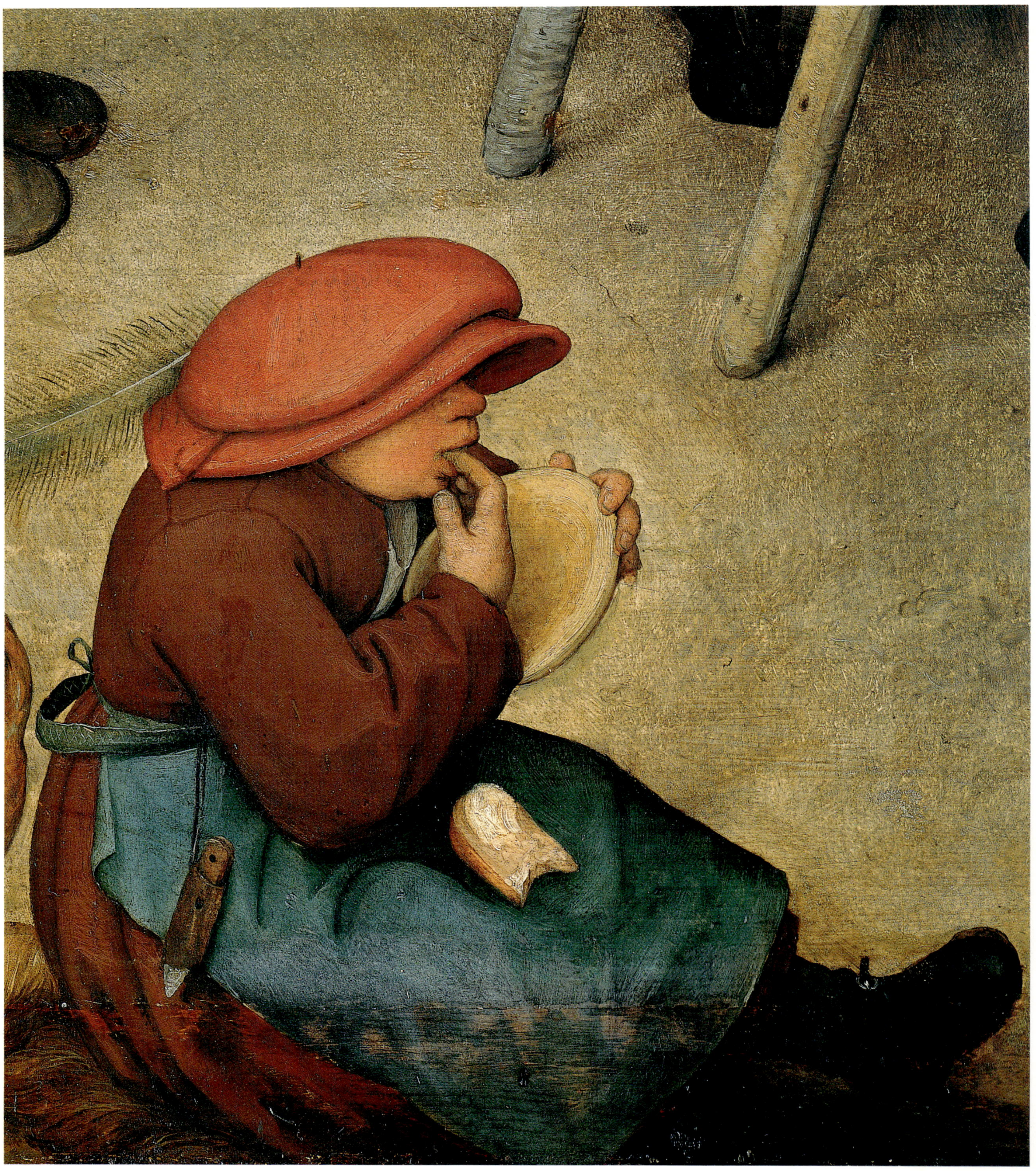

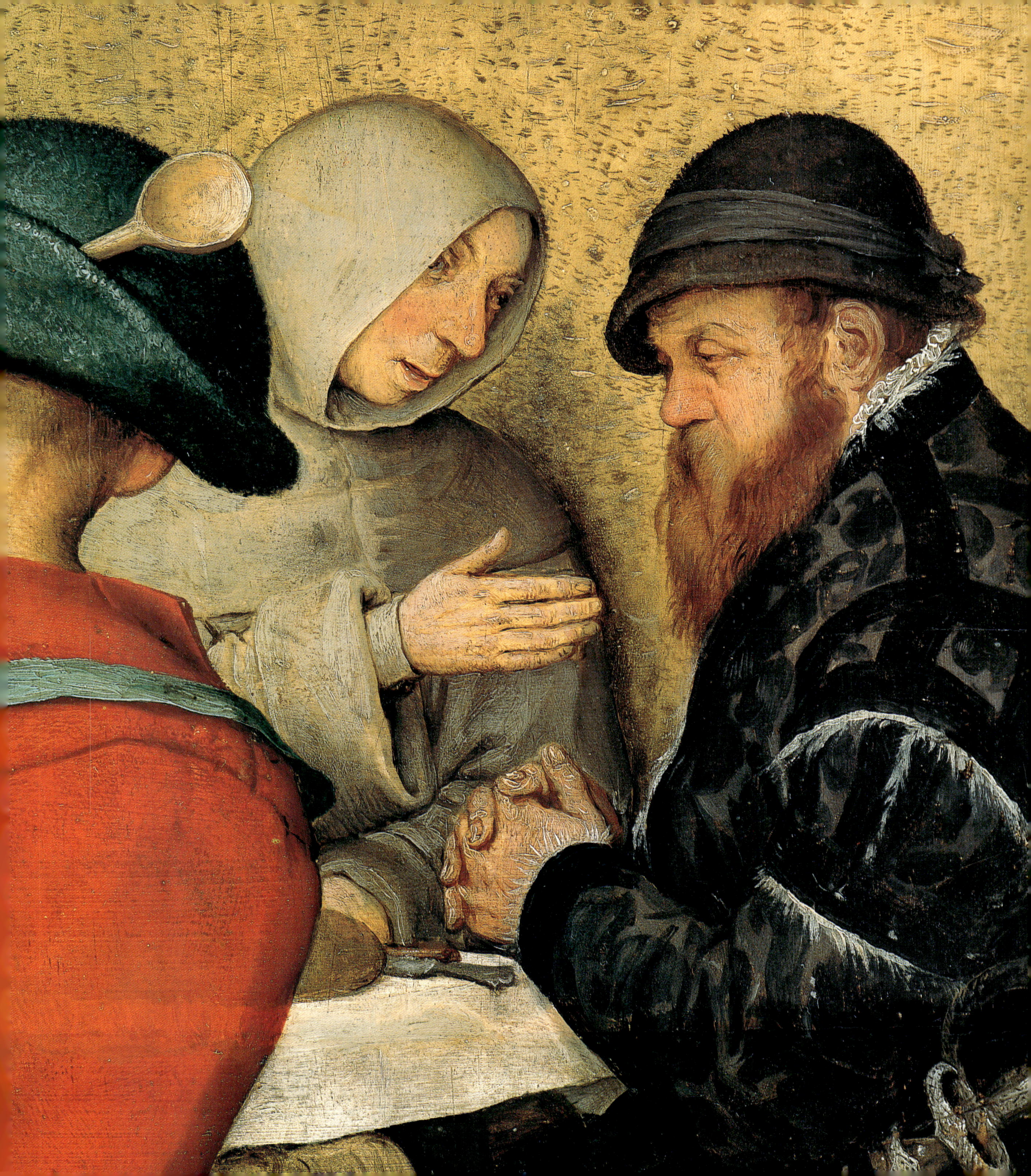

Peasant Dance (or Peasant Kermis)
Around 1568

Signed below right:
"BRVEGEL"
Woodcut 114 × 164 cm
Around 1610/19 in the Vienna
Gallery; Inv. No. 1059

The title "Peasant Dance" for the Vienna painting is not quite appropriate. For folk dancing is not shown here, as it is in a painting in Detroit (Bruegel never repeated himself, with one exception, which is not really an exception); rather, it is the opening of the village church fair with the presentation of the spring dance, traditionally performed by two couples. (Jan Bruegel the Elder's *Church Fair*, in the Vienna Gallery, shows the same scene likewise surrounded by spectators in the middle ground). The subject, still designated as "Bauernmusica" (Peasant Music) in the old inventories, is not so easily recognizable here as in the picture of the wedding feast, where it is immediately made completely comprehensible by the easy control of the space and diagonal perspectives. Here Bruegel has conspicuously dispensed with the didactic plan, the elevated view of an event (we will later investigate why), for the first and, as it was at the end of his life's work, only time. Standing on the same ground with his figures, the artist, and with him the observer, has the same view and horizon. What then appears from outside as a milling crowd can only be recognized from a closer perspective (like that of the couple in the foreground, hurrying over but not yet dancing at all) as the *res media*, the dramatic dance opening the church fair celebrations. It is not until after this performance that the man in the fool's costume will invite everyone else to enjoy the dancing. Thus, the couple in the foreground will make it in good time. A man is pulling his initially reluctant dancing partner out of the house flying the archers' guild flag. In the background the church fair stalls lie waiting, but in the foreground, where the space before the bagpipe player is "uncluttered", a frugal meal of bread, butter, salt and a small beer has already been begun at an improvised table outside of the inn. The festival has also begun for the children. Their emulation of the adults is probably their attempt to reach the first stage of the famous spring dance which demands some virtuosity. And the nasal tone of the bagpipes has lured yet another participant, the bareheaded, mute beggar or pilgrim entering the picture from the left. (His gesture attracts the attention of the man running by, thus creating a link between the two halves of the foreground.) The artist enjoyed such church fairs in the company of the businessman, Franckert, and it is all here, including the little burlesque at the table. (The scene is complicated but it should be explained for the benefit of the iconologists that three mortal sins have been illustrated here. Alongside *Gula* and *Ebrietas/Intemperantia* there also appears *Ira*: the figure with his hand outstretched, inviting the pilgrim to "share with him", has struck in the face the blind man — or is he a simpleton? — whose woeful lament arouses the woman's protectiveness. So there is no satire here, but humour!)

All in all, the kissing couple included, it is probably the most "respectable" of all church fair representations in Flemish painting. There is no trace of dissoluteness, everything is all quite respectable. Nevertheless scholars, embarrassed by the insipid nature of this "unfeeling" portrayal, wanted to highlight the naughty reputation peasant church fair celebrations generally enjoyed, proceeding with courageous intuition. The fact that Bruegel wanted to depict the happiest time for the church fair after the harvest with the blades of straw and nutshells strewn over the ground was simply overlooked. Yet the fact that the foot that, formally speaking, unites the crossed blades of straw and the ground necessarily tramples on them, just as the fact that the picture of the Madonna does not hang quite straight on the tree(!), is taken as a denouncement of the irreligiousness of peasant traditions. And so continues the catalogue of sins, analyzing them in minute detail!
It can, on the other hand, be established that the aim in this late work by the humorist is not only not satire, but not even mockery or laughter, or irony. To focus on catching traces of a deeper meaning and double meanings in the representation means missing out on the wonderful *ethos* by which objective realism is brought to the highest design. The picture possesses a full classical unity. And in the subject matter, theme and content are in harmony. The artistic form developed on the objective realism here reaches a purity and classical form that completely excludes every negative tendency as inferior subject bias. Bruegel's unique combination of a faithfulness obsessed with detail and love for the subject with a magnificently personal, fine and sharply stylizing formal art is shown here in its most mature and monumental form. It is art learned from the Renaissance experience, but which instead of ideal figurative beauty seeks to describe in a meaningful way the spontaneity, the non-classical barbarism of the indigenous race. It therefore stays with its national Flemish constant factor and so attains a classicism, perceived as the highest level of artistically developed form. (By the way, Bruegel is no Mannerist here either, and his form does not degenerate into the expressive. It is again individually stylized in harmony with the virtue of objective accuracy.) One may well ask why Bruegel has used the central perspective with the vanishing point at eye level only in this peasant picture, one of his last works. It would be legitimate to assume that the acceptance of all forms and aspects of human life, which Bruegel had so often shown from above, is the symbolic reason for this device of putting himself "on the same level". If this is the case, then it would be the most eloquent testimony of a humanity that has rejected, indeed abolished all "humanist" irony and detachment.

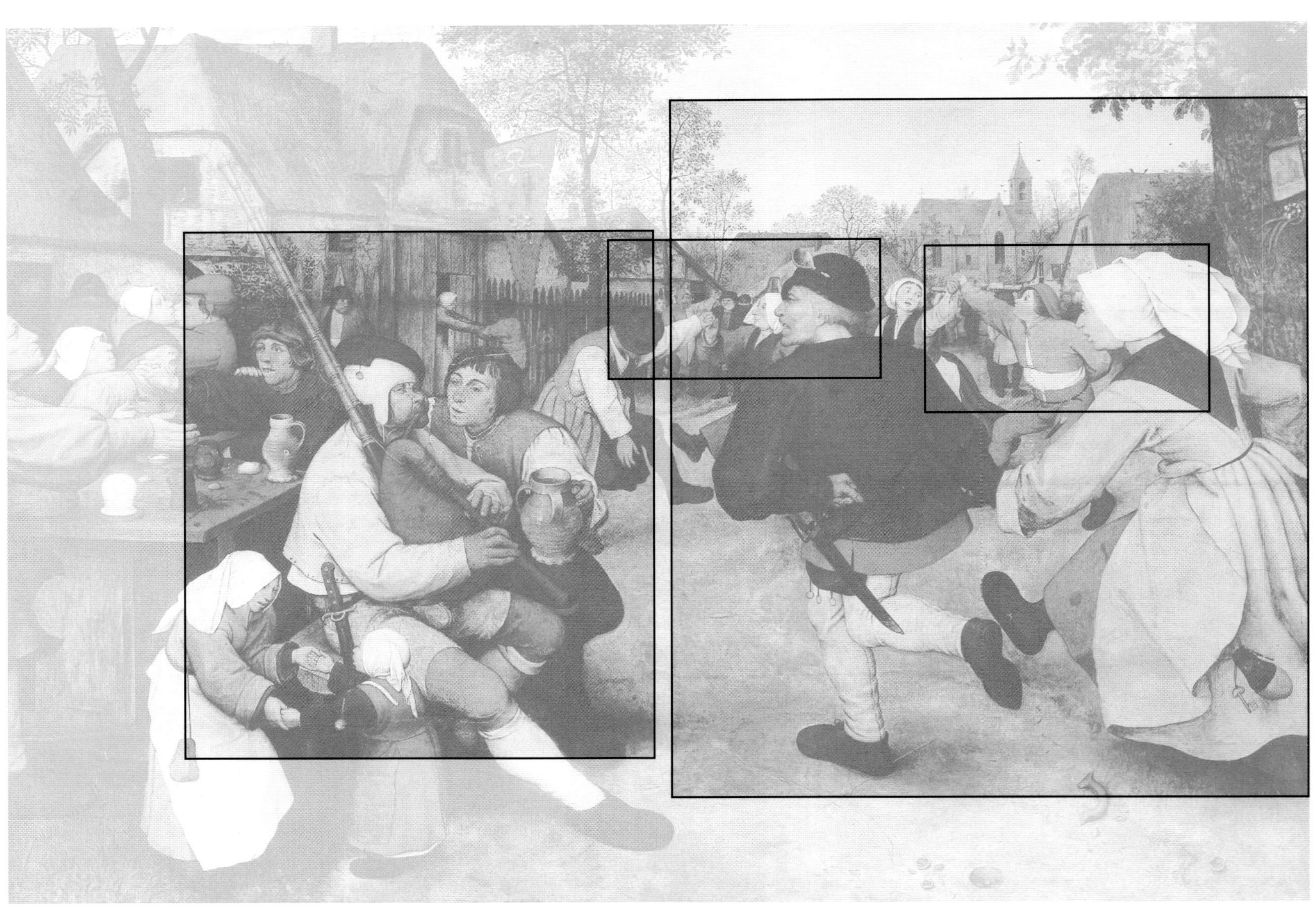

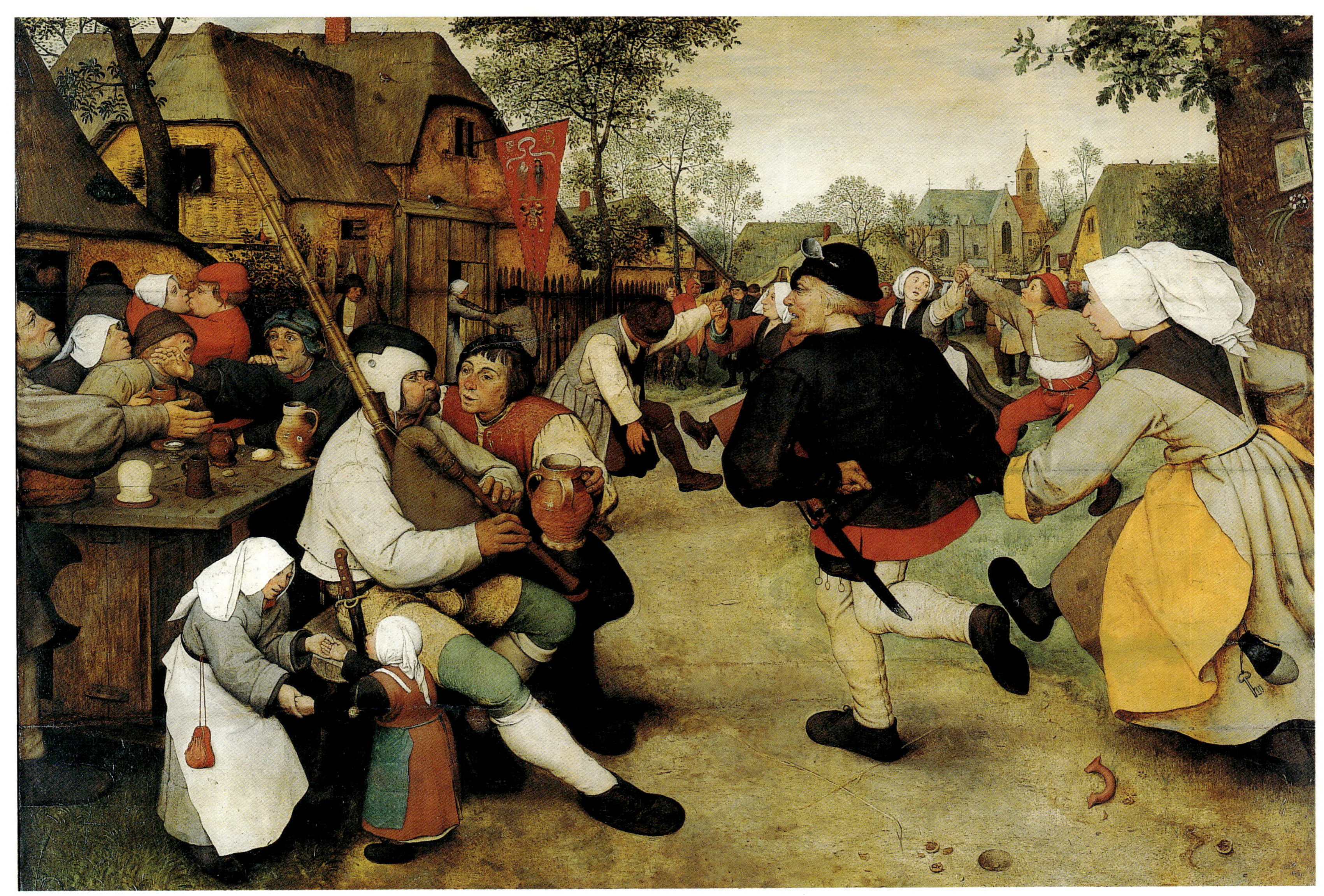

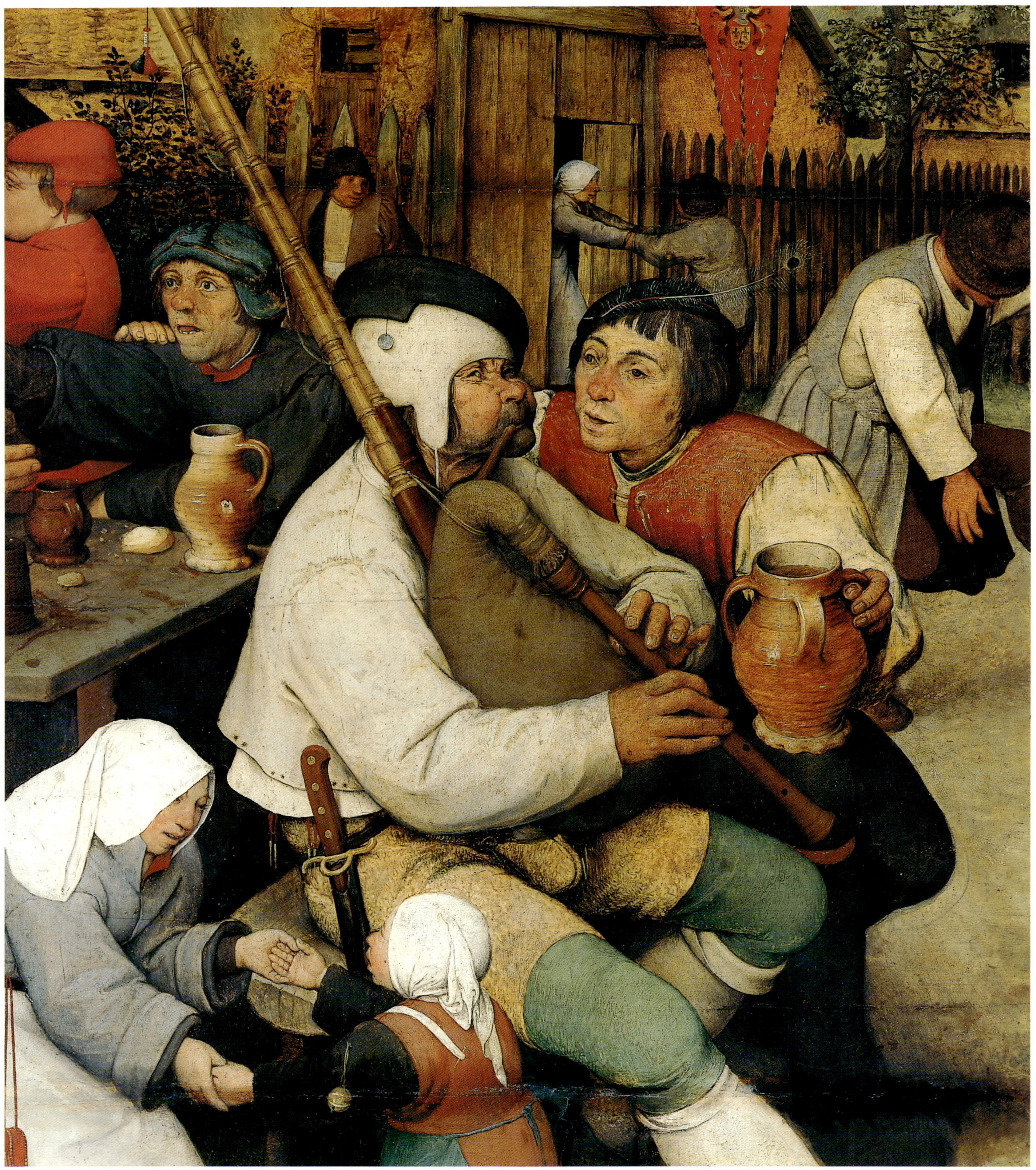

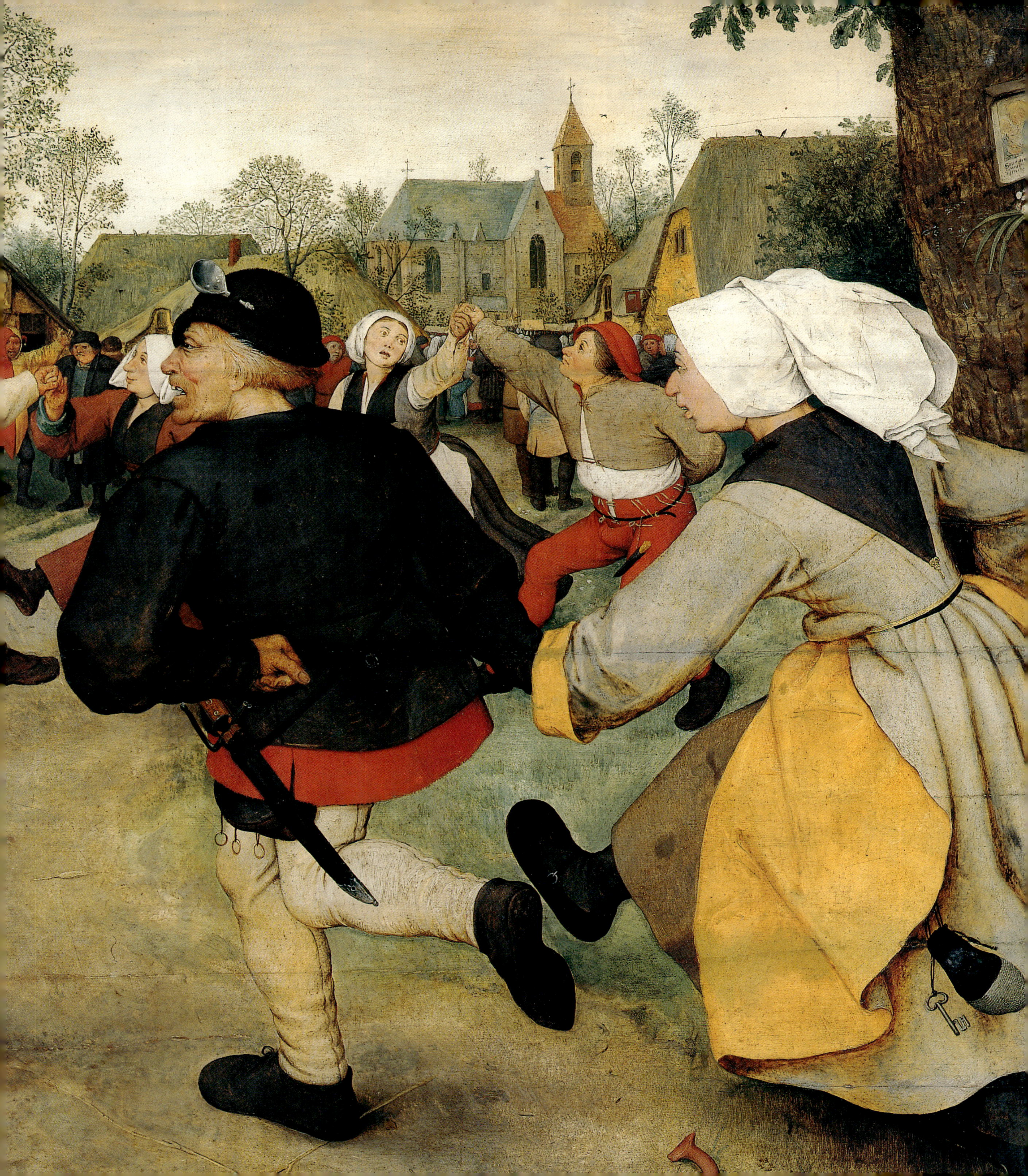

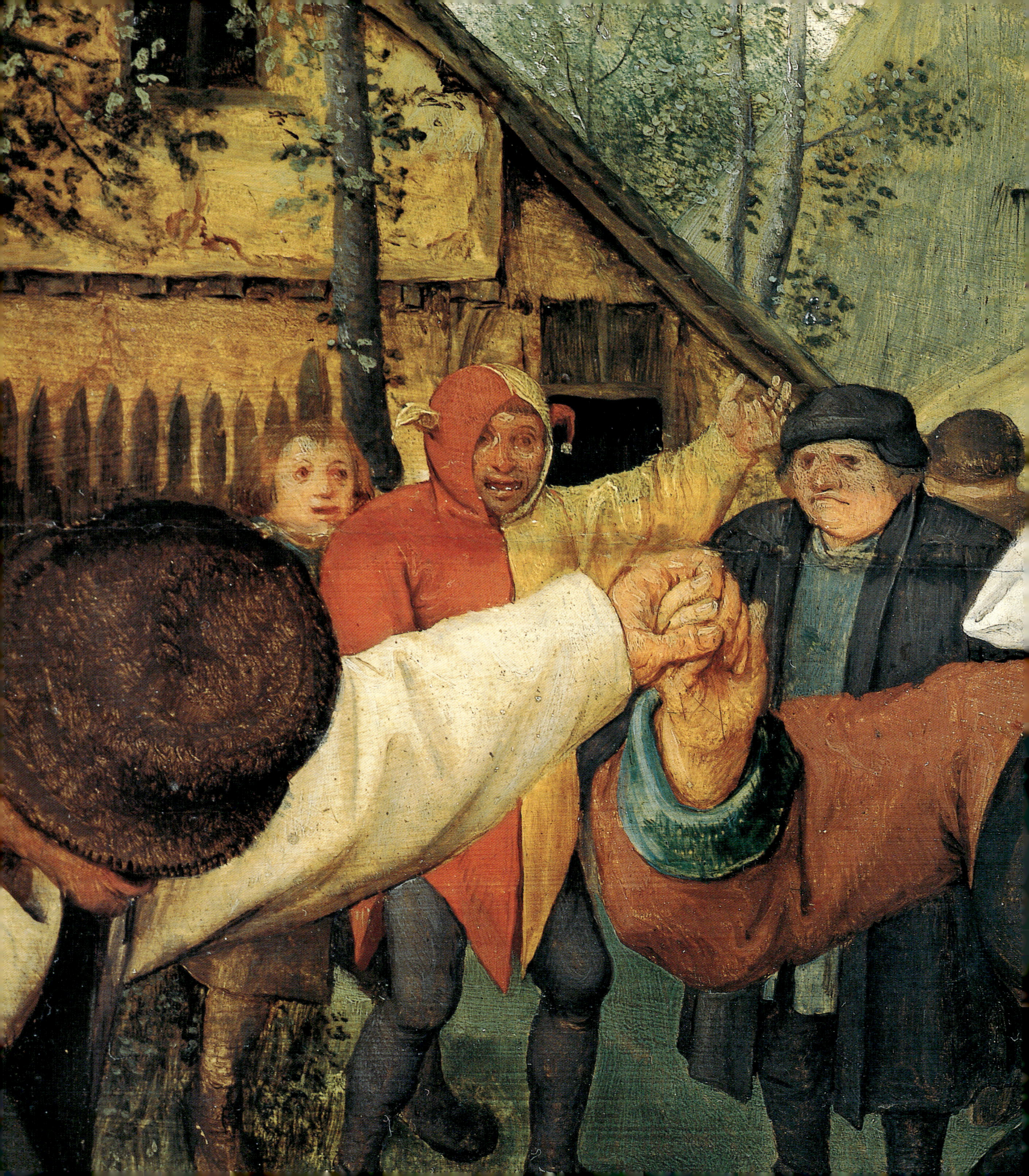

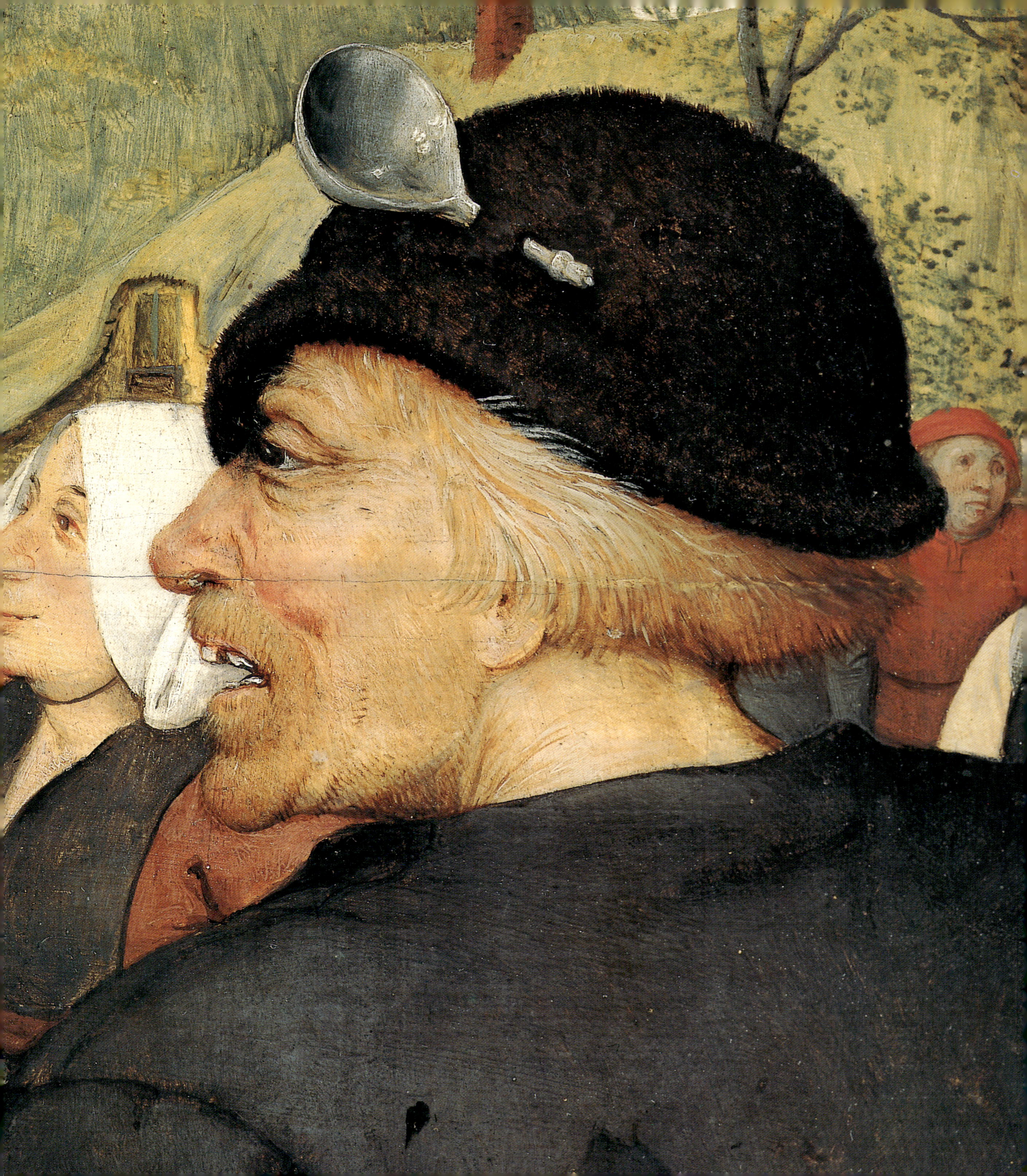

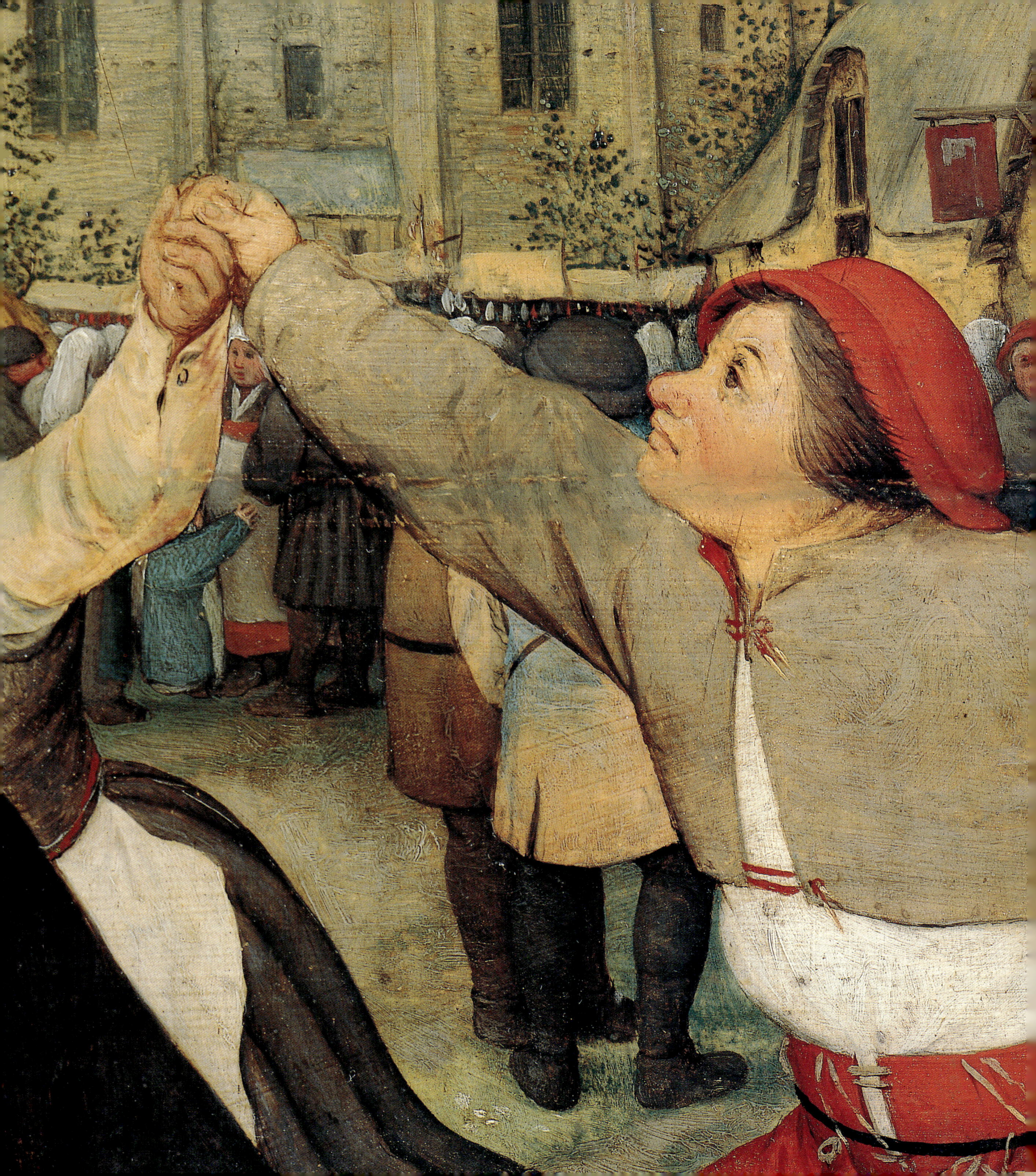

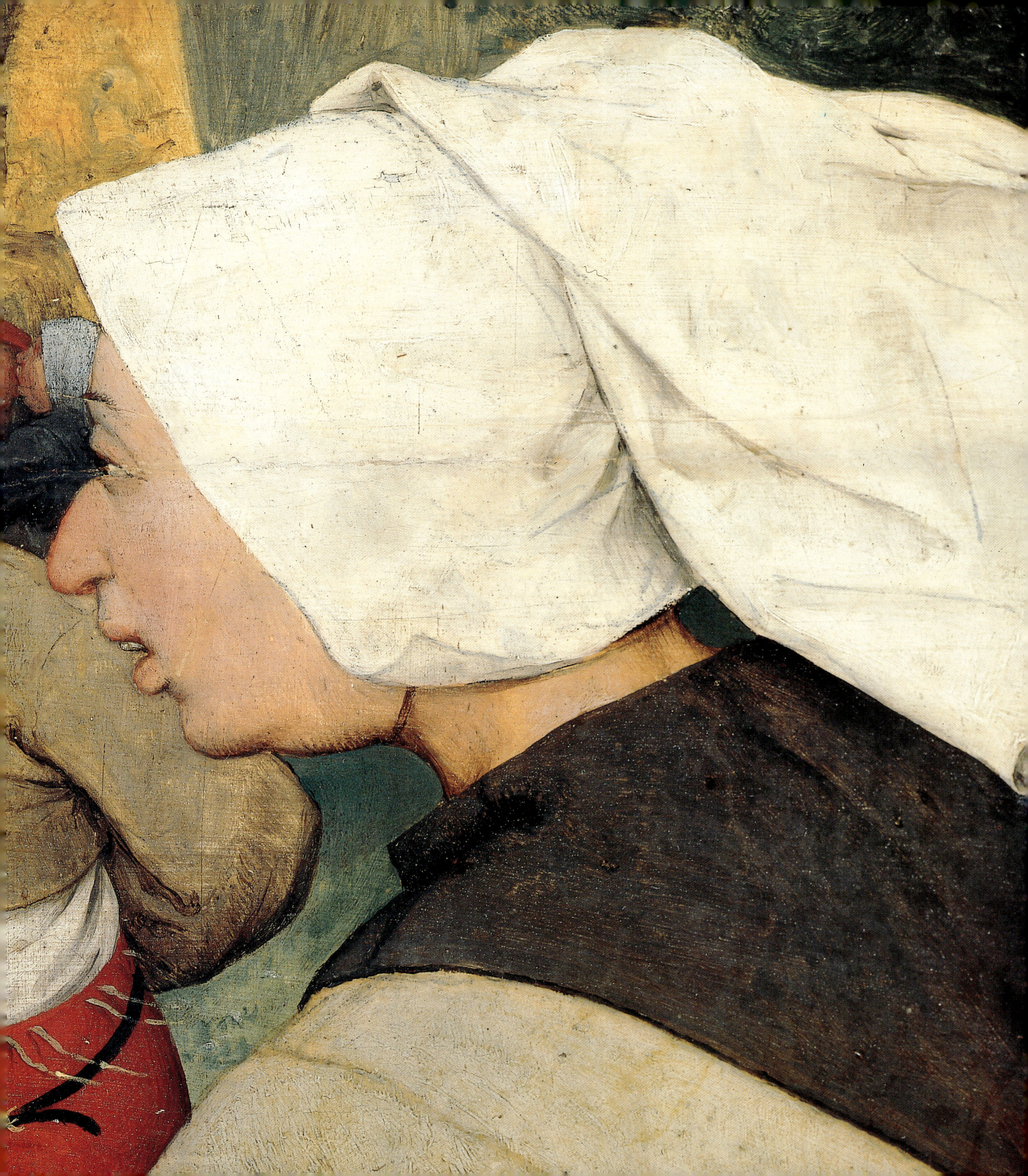

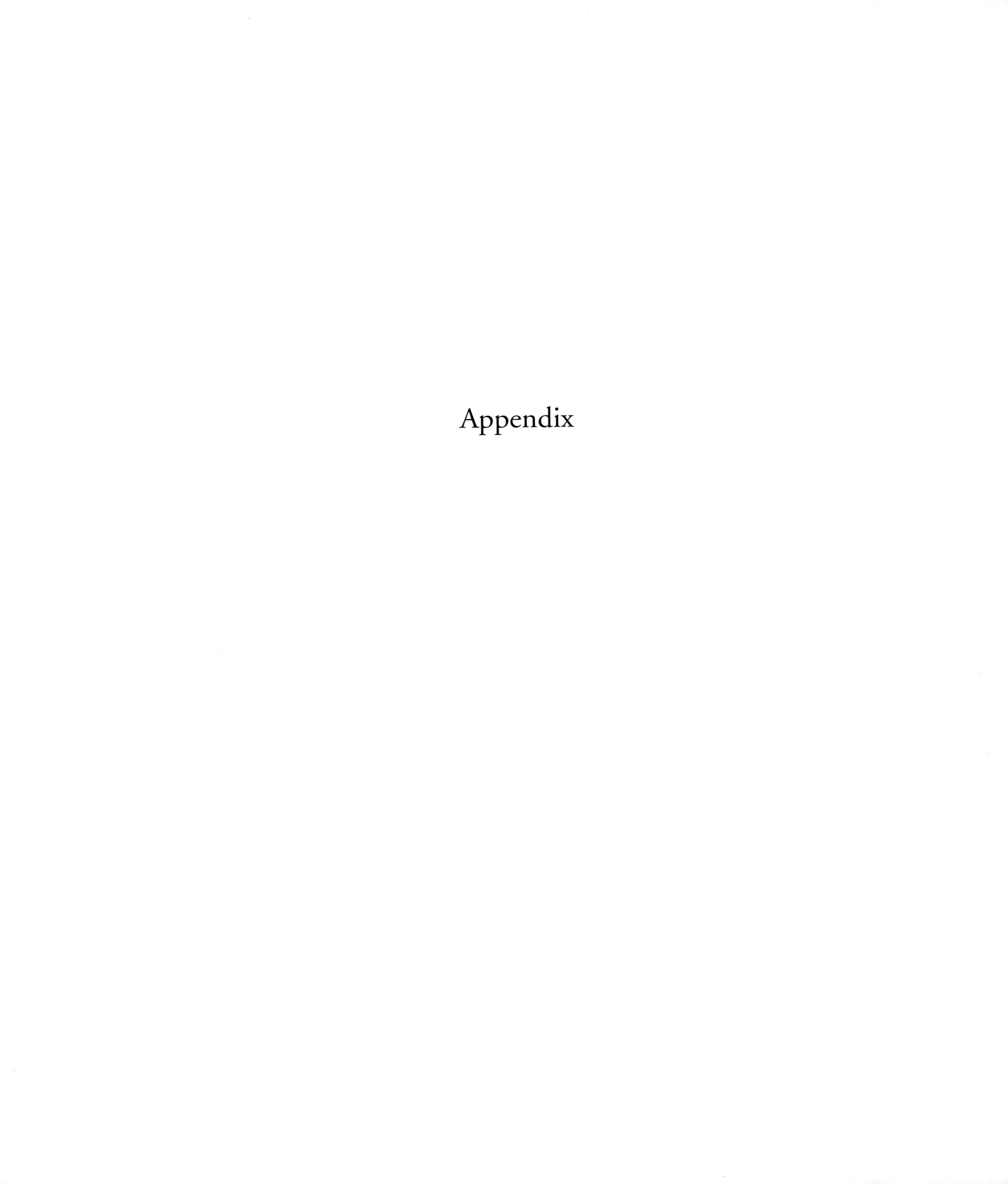

Appendix

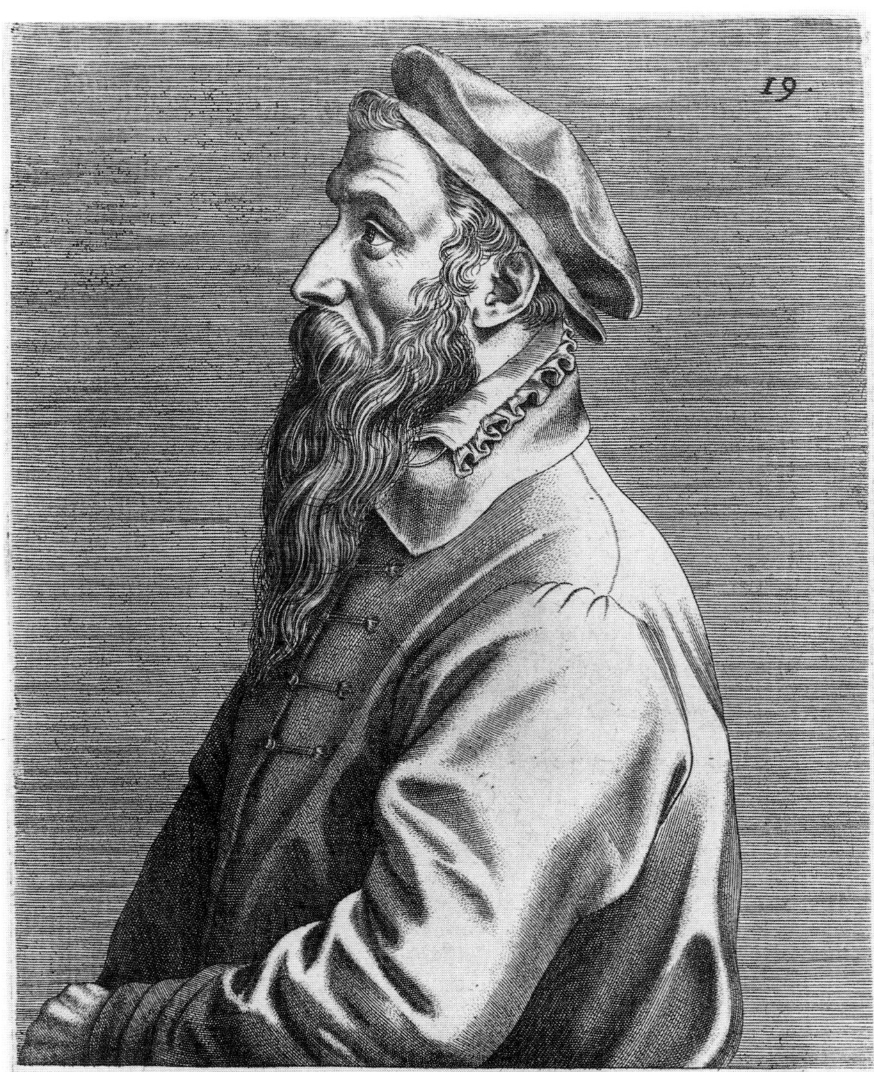

Portrait of Pieter Bruegel the Elder by H. Hondius, in: *Pictorum aliquot celebrium Germaniae inferioris effigies,* 1572

Biography of Pieter Bruegel the Elder

Around 1526/30
Birth of Pieter Bruegel the Elder. His biographer, Karel van Mander, reports in his *Schilderboek* of 1604 that Bruegel was born the son of a simple peasant in a village by the name of Brueghel close to Breda, a detail which cannot, of course, be verified. L. Guicciardini mentions "Pietro Brueghel di Breda" in the *Descrittione di tutti i Paesi Bassi.*
Van Mander names the Romanist Pieter Coecke van Aelst (c. 1550), then working in Antwerp and from 1554 in Brussels, as Bruegel's teacher, whose style, however, left no trace in Bruegel's art. Instead it was Joachim Patinir, Herri met de Bles, Matthys Cock and the so-called "Brunswick Monogrammist" who could be identified with Jan van Amstel, the brother-in-law of Pieter Coecke van Aelst who influenced his work.
1550/51
Bruegel's documented work in the workshop of Claude Dorizi in Mecheln and, to be precise, in connection with the execution of a retable for the town's glove makers' guild: Pieter Baltens paints the altar's centre piece, Bruegel portrays St. Gommarius and St. Rombaut on the outer wings in grisaille.
1551
Bruegel joins the Antwerp Guild of Painters and becomes free master of his craft outside his guild.
The approximate date of Bruegel's birth can be deduced from the fact that this usually happened between the ages of 21 and 25 years.
1552
The Italian journey also mentioned by van Mander begins, the route of which can be reconstructed from drawings and engravings. Bruegel travels via Lyon, Rome, Naples and Reggio di Calabria to Messina. The geographer Abraham Ortelius accompanies him, possibly together with the Antwerp painter, Marten de Vos. In 1552 two of Bruegel's earliest dated works known to us, two landscapes, appear (in Paris and Berlin).
1553
It can be proved that Bruegel was in Rome by two etchings by Joris Hoefnagel marked "Petrus Bruegel Fecit Romae Ao 1553". A series of (now missing) works by Bruegel is in the possession of the miniaturist Giulio Clovio, whom the artist got to know there. The earliest of Bruegel's signed and dated paintings known to us emerges: *Christ Appears to the Apostles at Lake Tiberias* (New York, in private ownership).
Around 1554/55
Returns from Italy to Antwerp. Numerous drawings with mountainous motifs, later used in some paintings, are evidence of his route over the Alps.
1555 onwards
The series of copper engravings of the *Great Landscape Sequence* appears as the first of a great number of prints done to Bruegel's drafts in the Antwerp printing works, "To the Four Winds", owned by Hieronymus Cock; the works are very distinguished from an artistic and culturally historical point of view.
1556 onwards
Hieronymus Cock publishes a series of engravings after Bruegel's drawings in which themed references to the art of Hieronymus Bosch are quite clearly identifiable, as in the *Temptation of St. Anthony.* Reminiscences of his work appear much more frequently in Bruegel's prints than in his paintings (in the painting, for example of *Mad Meg* in Antwerp and in the *Fall of the Rebellious Angel* in Brussels).
1559
The paintings of *The Flemish Proverbs* (Berlin) and *The Battle between Carnival and Lent* (Vienna) appear. Together with *Children's Games* (Vienna) dated 1560, they form a group of figuratively rich pictures, for which a profusion of details is characteristic (particularly interesting from a culturally historical point of view), shown scattered on a virtually "opened up" perspective plane with a raised horizon.
1559 onwards
Bruegel changes his signature from "Brueghel" in Gothic lowercase to "BRVEGEL" in Roman uppercase, probably in order to emphasize the humanist claim of his art.

1559/60
The sequence of the *Seven Deadly Sins* engraved by Philipp Galle after Bruegel's drawings is published by Hieronymus Cock.
1562
The painting of *The Suicide of Saul* (Vienna) appears. Along with the *Tower of Babel* of 1563 (likewise in Vienna), it is one of the few pictures by Bruegel with a subject from the Old Testament.
1563
Bruegel marries Maryken, the daughter of his teacher, Pieter Coecke van Aelst, in Notre-Dame-de-la-Chapelle in Brussels, of whom van Mander reports that Bruegel carried her as a child in his arms. Bruegel moves to Brussels.
1564
Christ Carrying the Cross (Vienna) appears during this year. In contrast to his other paintings, Bruegel follows an existing pictorial tradition here (Herri met de Bles, Pieter Aertsen, Jan van Amstel).
1564/65
Birth of Bruegel's first son, Pieter (Pieter Bruegel the Younger), who will continue the family's artistic tradition.
1565
Bruegel is mentioned in two letters by the Bolognese geographer, Scipio Fabius, to his Antwerp colleague, Abraham Ortelius.
The *Seasons* appear. Those surviving are *The Gloomy Day* (Vienna), *Haymaking* (Nelahozeves, Tchechen), *The Corn Harvest* (New York), *Return of the Herd* (Vienna) and *The Hunters in the Snow* (Vienna).
1566
The humanistically trained Antwerp businessman, Nicolas Jongelinck, stands surety to the City of Antwerp for another businessman.
On the list of his possessions, which he pledges as a guarantee, are 16 paintings by Pieter Bruegel, including *The Twelve Months*, a *Tower of Babel* and a *Christ Carrying the Cross*. The surety is then evidently forfeited to the City, which keeps the pictures. In 1594 *The Twelve Months* are cited as a gift to Archduke Ernst.
1567
Bruegel paints the *Conversion of Paul* (Vienna). In this picture, as in the *Suicide of Saul* (likewise in Vienna), recollections of Bruegel crossing the Alps are unmistakable.
1568
Birth of Bruegel's second son, Jan, who later gains fame as the "Flower Brueghel" or "Velvet Brueghel" particularly in the area of still life painting. *The Peasant and the Nest Robber* by Pieter Bruegel the Elder appears this year. The monumental main figure, a curious quotation after Michelangelo, probably represents an ironic allusion, which can be interpreted in relation to the tense contrast between the "classical" Italian and the "non-classical" Flemish art as being constantly reformulated by the art theoreticians of the time.
Around 1568
The Peasant Wedding Feast and *The Peasant Wedding Dance* (both in Vienna) are two examples of the stylistic change from paintings rich in detail around 1559/60 to later works in which few large figures define the picture. They are together nothing short of exemplary of the peasant genre which van Mander places at the very bottom of the hierarchy of genres and which thematically and stylistically (through an unadorned portrayal of reality) only serves to make the towndweller laugh (hence the name "Pieter the Comical" or "Peasant Bruegel" which for a long time determined how Bruegel was received).
1569
An archive report of January 1569 states that the Spanish soldiers in the house of "Peeteren van Breugel" are to withdraw and that Bruegel is to receive financial compensation. According to van Mander, he asks his wife to burn some of the drawings with a satirical content, perhaps in order to spare her any difficulties after his death.
Bruegel dies in September 1569 in Brussels and is buried in Notre-Dame-de-la-Chapelle.

The Life of the Outstanding Painter, Pieter Breughel of Breughel*

Karel van Mander

Nature struck lucky with her man who was to capture her again for his part most happily when she chose him who affords our Netherlands lasting fame, the witty and humorous Pieter Breughel, from the peasants of an unknown Brabant village and turned him into a painter so that he could depict peasants with the brush.

He was born not far from Breda in a village by the name of Breughel, the name of which he took and left behind to his descendants. He learnt to paint with Pieter Koeck van Aelst, whose daughter, whom he had often carried in his arms when she was small when staying with Pieter, he later married. From there he went to work with Hieronymus Kock and travelled to France and from there to Italy.

He had worked a great deal in the manner of Hieronymus Bosch and also painted many nightmarish pictures and humorous scenes, on account of which he was called by many Pieter the Comical. There are, indeed, few of his pictures which the observer can seriously look at without laughing, and however taciturn and grumpy he may be, he must at least smile. On his travels he drew so many lifelike vedutas that it is said that when he was in the Alps he swallowed up all the mountains and rocks and spewed them out again as painted epics, so close was he able to get to nature in this and other respects. He took up residence in Antwerp and there entered the Guild of Painters in the year of our Lord 1551.

He worked a great deal for a businessman by the name of Hans Franckert, a splendid fellow who liked to associate with Breughel and met with him socially on a daily basis. With this Franckert Breughel frequently went out amongst the peasants whenever there was a *Kirmes* (feast) or wedding. They would go disguised as peasants and took gifts just like the other guests, professing to be relations of the bride or groom. It gave Breughel great pleasure to observe the way in which the peasants ate, drank, danced, frolicked, courted and engaged in other humorous acts, ingenuous moments which he understood how to depict very prettily and comically with colour as well as with water and oils. He was able to handle both very well. He also understood above all how to paint these peasant men and women in the costume of the *Kampine* and other regions and how best to characterize the coarse peasant manners in dancing, walking, standing and other movements. He was wonderfully resolute in arranging his figures and drew very cleanly and prettily with the quill, especially many small vedutas.

When he was still living in Antwerp, he kept house with a house maid, whom he would gladly have married if he had not disapproved of her constant lying. He agreed with her that he would notch up all the lies on a stick (he chose a very long one for this purpose), and if the stick was full within a certain time, the wedding would be completely off, which came true in quite a short time.

Finally, when Pieter Koeck's widow was then living in Brussels, he fell in love with her daughter, whom he, as already mentioned, had frequently carried in his arms, and took her as his wife. The mother therefore demanded that he should leave Antwerp and move to Brussels so that he would get away from the other girl and forget her. And so it happened.

He was a very calm and understanding man of few words, but was very funny in company and loved to scare people, even his own companions, with hubbub and uproar, which he created.

Some of his most important works are now in the Emperor's possession, in particular a large picture representing the Tower of Babel, full of lovely detail. You can see into the tower from above. A picture also of the same subject, but smaller; two further pictures representing *Christ Carrying the Cross* make a very convincing impression, enlivened here and there with comical scenes. Also, a slaughter of the innocents with many scenes taken from reality, which I have described at another point, how a whole family is pleading for a peasant child, whom one of the murderous soldiers has seized to kill, as the despairing mother swoons, and other vividly depicted events. Finally, a *Conversion of Paul* in a very beautiful mountainous landscape. It would be difficult to list all that he has created in nightmarish pictures,

representations of hell, peasant scenes and the like. He has also painted a *Temptation of Christ*. The proceedings take place here in an Alpine landscape, and towns and fields can be seen from above in many places through splits in the clouds; also a tolle Griet (Mad Meg), plundering before Hell. She has quite a vacant stare and is strangely dressed in the Scottish manner. I believe that these and other pictures are likewise in the Emperor's possession.
A very beautiful peasant wedding feast painted in oil can be seen at the art lovers Mr Hermann Pilgrim's, in Amsterdam. The faces and other fleshy parts of the peasants are yellow and brown from sunburn, and their skin is portrayed as unsightly, quite different to that of town dwellers. Breughel has also painted a *Battle between Carnival and Lent*, a further picture showing how every means is turned against death, a further one showing all kinds of childrens games, and further innumerable other evocative small pictures.
Two water colours on canvas can also be seen at the art lover, Mr Willem Jacobsz, at the New Church in Amsterdam, in particular a *Peasant Kirmes* and a *Peasant Wedding Feast*, which show many comic figures and characterize superbly the peculiar features of the peasants. In a scene showing the bride being given gifts, an old peasant can also be seen with a small bag around his neck, busy counting money in his hands. These are quite outstanding pictures.
The masters of Brussels had commissioned him shortly before his death to depict the excavation of the Brussels-Antwerp canal in a few pictures. This, however, was never fulfilled due to his death. Many of his strangely devised evocative compositions are engraved in copper. He had his wife burn a large quantity of finely and cleanly drawn, inscribed satires, parts of which were especially biting and derisive, when he was mortally ill, either because he had regrets about them, or because he was afraid that something unpleasant could happen to his wife because of them. He left a picture to her in his will with a magpie on a gallows. With the magpie he intended the scandalmongers whom he surrendered to the gallows. He had also painted a *Triumph of Truth*, a picture which in his words was the best he had ever painted.
He left behind two sons, who are likewise good painters. One of them by the name of Pieter learnt with Gillis van Conincxloo and paints lifelike portraits. Jan, after he had learnt to paint water colours at his grandmother's, the widow of Pieter Koeck van Aelst, went to a certain Pieter Goetkindt, at whose home many beautiful things could be seen. He learnt to paint in oil there. He later travelled to Cologne and from there to Italy. He gained greatest attention with his small landscapes with tiny figures which he painted in quite a wonderful way.
Lampsonius spoke of Breughel in the following terms, where he asks:
Who is this new Hieronymus Bosch, reborn to the world, who brings back to life the brilliant flights of fantasy of his master with brush and style, that he even surpasses his model? Glory to you, Pieter, as Your Art is also glorious, like the Old Masters You deserve unqualified praise no less than all the other artists and, of course, for the fact that Your Painting is crammed with tasteful wit.

* From Karel van Mander, *Het Schilderboeck*, translated by Müller 1997, 42–44.

Index of the works of Pieter Bruegel the Elder

Alexander Wied

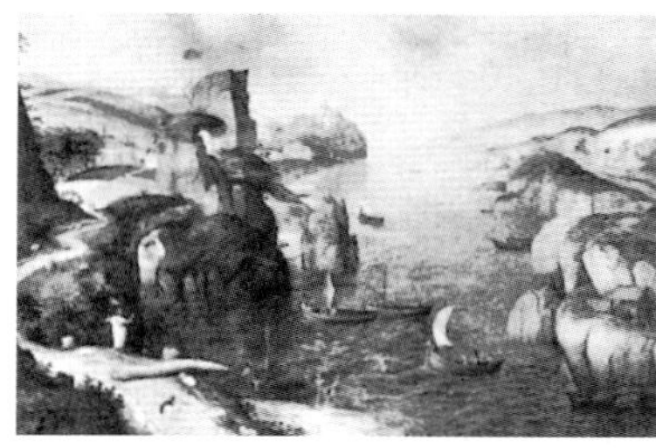

1
Christ appears to the Apostles at the Lake of Tiberias, 1553
Signed "P. BRVEGHEL 1553"
Oil/Wood, 67 × 100 cm
New York, Privately owned

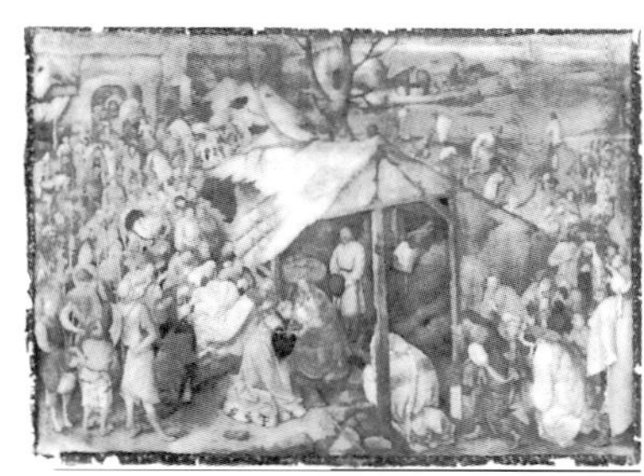

2
Adoration of the Magi, Around 1556
Tempera/Canvas, 115.5 × 163 cm
Brussels, Musées Royaux des Beaux-Arts

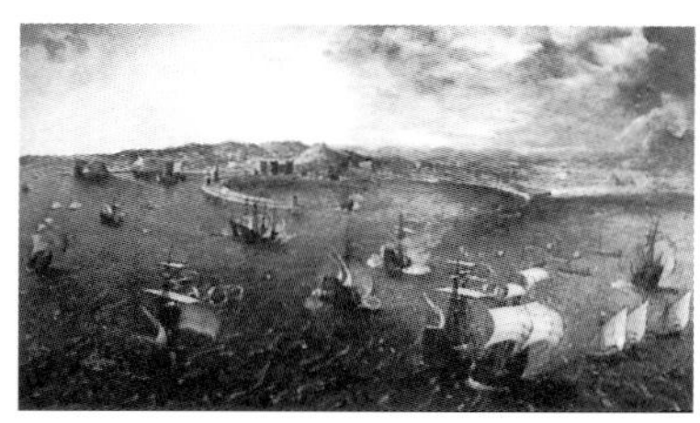

3
View of the Bay of Naples
Around 1556
Oil/Wood, 39.8 × 69.5 cm
Rome, Galleria Doria Pamphili

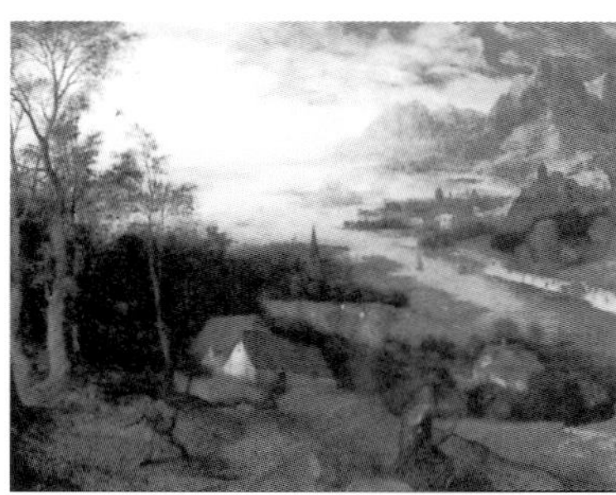

4
Landscape with the Parable of the Sower, 1557
Signed: "...VEGHEL 1557"
Oil/Wood, 74 × 102 cm
San Diego (California), Timken Art Gallery

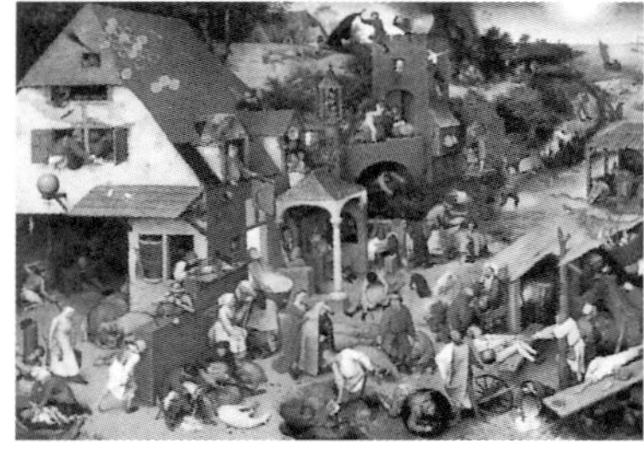

5
Netherlandish Proverbs, 1559
Signed.: "BRVEGEL 1559"
Oil/Wood, 117 × 163 cm
Berlin-Dahlem, Staatliche Museen

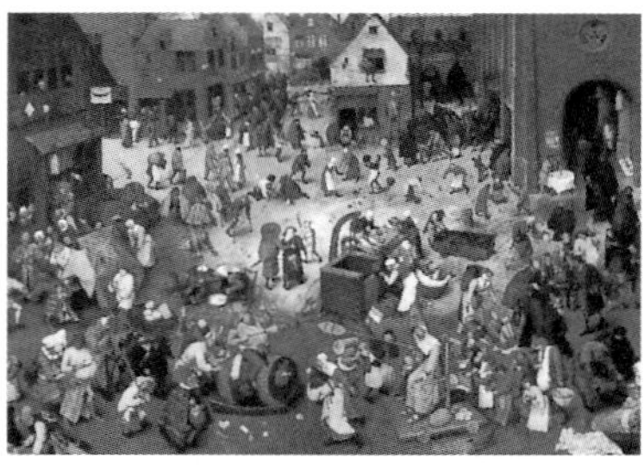

6
Battle between Carnival and Lent, 1559
Signed: "BRVEGEL 1559"
Oil/Wood, 118 × 164.5 cm
Vienna, Kunsthistorisches Museum

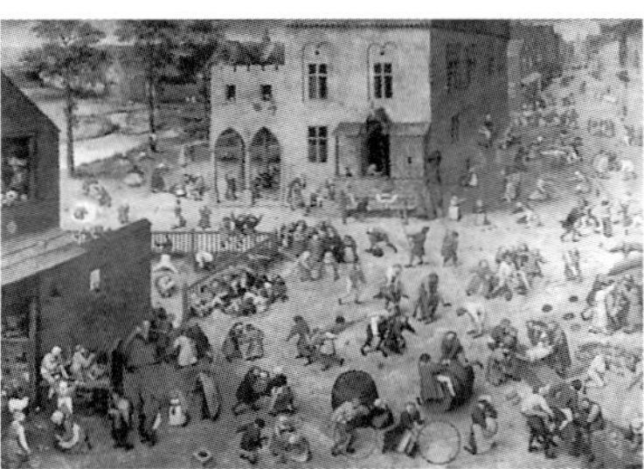

7
Children's Games, 1560
Signed: "BRVEGEL 1560"
Oil/Wood, 118 × 161 cm
Vienna, Kunsthistorisches Museum

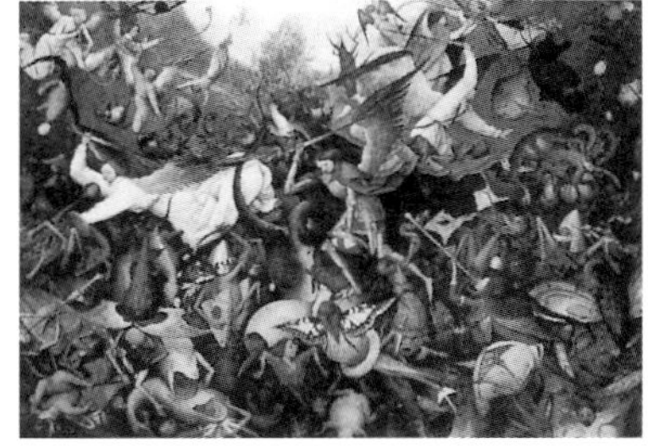

8
Fall of the Rebel Angels, 1562
Signed: "M.D.LXII BRVEGEL"
Oil/Wood, 117 × 162 cm
Brussels, Musées Royaux des Beaux-Arts

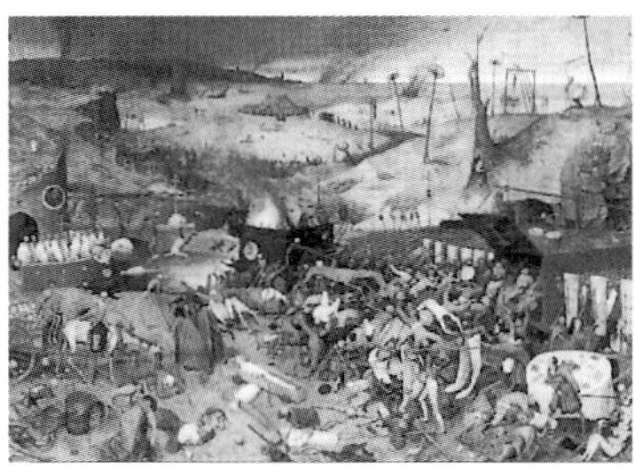

9
"Dulle Griet", 1561
Signed by: "[...] MDLXI"
Oil/Wood, 115 × 161 cm
Antwerp, Museum Mayer-van den Bergh

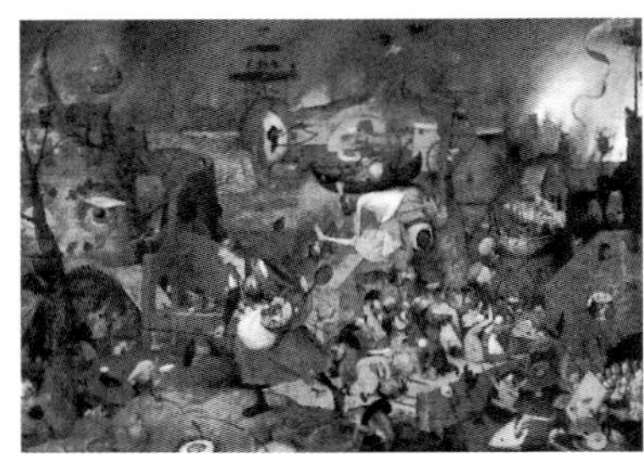

10
Triumph of Death
Around 1562
Oil/Wood, 117 × 162 cm
Madrid, Prado

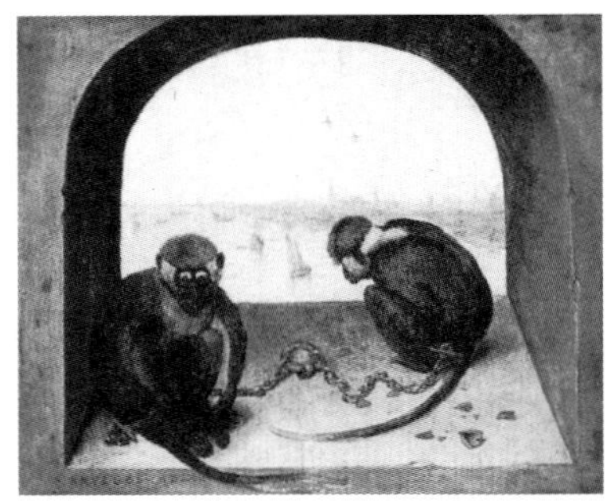

11
Two Monkeys, 1562
Signed: "BRVEGEL MDLXII"
Oil/Wood, 20 × 23 cm
Berlin-Dahlem, Staatliche Museen

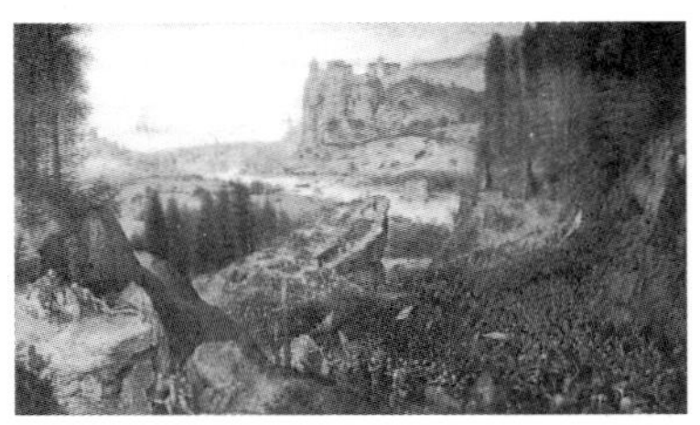

12
The Suicide of Saul, 1562
Signed by his own hand: "SAVL. XXXI. CAPIT. BRVEGEL. M.CCCCC.LXII"
Oil/Wood, 33.5 × 55 cm (top 4 cm, bottom 1 cm later added to)
Vienna, Kunsthistorisches Museum

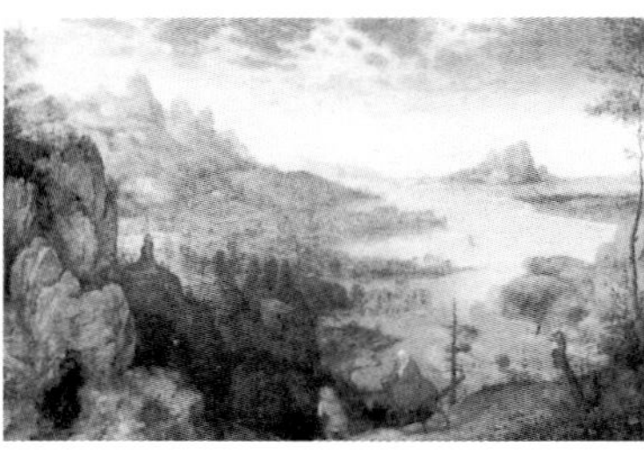

13
The Flight into Egypt, 1563
Signed: "BRVEGEL MDLXII"
Oil/Wood, 37.2 × 55.5 cm
London, Courtauld Institute (previously in the collection of A. Graf Seilern)

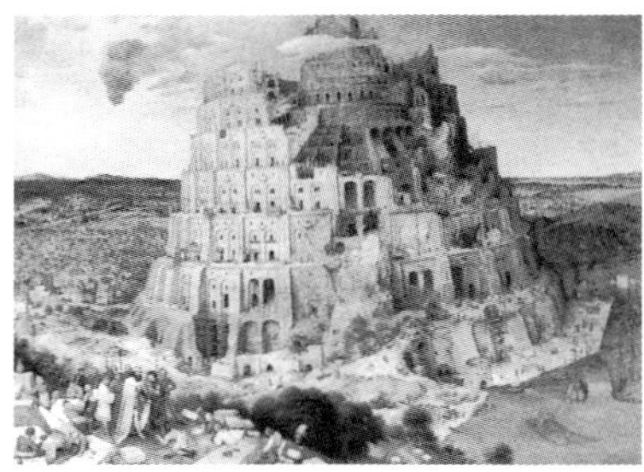

14
Tower of Babel, 1563
Signed: "BRVEGEL FE.M.CCCCC.LXIII"
Oil/Wood, 114 × 155 cm
Vienna, Kunsthistorisches Museum

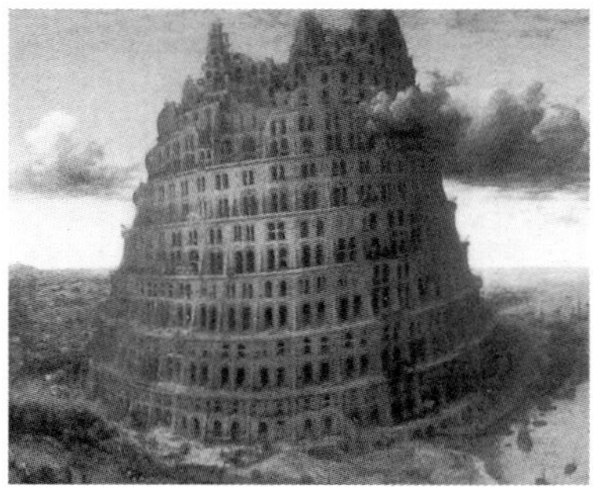

15
Tower of Babel
Unsigned, probably 1563
Oil/Wood, 60 × 74.5 cm
Rotterdam, Museum Boymans-van Beuningen

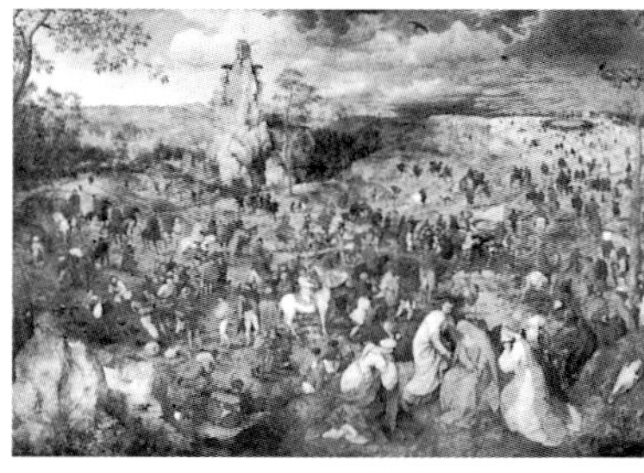

16
Christ Carrying the Cross, 1564
Signed: "BRVEGEL MD.LXIIII"
Oil/Wood, 124 × 170 cm
Vienna, Kunsthistorisches Museum

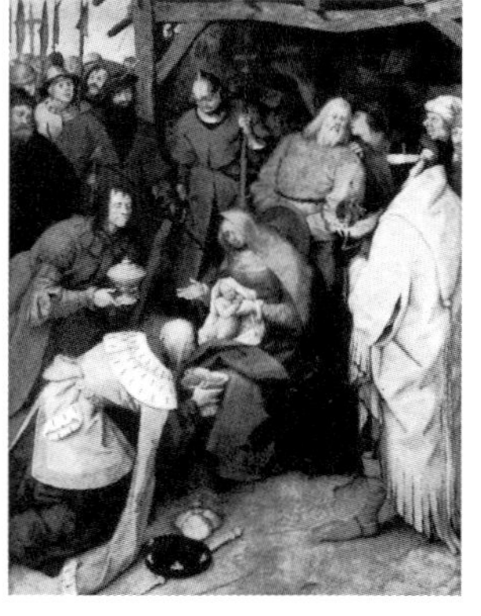

17
Adoration of the Magi, 1564
Signed: "BRVEGEL M.D.LXIIII"
Oil/Wood, 111 × 83.5 cm
London, National Gallery

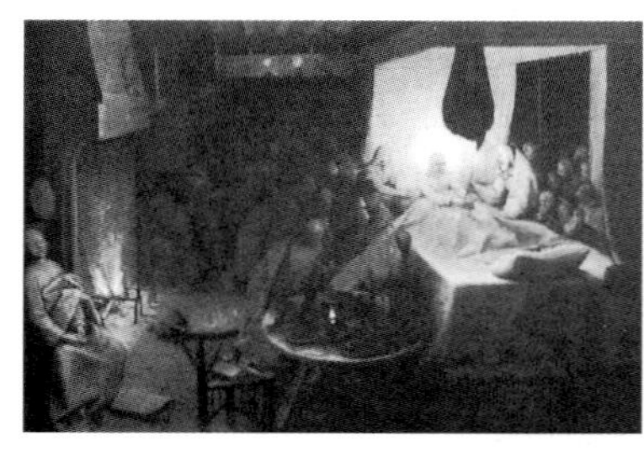

18
Death of the Virgin
Around 1564 (illegible traces of a date)
Signed: "BRVEGEL"
Grisaille/Wood, 36 × 55 cm
Banbury, Upton House, National Trust

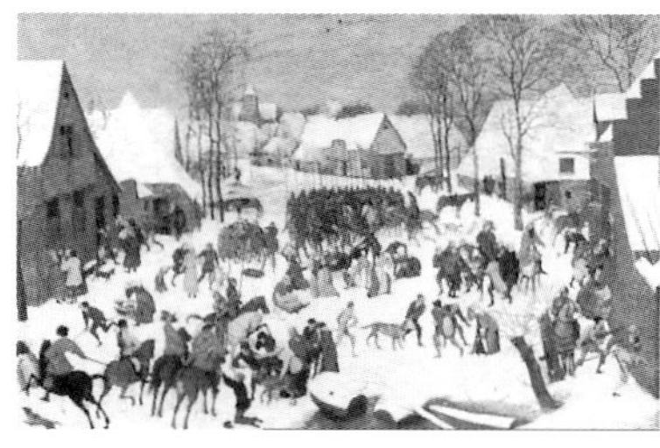

19
Slaughter of the Innocents in Bethlehem
Around 1564; unsigned
Oil/Wood, 109.2 × 154.9 cm
Hampton Court Palace, Collection of Queen Elizabeth II of England

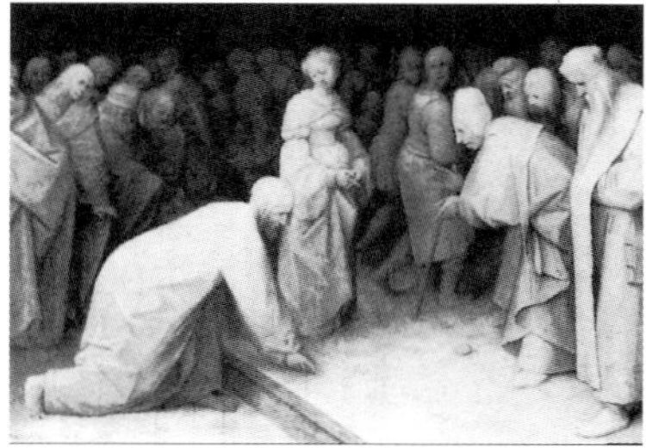

20
Christ and the Woman Taken in Adultery, 1565
Signed: "BRVEGEL.M.D.LXV"
Grisaille/Wood, 24.1 × 34 cm
London, Courtauld Institute (previously in the collection of A. Graf Seilern)

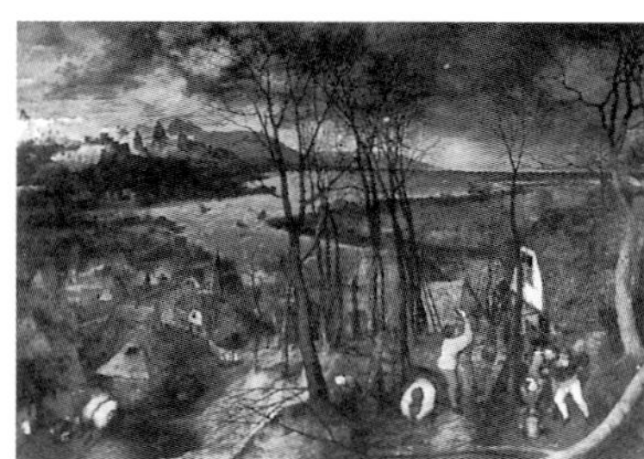

21
Gloomy Day (Early Spring), 1565
Remains of a Sig.: "[MDLX]V"
Oil/Wood, 118 × 163 cm
Vienna, Kunsthistorisches Museum

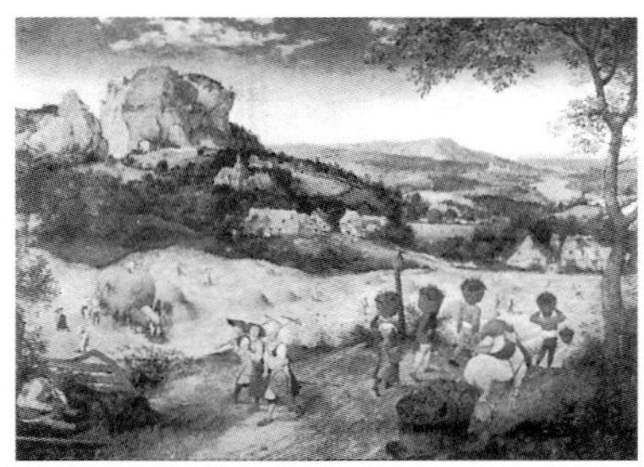

22
Haymaking, 1565; unsigned
Oil/Wood, 117 × 161 cm
Prague, Nationalgalerie

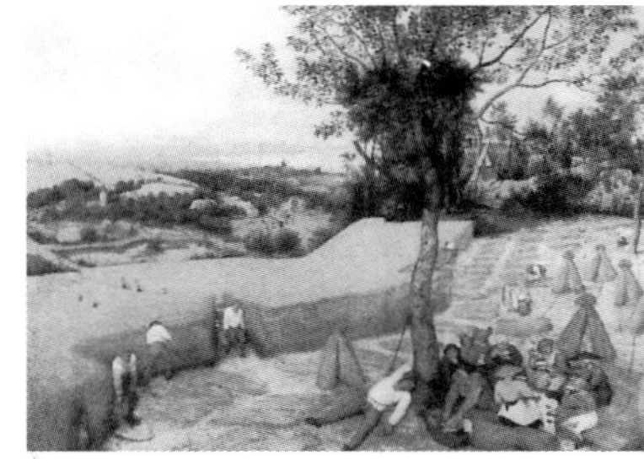

23
Wheat Harvest, 1565
Signed: "BRVEGEL [...] LXV" [1565]
Oil/Wood, 118 × 160.7 cm
New York, The Metropolitan Museum of Art

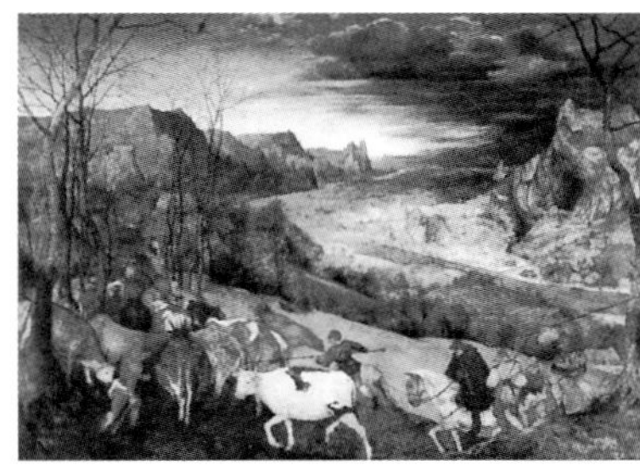

24
Return of the Herd (Autumn), 1565
Signed: "BRVEGEL MDLXV"
Oil/Wood, 117 × 159 cm
Vienna, Kunsthistorisches Museum

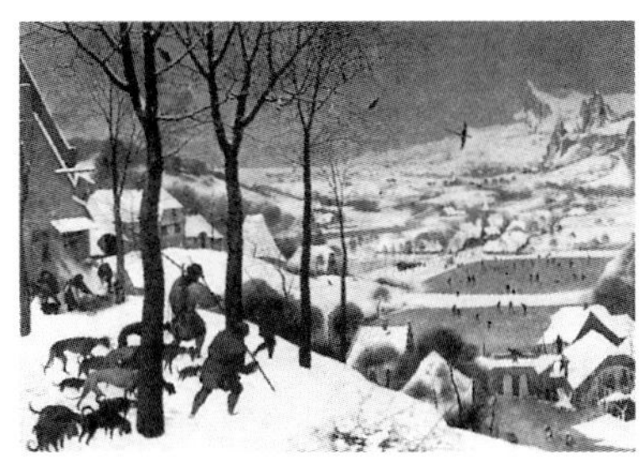

25
Hunters in the Snow (Winter), 1565
Signed: "BRVEGEL. M.D.LXV."
Oil/Wood, 117 × 162 cm
Vienna, Kunsthistorisches Museum

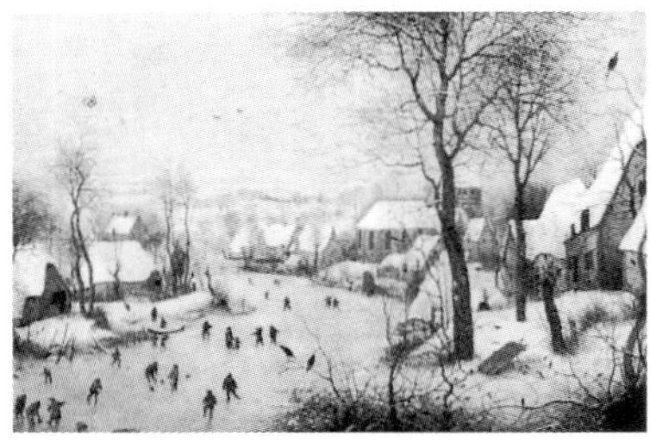

26
Winter Landscape with Ice Skaters and Bird Trap, 1565
Signed: "BRVEGEL.M.D.LXV."
Oil/Wood, 38 × 56 cm
Brussels, Dr. F. Delporte's Collection

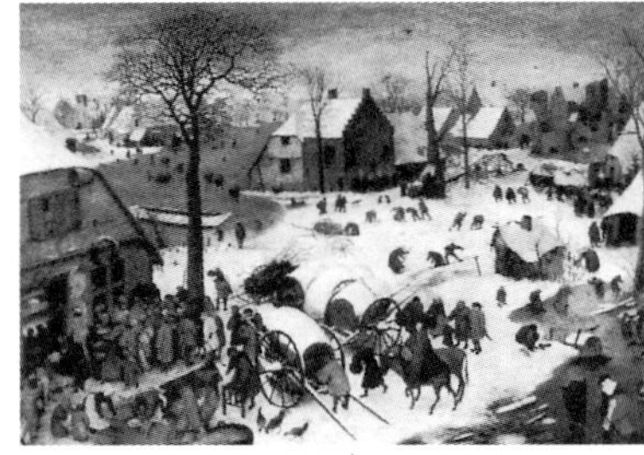

27
Census at Bethlehem, 1566
Signed: "BRVEGEL 1566"
Oil/Wood, 115.5 × 163.5 cm
Brussels, Musées Royaux des Beaux-Arts

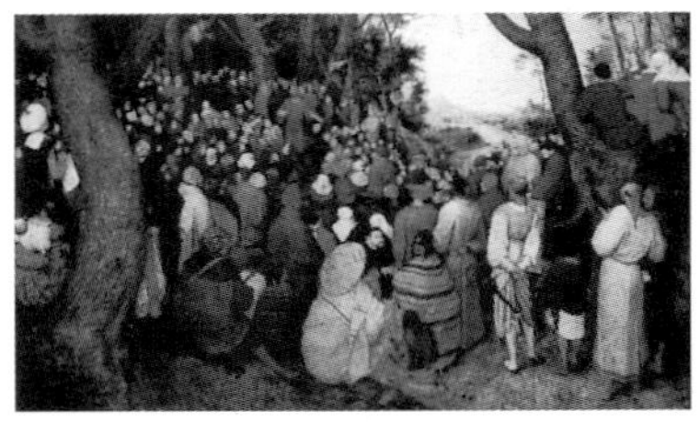

28
Sermon of St John the Baptist, 1566
Signed: "BRVEGEL.M.D.LXVI."
Oil/Wood, 95 × 160,5 cm
Budapest, Museum of Fine Arts

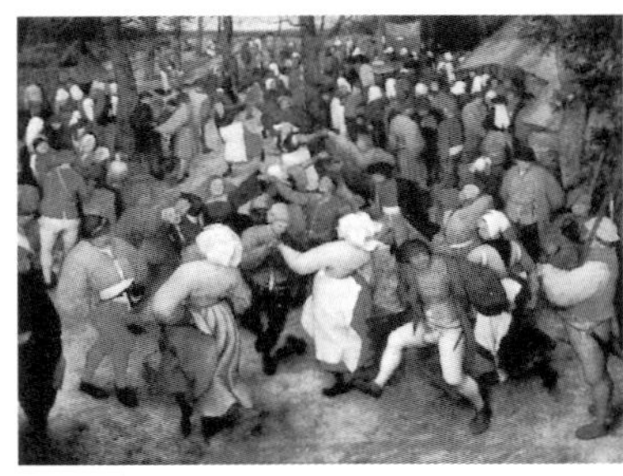

29
Peasant Wedding Dance, 1566
Signed: "M.D.LXVI."
Oil/Wood, 119 × 157 cm
Detroit, Institute of Arts

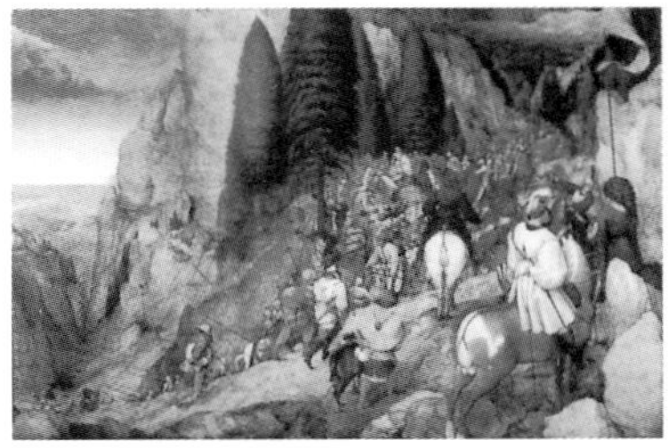

30
Conversion of Paul, 1567
Signed: "BRVEGEL. M.D.LXVII"
Oil/Wood, 108 × 156 cm
Vienna, Kunsthistorisches Museum

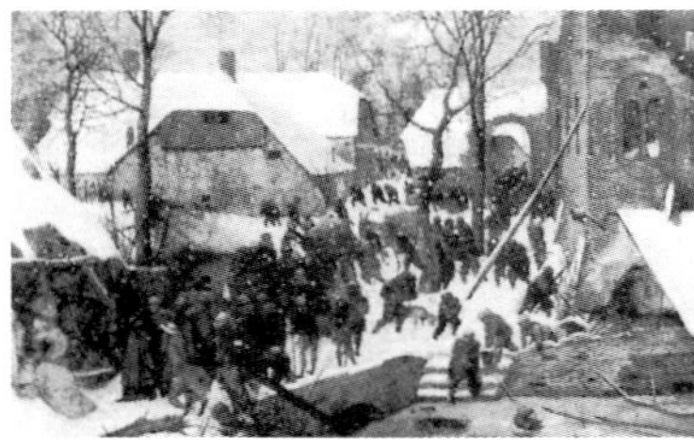

31
Adoration of the Magi in the Snow, 1567
Signed: "M.D.LXVLL/BRVEGEL"
Oil/Wood, 35 × 55 cm
Winterthur, Dr. Oskar Reinhart Collection

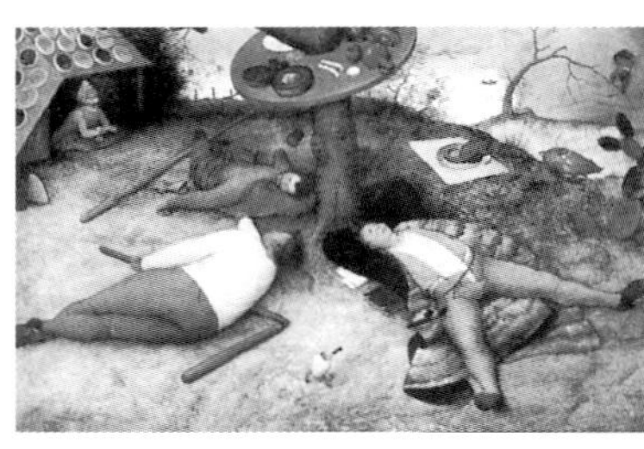

32
Land of Cockaigne, 1567
Signed: "M.DLXVII.BRVEGEL."
Oil/Wood, 52 × 78 cm
Munich, Alte Pinakothek

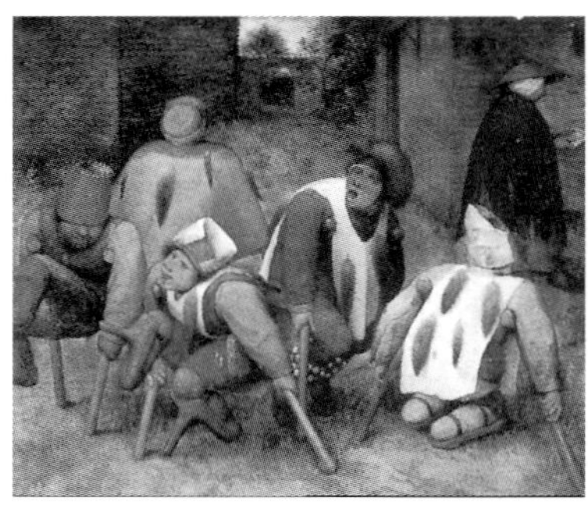

33
The Cripples, 1568
Signed: "BRVEGEL M.D.LVIII."
Oil/Wood, 18 × 21.5 cm
Paris, Louvre

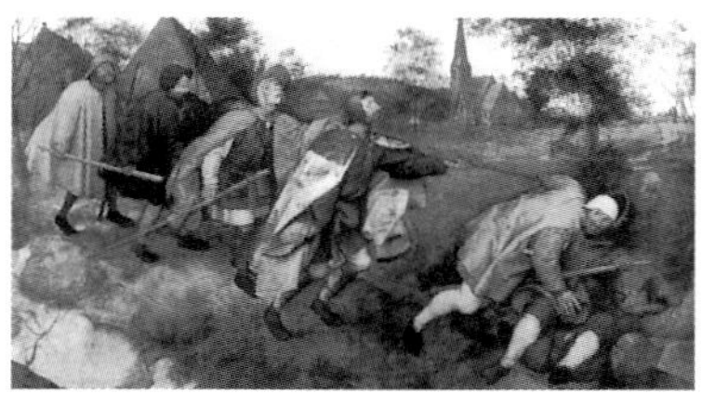

34
Parable of the Blind, 1568
Signed: "BRVEGEL.M.D.LX.VIII."
Tempera/Canvas, 86 × 154 cm
Naples, Museo Nazionale di Capodimonte

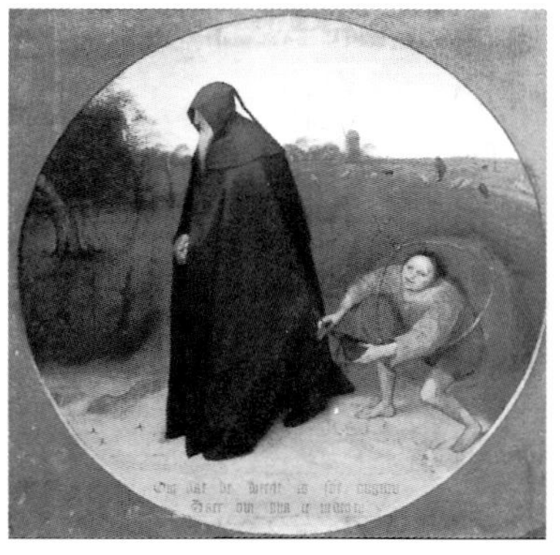

35
The Misanthrope, 1568
Signed on the painted border: "BRVEGEL 1568"
Tempera/Canvas, 86 × 85 cm
Naples, Museo Nazionale di Capodimonte

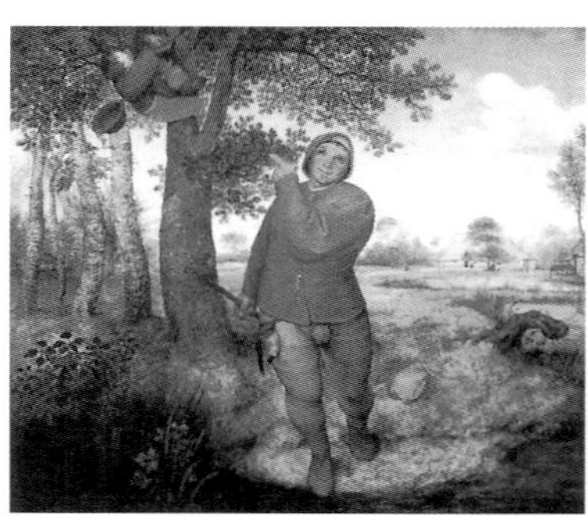

36
Peasant and the Nest Robber, 1568
Signed: "BRVEGEL M.D.LXVIII"
Oil/Wood, 59.3 × 68.3 cm
Vienna, Kunsthistorisches Museum

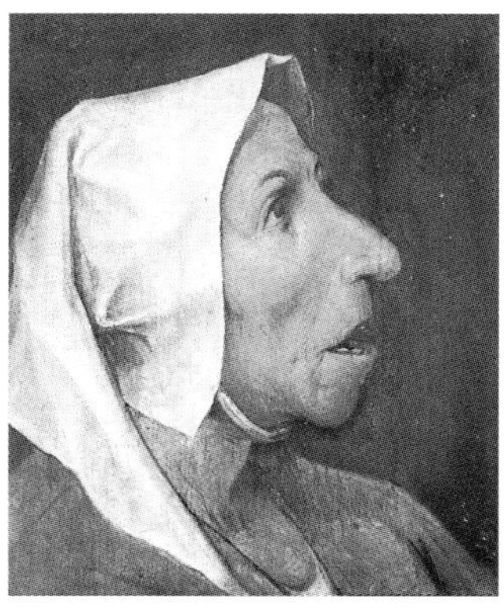

37
Head of an old Peasant Woman
Around 1568; unsigned
Oil/Wood, 22 × 18 cm
Munich, Alte Pinakothek

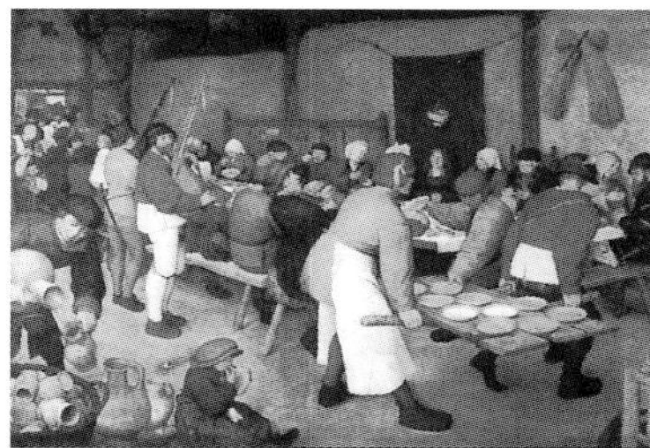

38
Peasant Wedding
Around 1568; unsigned
Oil/Wood, 114 × 164 cm
Vienna, Kunsthistorisches Museum

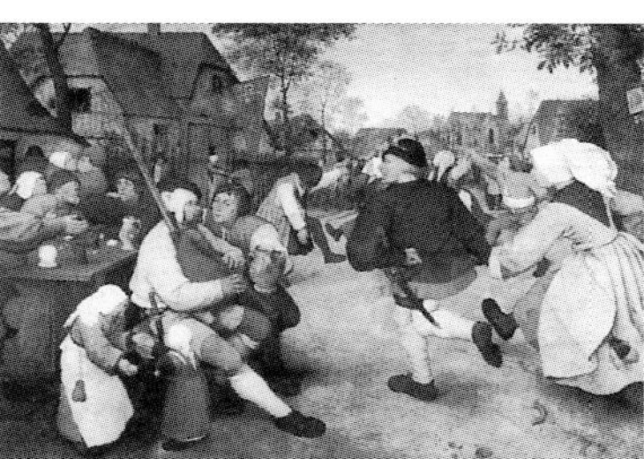

39
Peasant Dance
Signed: "BRVEGEL"
Oil/Wood, 114 × 164 cm
Vienna, Kunsthistorisches Museum

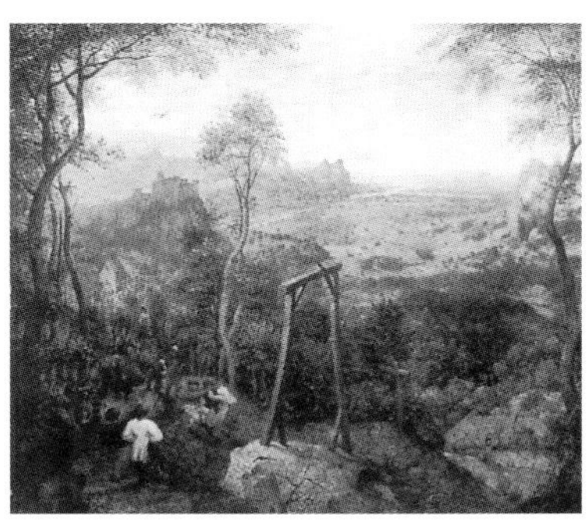

40
Magpie on the Gallows, 1568
Signed: "BRVEGEL 1568"
Oil/Wood, 45.9 × 50.8 cm
Darmstadt, Hessisches Landesmuseum

Works not universally acknowledged

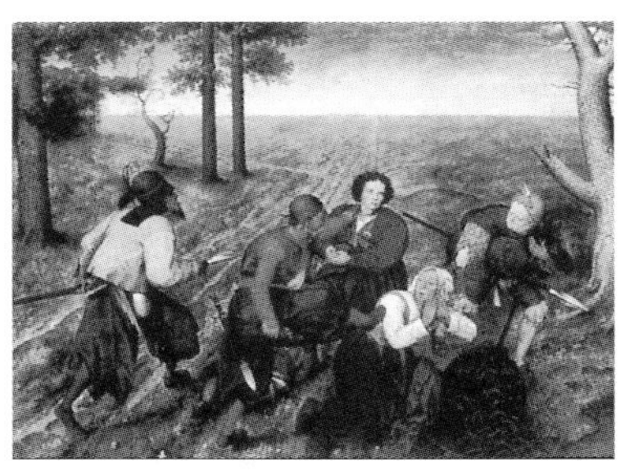

41
The Ambush
Signed: "M.D.LX VII BRVEGEL"
Oil/Oak, 96 × 128 cm
Stockholm, Stockholms Universitets Konstsamling

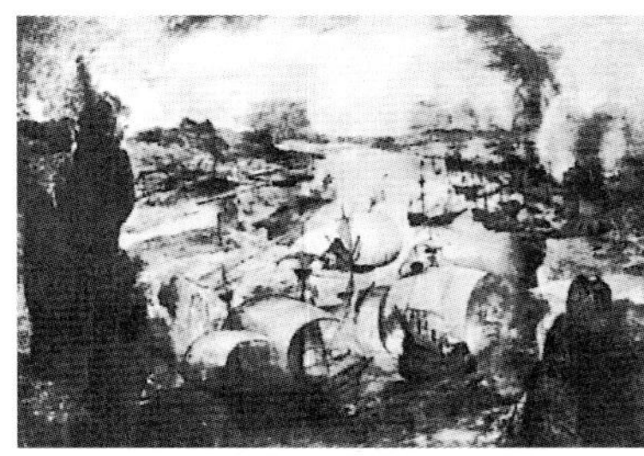

42
Landscape with Sailing Ships and a Burning Town
Around 1552/53
Oil/Wood, 24.4 × 34.8 cm
Dortmund, previously in the Becker Collection

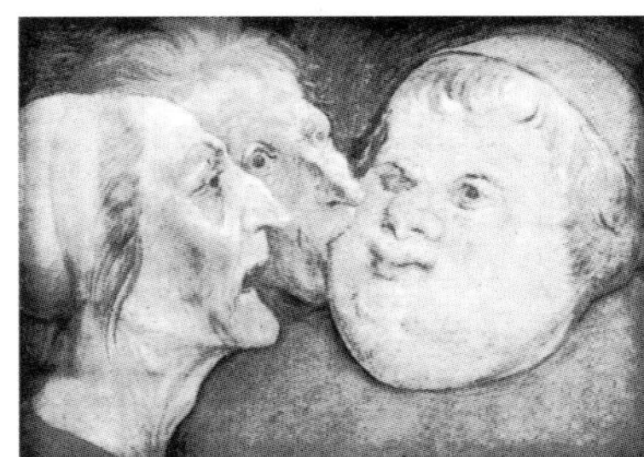

43
Three Heads
Around 1560?
Oil/Wood, 24.7 × 33.6 cm
Kopenhagen, Statens Museum for Kunst

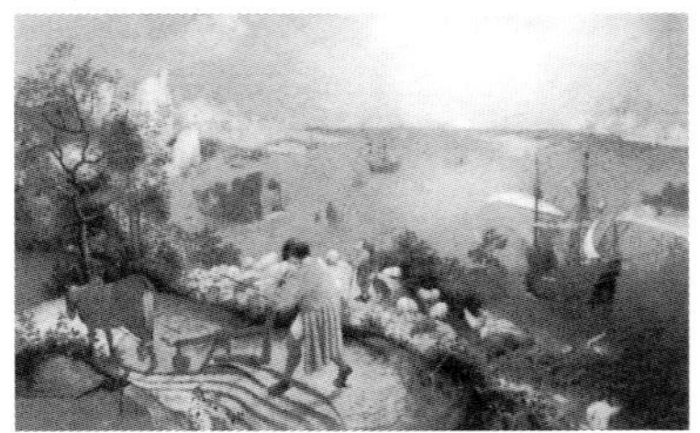

44
The Fall of Icarus
Oil, transferred from wood to canvas, 73.5 × 112 cm
Brussels, Musées Royaux des Beaux-Arts

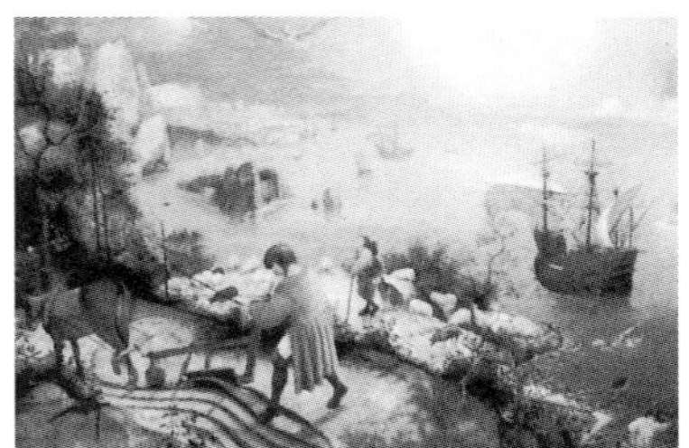

45
The Fall of Icarus
Oil/Wood, 63 × 90 cm
New York and Brussels, D. M. van Buuren Collection

Questionable works or copies

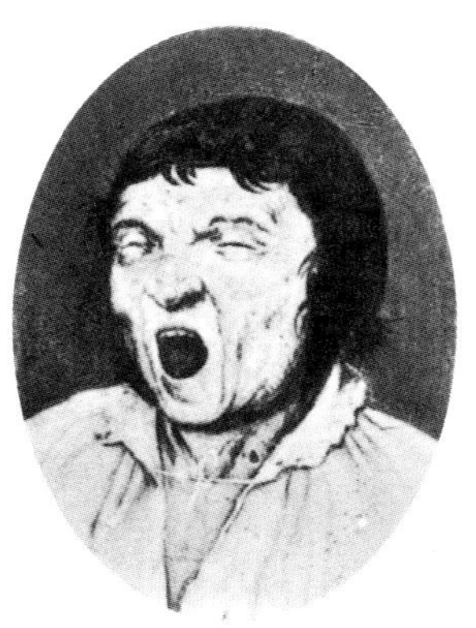

46
Yawning Man
Signed: "P"
Oil/Wood, oval, 12.6 × 9.2 cm
Brussels, Musées Royaux des Beaux-Arts

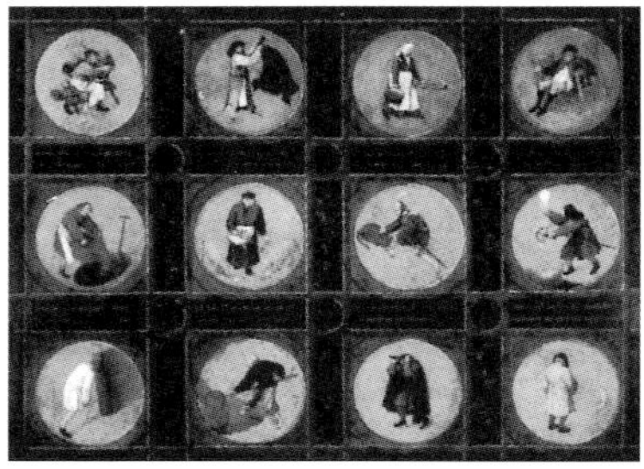

47
Twelve Proverbs
Oil/Wood, 74.5 × 98.4 cm
Antwerp, Museum Mayer-van den Bergh

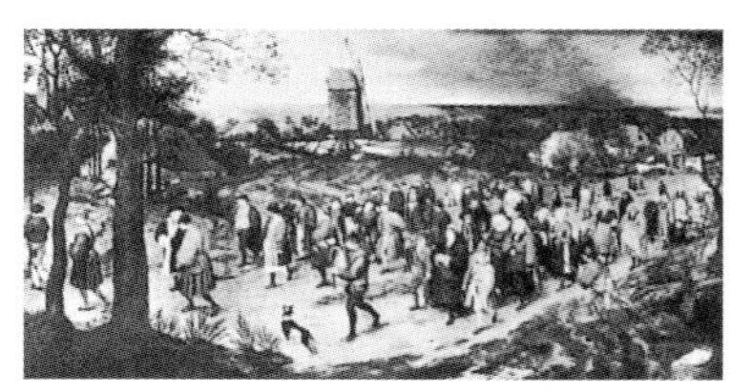

48
Wedding Procession
(now attributed to Jan Bruegel the Elder)
Oil/Wood, 61.5 × 114.5 cm
Brussels, City Museum

Omitted:

Storm at See
Oil/Wood, 71 × 97 cm
Identified as the work of Joos de Momper by Demus 1981, 128 ff.; this was confirmed by Ertz in 1986.
Vienna, Kunsthistorisches Museum

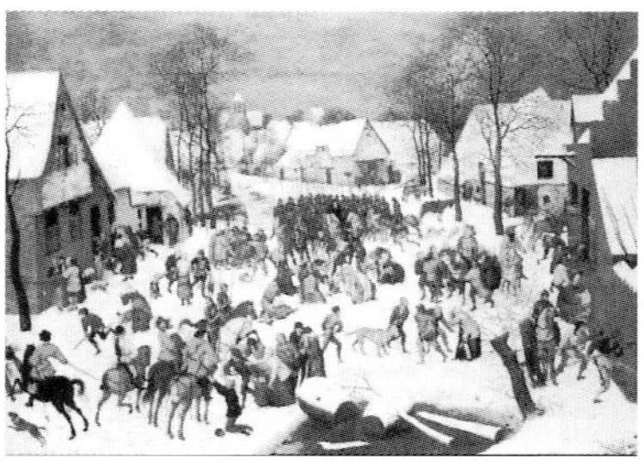

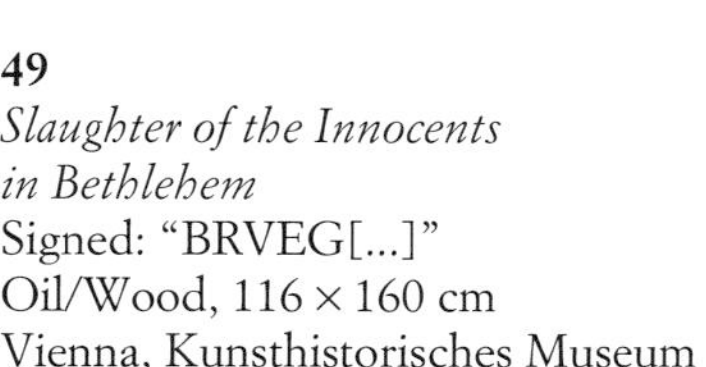

49
Slaughter of the Innocents in Bethlehem
Signed: "BRVEG[...]"
Oil/Wood, 116 × 160 cm
Vienna, Kunsthistorisches Museum

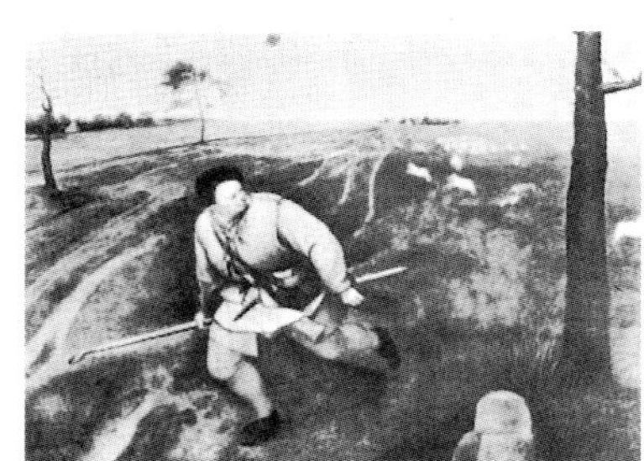

50
The Unfaithful Shepherd
Oil/Wood, 61.6 × 86 cm
Philadelphia, John J. Johnson Collection

51
The Feast of St Martin
(Fragment)
Tempera on canvas, 92.5 × 73.5 cm
Vienna, Kunsthistorisches Museum
See Marlier 1969 for further copies after Pieter Bruegel I.

Bibliography (Selection)

Today it is almost impossible to assess the extent of the literature on Bruegel. It is no longer limited to our continent alone. There are already books in Japanese on Bruegel, and the number of individual studies is understood to be constantly increasing. The selection offered here begins with a few short remarks.

F. Grossmann provides an extensive bibliography in his article on Bruegel in the Enciclopedia Universale dell'arte, Vol. II, Venice – Rome 1958, p. 794 ff.. R. L. Delevoy's, *Pieter Brueghel,* Geneva 1959, 133 ff. also contains an interesting bibliography. There are further, more recent bibliographies by W. Stechow, 1970, and R. H. Marijnissen, 1969. The seminal standard work is still the great work written jointly by R. van Bastelaer und G. Hulin de Loo, *Peter Bruegel l'Ancien, son oeuvre et son temps,* Brussels 1907. Bastelaer edited the graphics, de Loo the painting. In 1908 Bastelaer also drew up the first detailed index of graphic reproductions after Bruegel.

Significantly, the monographs by G. Jedlicka and F. Grossmann also appeared in 1938 (1966 und 1973 editions; work is continuing on a posthumous issue of the catalogue). Grossmann also describes the sources and provides a history of opinion on Bruegel from the 16th century onwards.

Particularly indispensable for the drawings, along with Münz 1962, is the 1975 Berlin Exhibition Catalogue, *Pieter Bruegel d. Ä. als Zeichner (Pieter Bruegel the Elder as a Graphic Artist),* Berlin (Kupferstichkabinett) 1975, which has many new conclusions and an outstanding bibliography. Following this exhibition in Berlin, a seminar on Bruegel took place, and the papers presented at it appeared in an anthology in 1979. The extensive article by Justus Müller Hofstede 1979 is outstanding and indispensable with its abundance of cross-references and further literature. Müller Hofstede looks for Bruegel‘s conception of landscapes (refuting Tolnay‘s pantheistic interpretation) as the basis for proving the stoic philosophy conveyed by Abraham Ortelius on Bruegel. This was contradicted by K. Demus in 1981 in the Catalogue of the Kunsthistorisches Museum in Vienna, who very convincingly liberated the later works from any iconological overload (with a large, detailed bibliography).

Finally, the Exhibition Catalogue, *The Age of Bruegel,* Washington (National Gallery) 1987, by J. O. Hand, J. R. Judson, W. W. Robinson and M. Wolff is important for the graphics. A new, complete catalogue of the drawings (with radical amendments of attributions) by H. Mielke (†) appeared in 1996 by Brepols in Turnhout.

Sources:

L. Guicciardini, *Descrittione di tutti i Paesi Bassi,* Antwerp 1567 (abbreviated as: Guicciardini 1567); appeared in French in 1568

G. Vasari, *Le Vite dei più eccellenti Pittori, Scultori e Architettori,* second edition, Florence, 1568 (abbreviated as: Vasari 1568)

D. Lampsonius, *Pictorum aliquot celebrium Germaniae inferioris effigies,* Antwerp 1572 (critical edition by J. Puraye, *Les effigies des Peintres célèbres des Pays-Bas,* Bruges 1956)

A. Ortelius, *Album Amicorum,* Antwerp 1574–1596 (Manuscript in Pembroke College, Cambridge); Translation by F. Grossmann, published by A. E. Popham, in: The Burlington Magazine LIX, London 1931, 184 ff., and in: W. Stechow, *Northern Renaissance Art 1400–1600, Sources and Documents,* Englewood Cliffs, N. J., Prentice Hall 1966, 38 ff.; French edition by J. Puraye, in: De gulden Passer, Bulletin van de 'Vereeniging der Antwerpsche Bibliophielen', XLV, 1967, 1–125, XLVI, 1968, Nos.1–3, 1–99, with illustrations on every page of the album, but incorrect

A. Coremans, *L'archiduc Ernest, sa cour, ses dépenses 1593–1595, D'après les comptes de Blaise Hütter, son secrétaire intime et premier valet de chambre* (Académie royale de Belgique, Compte-rendu des séances de la Commission royale d'histoire, Bd. 13), Brussels 1847, 85–125 (abbreviated as: Coremans 1847)

K. van Mander, *Het Schilderboeck,* Haarlem 1604; French edition by H. Hymans 1885; Edition with German commentary by H. Floerke 1906. The large, new critical edition with commentary of the *Schilder-Boeck* by H. Miedema: *Karel van Mander. The Lives of the Illustrious Netherlandish and German Painters,* Vol. I–III, Doornspijk 1994–1996; Vol. III: *Lives/fol. 211r36 – 236v36,* Doornspijk 1996, abbreviated as: Miedema 1996 is extremely important. Finally, W. S. Melion, *Shaping the Netherlandish Canon. Karel van Mander's Schilder-Boeck,* Chicago – London 1991, and J. Müller, *Concordia Pragensis. Karel van Manders Kunsttheorie im Schilder-Boeck,* Munich 1993 dealt in a speculative manner with van Mander (Martin Raspe wrote extremely critical reviews in: Journal of Art History, 1st set of issues, 1997, Issue 1, 70–81)

Inventarium aller vnndt jeder Ihrer hochfürstlichen Durchleücht Herrn Herrn Leopoldt Wilhelmen […] zue Wienn vorhandenen Mahllereyen, publ. by A. v. Berger, in: Yearbook of the art history collections of the very highest imperial house 1, 1883 (abbreviated as: Berger 1883)

Ph. Rombouts – Th. van Lerius, *De Liggeren en andere historische Archieven der Antwerpsche Sint-Lucasgilde* I, The Hague 1872

H. Zimmermann, in: Yearbook of the art history collections of the very highest imperial house 25, 1905, S. XX (abbreviated as: Zimmermann 1905)

W. Köhler, *Aktenstücke zur Geschichte der Wiener Kunstkammer in der herzoglichen Bibliothek zu Wolfenbüttel,* in: Yearbook of the art history collections of the very highest imperial house 26, 1906/07 (abbreviated as: Köhler 1906/07)

J. Denucé, *De Antwerpsche 'Konstkamers'. Inventarissen van Kunstverzamelingen te Antwerpen in de 16e en 17e eeuwen,* Amsterdam 1932; German edition: J. Denucé, *Inventare von Kunstsammlungen zu Antwerpen im 16. und 17. Jahrhundert* (Sources on the History of Flemish Art 2), Antwerp 1932 (abbreviated as: Denucé 1932)

J. Briels, *Amator Pictoriae Artis. De Antwerpsche Kunsthandelaer Peeter Stevens (1590–1668) in zijn Constkamer,* in: Jaarboek van het koninklijk Museum voor schone Kunsten, Antwerpen 1980, 137–226 (abbreviated as: Briels 1980)

On the history:

H. Pirenne, *Geschichte Belgiens,* Gotha 1899–1907

J. Huizinga, *Herbst des Mittelalters,* Stuttgart 1975, second edition in German; Dutch edition 1941

G. Parker, *The Dutch Revolt,* London 1977; German edition Munich 1979

On his life and work
(General descriptions):

H. Hymans, *Pierre Brueghel le*

Vieux, in: Gazette des Beaux-Arts 32, 1890/I, 361–375; 1890/II, 361–373; 33, 1891/I, 20–40
A. L. Romdahl, *Pieter Brueghel der Ältere und sein Kunstschaffen,* in: Yearbook of the art history collections of the very highest imperial house 25, 1905, 85–169
R. van Bastelaer – G. Hulin de Loo, *Peter Bruegel L'Ancien, son oeuvre et son temps,* Brussels 1907
V. Barker, *Peter Bruegel the Elder. A study of his paintings,* New York 1926 – London 1927
E. Michel, *Bruegel,* Paris 1931
G. Glück, *Bruegels Gemälde,* Vienna 1932
C. de Tolnay, *Pierre Bruegel L'Ancien,* Brussels 1935
M. J. Friedländer, *Die altniederländische Malerei, XIV., Pieter Bruegel und Nachträge zu den früheren Bänden,* Leiden 1937; 2nd edition in English: Leiden – Brussels 1976
G. Jedlicka, *Pieter Bruegel. Der Maler in seiner Zeit,* Erlenbach – Zürich 1938 (abbreviated as: Jedlicka 1938)
M. Dvorák, *Die Gemälde Pieter Bruegels d. Ä.,* Vienna 1941
J. B. Knipping O.F.M., *Pieter Bruegel de Oude,* Amsterdam 1945
A. L. Romdahl, *Pieter Bruegel den äldre,* Stockholm 1947
G. Glück, *Das große Bruegel-Werk,* Vienna 1951
V. Denis, *Tutta la pittura di Pieter Bruegel,* Milan 1952
F. Grossmann, *Bruegel. The Paintings,* London 1955 (abbreviated as: Grossmann 1966); 2nd extended edition 1966
M. Auner, *Pieter Bruegel. Umrisse eines Lebensbildes,* in: Yearbook of the art history collections in Vienna 52, 1956, 51–122 (abbreviated as: Auner 1956)
C. G. Stridbeck, *Bruegelstudien,* Stockholm 1956 (abbreviated as: Stridbeck 1956)
F. Grossmann, *Pieter Bruegel il Vecchio,* in: Enciclopedia Universale dell'Arte, Vol. 2, Venice – Rome 1958, 794 ff. (with a bibliography)
R. L. Delevoy, *Brueghel,* Geneva 1959
F. Grossmann, *Bruegel,* in: Encyclopedia of World Art II, New York – Toronto – London 1960 (with a bibliography)
M. Fryns, *Pierre Brueghel l'Ancien,* Brussels 1964
G. W. Menzel, *Pieter Bruegel der Ältere,* Leipzig 1966
G. Arpino – P. Bianconi, *L'opera completa di Bruegel* (= Classici dell'arte 7), Milan 1967
H. A. Klein – M. C. Klein, *Pieter Bruegel the Elder,* New York 1968
B. Claessens – J. Rousseau, *Unser Bruegel,* Antwerp 1969
R.-H. Marijnissen, *Bruegel,* Stuttgart 1969
W. Stechow, *Pieter Bruegel the Elder,* New York 1970
E. G. Grimme, *Pieter Bruegel d. Ä. Leben und Werk,* Cologne 1973
F. Grossmann, *Pieter Bruegel. Complete edition of the paintings,* third checked edition London 1973
C. Brown, *Bruegel,* London 1975
W. S. Gibson, *Bruegel,* London 1977; French edition Paris 1980
A. Wied, *Bruegel,* Italian edition Milan 1979; English edition Sydney 1980; French edition Paris 1980
R. H. Marijnissen, *Bruegel. Tout l'Œuvre peint et dessiné,* Antwerp 1988
R. M. und R. Hagen, *Bruegel. Sämtliche Gemälde,* Cologne 1994
A. Wied, *Bruegel,* Milan 1994

Drawings:
L. Burchard, *Pieter Bruegel im Kupferstichkabinett zu Berlin,* in: Official reports from the royal art collections 34, No. 11, August 1913, 223–234
K. Tolnai, *Die Zeichnungen Pieter Bruegels,* Munich 1925
O. Benesch, *Die Zeichnungen der niederländischen Schulen des 15. und 16. Jahrhunderts* (= Descriptive Catalogue of the sketches in the Albertina Graphics Collection, publ. by A. Stix, Vol. 2), Vienna 1928
K. Tolnai, *Beiträge zu Bruegels Zeichnungen,* in: Yearbook of the Prussian Art Collections 50, 1929, 195–216
A. E. Popham, *Dutch and Flemish Drawings of the 15th and 16th Centuries* (= Catalogue of Drawings by Dutch and Flemish Artists preserved in the British Museum 5), London 1932
J. G. van Gelder – J. Borms, *Brueghels deugden en hoofdzonden,* Amsterdam 1939
A. E. Popham, *Two landscape drawings by Pieter Bruegel the Elder,* in: The Burlington Magazine 91, 1949, 319 f.
H. Gerson, *De "Ripa Grande" te Rome,* in: Oud Holland 66, 1951, 65
C. de Tolnay, *Die Zeichnungen Pieter Bruegels,* Zürich 1952
O. Benesch, Besprechung von Tolnay 1952, in: Kunstchronik 6, 1953, 76–82
F. Grossmann, *The Drawings of Pieter Bruegel the Elder in the Museum Boymans,* in: Bulletin Museum Boymans, Rotterdam, July 1954, Part 5, No. 2, 41–63
O. Benesch, *Zur Frage der Kopien nach Pieter Bruegel,* in: Bulletin des Musées Royaux des Beaux-Arts de Belgique 8, 1959, 35–42
C. de Tolnay, *Remarques sur quelques dessins de Bruegel l'ancien sur un dessin de Bosch récemment réapparus,* in: Bulletin des Musées Royaux des Beaux-Arts de Belgique 9, 1960, 3 ff.
L. Münz, *Bruegel, Zeichnungen,* complete edition, London – Cologne 1962 (abbreviated as: Münz)
K. Arndt, *Unbekannte Handzeichnungen von Pieter Bruegel d. Ae.,* in: Pantheon XXIV, 1966, 207–216
I. L. Zupnick, *The meaning of Bruegel's "Nobody" and "Everyman",* in: Gazette des Beaux-Arts 67, 1966/I, 257–270
K. Arndt, *Frühe Landschaftszeichnungen von Pieter Bruegel d. Ae.,* in: Pantheon XXV, 1967, 97–104
C. de Tolnay, *A Contribution to Pieter Bruegel the Elder as Draughtsman,* in: Miscellanea I. Q. van Regteren Altena, Amsterdam 1969, 61–63
F. van Leeuwen, *Jets over het handschrift van de "naar het leven"-tekenaar,* in: Oud Holland 85, 1970, 25–32
J. A. Spicer, *The "Naer het Leven" Drawings: by Pieter Bruegel or Roelandt Savery?,* in: Master Drawings VIII, 1, Spring 1970, 3–30
J. A. Spicer, *Roelandt Savery's studies in Bohemia,* in: Umení 18, 1970, 270–275
F. van Leeuwen, *Figuurstudies van „P. Bruegel",* in: Simiolus 5, 1971, No. 3/4, 139–149
K. Arndt, *Pieter Bruegel d. Ä. und die Geschichte der Waldlandschaft,* in: Yearbook of the Berliner Museums 14, 1972, 69–121
E. Haverkamp Begeman, *Joos van Liere,* in: *Pieter Bruegel und seine Welt. Ein Colloquium,* publ. by O. v. Simson and M. Winner, Berlin 1979, 17–28
L. De Pauw-De Veen, *Das Brüsseler Blatt mit Bettlern und Krüppeln: Bosch oder Bruegel?,* in: *Pieter Bruegel und seine Welt. Ein Colloquium,* publ. by O. v. Simson and M. Winner, Berlin 1979, 149–158
H. Mielke, Besprechung des Ausstellungskataloges: K. G. Boon, *L'Epoque de Lucas van Leyde et Pierre Bruegel: Dessins des anciens Pays-Bas: Collection Frits Lugt,* in: Master Drawings 23–24, 1986, 75–90
H. Mielke, *Pieter Bruegel. Probleme seines zeichnerischen Oeuvres,* in: Jahrbuch der Berliner Museen 1991, N. F. Bd. 33, 129–134
H. Mielke, *Noch einmal zum Problem von Pieter Bruegels Landschaftszeichnungen. Eigene Studien oder Ableitungen?,* in: Munich Yearbook of the Plastic Arts 3 Vol. XLII. 1991, 137–147
H. Mielke, *Pieter Bruegel. Die Zeichnungen,* Turnhout 1996 (abbreviated as: Mielke 1996)

Druckgraphik:
R. van Bastelaer, *Les estampes de Peter Bruegel l'Ancien,* Brussels 1908
E. Feinblatt, *Prints and Drawings of Pieter Bruegel the Elder,* Los Angeles Exhibition Catalogue (Country Museum) 1961
H. A. Klein, *Graphic Worlds of Peter Bruegel the Elder,* New York 1963
J. Lavalleye, *Lucas van Leyden, Peter Bruegel d. Ä. Das gesamte graphische Werk,* Vienna – Munich 1966; English edition: J. Lavalleye, *Pieter Bruegel the Elder and Lucas van Leyden. The Complete Engravings, Etchings and Woodcuts,* New York 1967
L. Lebeer, *Bruegel. Le Stampe,* Florence 1967
H. Mielke, *Radierer um Bruegel,* in: *Pieter Bruegel und seine Welt. Ein Colloquium,* publ. by O. v. Simson and M. Winner, Berlin 1979, 43–49
K. Oberhuber, *Pieter Bruegel und die Radierungsserie der Bauernköpfe,* in: *Pieter Bruegel und seine Welt. Ein Colloquium,* publ. by O. v. Simson and M. Winner, Berlin 1979, 143–147
T. A. Riggs, *Hieronymus Cock (1510–1570). Printmaker and Publisher in Antwerp at the Sign of the Four Winds,* phil. Diss. Yale University, New Haven/Conn. 1971
T. A. Riggs, *Bruegel and his Publisher,* in: *Pieter Bruegel und seine Welt. Ein Colloquium,* publ. by O. v. Simson and M. Winner, Berlin 1979, 165–174

Individual studies, miscellaneous:
E. R. v. Engerth, *Kunsthistorische Sammlungen des Allerhöchsten Kaiserhauses, Gemälde. Beschreibendes Verzeichnis,* Vol. II, Dutch Schools, Vienna, 1884 (abbreviated as: Engerth 1884)
W. Fraenger, *Der Bauern-Bruegel und das deutsche Sprichwort,* Erlenbach – Zürich 1923
F. Lugt, *Pieter Bruegel und Italien,* in:

Commemorative volume for Max Friedländer, Leipzig 1927, 111 ff.
A. Haberlandt, *Volkskundliches zur "Bauernhochzeit" P. Brueghels d. Ä.,* in: Folk Art Periodical 40, N. F. 2, 1930, H. 1–2, 10–16
E. Michel, *Pierre Bruegel le Vieux et Pieter Coecke d'Alost,* in: Mélanges Hulin de Loo, Brussels 1931, 266–271
A. Haberlandt, *Das Faschingsbild des Pieter Bruegel d. Ä.,* in: Folk Art Periodical 43, N. F 5, 1933, H. 3, 237–250
H. Sedlmayr, *Die "macchia" Bruegels,* in: Yearbook of the Art History Collections in Vienna, N. F. 8, 1934, 137–159 (reprinted in: H. Sedlmayr, *Epochen und Werke* I, Vienna-Munich 1959, 274–318)
E. Tietze-Conrat, *Pieter Bruegels Kinderspiele,* in: Oudheidkundig Jaarboek 2, 1934, 127–130
K. von Tolnai, *Studien zu den Gemälden Pieter Bruegels d. Ä.,* in: Yearbook of the Art History Collections in Vienna, N. F. 8, 1934, 105–135
G. Glück, *Über einige Landschaftsgemälde Pieter Bruegels des Älteren,* in: Yearbook of the Art History Collections in Vienna, 1935, 151–165
E. Michel, *Bruegel le Vieux a-t-il passé par Genève,* in: Gazette des Beaux-Arts 78, 1936/I, 105–108
J. Grauls, *De Spreekworden van P. Bruegel den Oude verklaard,* Antwerp 1938
E. Michel, *Bruegel et la critique moderne,* in: Gazette de Beaux-Arts 80, 1938/I, 27–46
C. de Tolnay, *La seconde Tour de Babel de Pierre Bruegel l'Ancien,* in: Annuaire des Musées Royaux des Beaux-Arts de Belgique 1938, 113–121
J. G. Gelder – J. Borms, *Brueghels Deugden en hoofdzonden,* Amsterdam 1939
F. Würtenberger, *Zu Bruegels Kunstform, besonders ihr Verhältnis zur Renaissancekomposition,* in: Art History Periodical 9, 1949, 30–48
V. De Meyere, *De kinderspelen van Pieter Bruegel den Oude verklaard,* Antwerp 1941
A. Lhotsky, *Festschrift des Kunsthistorischen Museums in Wien 1891–1941, 2. Teil, Die Geschichte der Sammlungen,* Vienna 1941–45 (abbreviated as: Lhotsky 1941–45)
C. Terlinden, *Pierre Bruegel le Vieux et l'histoire,* in: Revue belge d'architecture et d'histoire de l'art 12, 1942, 229–257
D. Bax, *Over allerhand bisschoppen en Bruegels kreupelen in het Louvre,* in: Historia 9, 1943, 241–248
G. Glück, *Peter Brueghel the Elder and classical antiquity,* in: The Art Quarterly 6, 1943, 167–186
F. Baumgart, *Zusammenhänge der niederländischen mit der italienischen Malerei der zweiten Hälfte des 16. Jahrhunderts,* in: Marburg Yearbook for Aesthetics and Art History 13, 1944, 187–250
J. Bakker, *De humor van Pieter Brueghel den Ouden,* in: Historia 10, 1944–1945, 277–283
L. Baldass, *Les paysanneries de Pierre Bruegel,* in: Les Arts Plastiques 1948, 11/12, 471–484
F. Novotny, *Die Monatsbilder Pieter Bruegels des Älteren,* Vienna 1948
D. Bax, *Pieter Bruegel. De jongen met het vogelnest,* in: Historia 14, 1949, 55–57
K. Boström, *Das Sprichwort vom Vogelnest,* in: Konsthistorisk Tidskrift 18, 1949, H. 2–3, 77–98
B. Lagercrantz, *Pieter Bruegel und Olaus Magnus,* in: Konsthistorisk Tidskrift 18, 1949, H. 2–3, 71–76
G. Glück, *Peter Bruegel the Elder and the Legend of St. Christopher in Early Flemish Painting,* in: The Art Quarterly 13, 1950, 37–47
F. Novotny, *Volkskundliche und kunstgeschichtliche Betrachtungsweise. Zu Pieter Bruegels "Heimkehr der Herde",* in:Austrian Folk Art Periodical, N. S. 4, 1950, No. 1–2, 42–53
H. Swarzenski, *The battle between Carnival and Lent,* in: Bulletin of the Museum of Fine Arts Boston 49, February 1951, 2–11
C. de Tolnay, *Bruegel et l'Italie,* in: Les Arts Plastiques, September 1951, 121–130
A. Haberlandt, *Volksbrauch im Jahreslauf auf den "Monatsbildern" Pieter Bruegels d. Ä.,* in: Austrian Folk Art Periodical 6, 1952, 43 ff.
C. Linfert, *Die Vermummung, eine Figuration der Angst (in Bildern von Bosch, Bruegel und Max Beckmann),* in: Centro internazionale di studi umanistici etc. (Atti del II Congresso internazionale di studi umanistici a cura di E. Castelli), Milan – Rome 1953, 263–268
O. Buyssens, *De schepen by Pieter Bruegel de Oude, proeve van identificatie,* in: Mededelingen van de Academie van Marine van België 8, 1954, 159–191
J. Avalon, *Bataille de Carnaval et de Carême,* in: Aesculape 37, 1955, 67–71
M. De Maeyer, *Albrecht en Isabella en de Schilderkunst. Bijdrage tot de geschiedenis van de XVIIe eeuwse schilderkunst in de zuidelijke Nederlanden,* Brussels 1955 (abbreviated as: De Maeyer 1955)
K. C. Lindsay – B. Huppé, *Meaning and method in Bruegel's painting,* in: Journal of Aesthetics and Art Criticism 14, 1956, 376–386
C. G. Stridbeck, *"Combat between Carnival and Lent" by Pieter Bruegel the elder. An allegorical picture of the sixteenth century,* in: Journal of the Warburg and Courtauld Institutes 19, 1956, 96–109
F. Anzelewsky, Besprechung von Grossmann 1955, in: Art Chronicle 10, 1957, 19 ff.
H. Bauer, Besprechung von Stridbeck 1956 und Würtenberger 1957, in: Art Chronicle 10, 1957, 235–240
J. Grauls, *Volkstaal en volksleven in het werk van Pieter Bruegel,* Antwerp – Amsterdam 1957
J. Hills, *Das Kinderspielbild von Pieter Bruegel d. Ä. Eine volkskundliche Untersuchung* (Publications of the Austrian Museum for Folk Art X), Vienna 1957
H. Sedlmayr, *Pieter Bruegel: der Sturz der Blinden, Paradigma einer Strukturanalyse,* in: Issues of the Art History Seminar of the University of Munich 2, 1957 (reprinted in: H. Sedlmayr, Epoques and Works I, Vienna-Munich 1959, 319–357
Würtenberger, *Pieter Bruegel d. Ä und die deutsche Kunst,* Wiesbaden 1957
P. J. Vinken, *De betekenis van Pieter Bruegel's –Nestroverì,* in: Het Bok 33, 1958, No. 2, 106–115
Grossmann, *New light on Bruegel,* in: The Burlington Magazine 101, 1959, 341–346
A. Monballieu, *P. Bruegel en het altaar van de Mechelse handschoenmakers (1551),* in: Handelingen van de koninklijke kring voor oudheidkunde, letteren en kunst van Mechelen 68, 1964, 92–110
J. Briels, *Amator Pictoriae Artis. De Antwerpse Kunsthandelaar Peeter Stevens (1590–1668) en zijn Constkamer,* in: Jaarboek van het koninklijk Museum voor schone Kunsten, Antwerp 1980, 137–226
F. Grossmann, *Bruegels Verhältnis zu Raffael und zur Raffael-Nachfolge,* in: Kurt Badt Commemorative Volume, Berlin 1961, 135–143
Portmann, *Die Kinderspiele Pieter Bruegels d.Ä.,* Bern 1961
H. Bartlett Wells, *Arms in Bruegel's "Slaughter of the Innocents",* in: The Journal of Arms and Armour's Society IV, Nr. 10, 1964, 193–209
E. Brochhagen, Besprechung der Ausstellung *Le siècle de Bruegel,* in: Art Chronicle 17, 1964, 1–7
I. L. Zupnick, *Bruegel and the revolt of the Netherlands,* in: Art Journal 23, 1964, 283–289
S. Gibson, *Some notes on Pieter Brueghel the Elder's Peasant Wedding Feast,* in: The Art Quarterly 28, 1965, 194–208
J. van Lennep, *L'alchimie et Pierre Brueghel l'ancien,* in: Bulletin des Musées Royaux des Beaux-Arts de Belgique 14, 1965, 105–126
C. de Tolnay, *Newly discovered miniatures by Pieter Bruegel the Elder,* in: The Burlington Magazine 107, 1965, 110–111 (abbreviated as: Tolnay 1965)
C. Van de Velde, *The Labours of Hercules, a lost series of paintings by Frans Floris,* in: The Burlington Magazine 107, 1965, 114–123 (abbreviated as: Van de Velde 1965)
S. Ferber, *Pieter Bruegel and the Duke of Alba,* in: Renaissance News 19, No. 3, Herbst 1966, 205–219
Dene, *Un paysage de Pieter Brueghel le Jeune d'après celui de Pieter Bruegel le Vieux dans la collection du Musée d'art de Bucarest,* in: Miscellanea Jozef Duverger, Geneva 1968, I, 269–274
P. Thon, *Bruegel's "The Triumph of Death" reconsidered,* in: Renaissance Quarterly 21, Nr. 3, 1968, 289–297
A. Deblaere, *Erasmus, Bruegel en de humanistische visie,* in: Vlaanderen 1969, No. 103
G. Marlier, *Peeter Balten, copiste ou créateur?,* in: Bulletin des Musées Royaux des Beaux-Arts de Belgique 14, 1969, 127–141 (abbreviated as: Marlier 1969)
G. Marlier, *Pierre Brueghel le Jeune,* posthumous edition, checked with comments by J. Folie, Brussels 1969
J. Weyns, *Bij Bruegel in de leer voor honderd-en-een dagelijkse dingen,* in: Bokrijkse berichten, Ons Heem, Tijdschrift van het Verbond voor Heemkunde 23, 1969, No. 3, 97–113
D. Schubert, *Die Gemälde des Braunschweiger Monogrammisten. Ein Beitrag zur Geschichte der Niederländischen Malerei des 16. Jahrhunderts,* Cologne 1970 (abbreviated as: Schubert 1970)
S. Alpers, *Bruegel's festive peasants,* in: Simiolus 4, 1972/73, 163–176
C. Gaignebet, *Le combat de Carnaval et de Carême de P. Bruegel,* in: Annales, Economies Sociétés Civilisations 27, 1972, 313–345

K. Renger, *Bettler und Bauern bei Pieter Bruegel d. Ä.,* in: Berlin Art History Association, Minutes, N. F. 20, 1971/72, 9–16
C. de Tolnay, *Pierre Bruegel l'Ancien,* in: Actes du XXIIe Congrès international d'histoire de l'art, Budapest 1969 (1972), Vol. I, 31–44
F. Grossmann, *Notes on some sources of Bruegel's art,* in: Album Amicorum J. G. van Gelder, Den Haag 1973, 147–158
J. B. Bedaux – A. van Gool, *Bruegel's birthyear, motive of an ars of natura transmutation,* in: Simiolus 7, 1974, 133–156 (abbreviated as: Bedaux 1974)
A. Monballieu, *De "Kermis van Hoboken" bij P. Bruegel, J. Grimmer en G. Mostaert,* in: Jaarboek van het koninklijk Museum voor schone Kunsten, Antwerp 1974, 139–169
W. Mössner, *Studien zur Farbe bei Pieter Brueghel d. Ä.,* phil. Diss. Würzburg 1975
S. Karling, *The Attack by Pieter Bruegel the Elder in the Collection of the Stockholm University,* in: Konsthistorisk Tidskrift 15, 1976, 1–18
D. Mattioli, *Nuove ipotesi su i quadri di "Bruol Vecchio" appartenuti ai Gonzaga,* in: Civiltà Mantovana 10, 1976, Quaderno 55–56, 32–43
Y. Mori, *The influence of German and Flemish prints on the works of Pieter Bruegel,* in: Bulletin of Tama Art School 1976, Bd. 2, Kawasaka-City 1976, 17–60
P. Dreyer, *Bruegels Alchimist von 1568. Versuch einer Deutung ad usum mysticum,* in: Yearbook of the Berlin Museums 19, 1977, 69–113
D. Kunzle, *Bruegel's proverb painting and the world upside down,* in: The Art Bulletin 59, 1977, 197–202
M. A. Sullivan, *Madness and Folly: Pieter Bruegel the Elder's "Dulle Griet",* in: The Art Bulletin 59, 1977, 55–66
F. Klauner, *Die Gemäldegalerie des Kunsthistorischen Museums in Wien,* Salzburg – Vienna 1978
Urbach, *Notes on Bruegel's Archaism,* in: Acta Historiae Artium Bd. XXIV, H. 1–4, Budapest 1978, 237–256
H. D. III Brumble, *Peter Brueghel the Elder: The allegory of landscape,* in: The Art Quarterly, N. S. 2, 1979, 125–139
M. Jaffé, *Rubens and Bruegel,* in: *Pieter Bruegel und seine Welt. Ein Colloquium,* publ. by O. v. Simson and M. Winner, Berlin 1979, 37–42
J.-C. Klamt, *Anmerkungen zu Pieter Bruegels Babel-Darstellungen,* in: *Pieter Bruegel und seine Welt. Ein Colloquium,* publ. by O. v. Simson and M. Winner, Berlin 1979
A. Monballieu, *De "Hand als teken op het kleed" bij Bruegel en Baltens,* in: Jaarboek van het koninklijk Museum voor schone Kunsten, Antwerp 1979, 197–209
Müller Hofstede, *Zur Interpretation von Pieter Bruegels Landschaft. Ästhetischer Landschaftsbegriff und stoische Weltbetrachtung,* in: *Pieter Bruegel und seine Welt. Ein Colloquium,* publ. by O. v. Simson and M. Winner, Berlin 1979, 73-142 (abbreviated as: Müller Hofstede 1979)
E. K. J. Reznicek, *Bruegels Bedeutung für das 17. Jahrhundert,* in: *Pieter Bruegel und seine Welt. Ein Colloquium,* publ. by O. v. Simson and M. Winner, Berlin 1979, 159–164
M. Walder, *Die Heimkehr der Herde,* in: Terra Plana 1979, No. 3, 5–6
J. Theuwissen, *Volkskundliche Aspekte im Werke Pieter Bruegels,* in: *Pieter Bruegel und seine Welt. Ein Colloquium,* publ. by O. v. Simson and M. Winner, Berlin 1979, 175–192
C. White, *"The Rabbit Hunters" by Pieter Bruegel the Elder,* in: *Pieter Bruegel und seine Welt. Ein Colloquium,* publ. by O. v. Simson and M. Winner, Berlin 1979, 187–192
R. Genaille, *La Montée au Calvaire de Bruegel l'Ancien*, in: Jaarboek van het koninklijk Museum voor schone Kunsten, Antwerp 1980, 61–97
C. de Tolnay, *Further miniatures by Pieter Bruegel the Elder,* in: The Burlington Magazine 122, 1980, 616–623
K. Demus, in: *Kunsthistorisches Museum, Wien. Katalog der Gemäldegalerie. Flämische Malerei von Jan van Eyck bis Pieter Bruegel d. Ä.,* Catalogue Editor: K. Demus, F. Klauner, K. Schütz, Vienna 1981, 61–138 (abbreviated as: Demus 1981)
S. Hindman, *Pieter Bruegel's "Children Games" and the Folly of Man,* in: The Art Bulletin, Sept. 1981, Vol. LXIII, No. 3, 447–475
S. A. Mansbach, *Pieter Bruegel's Towers of Babel,* in: Art History Periodical 45, 1982, 43–56
P. Vandenbroeck, *Laatmiddeleeuwse doekschilderkunst in de Zuidelijke Nederlanden. Repertorium der nog bewaarde werken,* in: Jaarboek van het koninklijk Museum vor schone Kunsten, Antwerp 1982, 29–61 (abbreviated as: Vandenbroeck 1982)
E. Snow, *"Meaning" in Children's Games: On the Limitations of the Iconographic Approach to Bruegel,* in: representations 2, University of California Press, Spring 1983
E. M. Schutt-Kehm, *Pieter Bruegels d. Ä. "Kampf des Karnevals gegen die Fasten" als Quelle volkskundlicher Forschung,* (Artes Populares Studia ethnographica et folkloristica 7), Frankfurt a. M. – Bern – New York 1983
S. Elliston Weiner, *The Tower of Babel in Netherlandish Painting,*, Diss. Columbia University (Ann Arbor) 1985
R. an der Heiden, *Pieter Bruegel d. Ä., "Das Schlaraffenland" und der "Kopf einer Bäurin" in der Alten Pinakothek,* Munich 1985
H. J. van Miegroet, *The twelve months reconsidered: how a drawing by Pieter Stevens clarifies a Bruegel enigma,* in: Simiolus 16, 1986, No. 1, 29–35
H.-J. Raupp, *Bauernsatiren. Entstehung und Entwicklung des bäuerlichen Genres in der deutschen und niederländischen Kunst ca. 1470–1570,* Niederzier 1986
M. Rumpf, *Der "Kampf des Karnevals gegen die Fasten" von Pieter Bruegel d. Ä. Volkskundlich-kulturhistorisch-medizingeschichtlich interpretiert,* in: Austrian Folk Art Periodical, N. S. Vol. XL (Complete Series Vol. 89), H. 2, Vienna 1986, 129
K. Ertz, *Joos de Momper der Jüngere,* Freren 1986 (Ertz 1986)
K. Renger, *Karneval und Fasten. Bilder vom Fressen und Hungern,* in: World Art 58, 1988, 184–189
St. Grieten, *De iconografie van de toren van Babel bij Pieter Bruegel: traditie, vernieuwing en navolging,* in: Jaarboek van het koninklijk Museum voor schone kunsten, Antwerp 1988, 97–136
K. Demus, in: *Flämische Malerei im Kunsthistorischen Museum Wien,* Zurich 1989 (Demus 1989)
I. Buchanan, *The collection of Niclaes Jongelinck: II, the "Months" by Pieter Bruegel the Elder,* in: The Burlington Magazine 132, 1990, 541–550
L. S. Milne, *Dreams and popular Beliefs in the Imagery of Pieter Bruegel the Elder,* Vol. I–III, Phil. Diss. Boston 1990
S. Ferino Pagden, W. Prohaska, K. Schütz, *Die Gemäldegalerie des Kunsthistorischen Museums in Wien. Verzeichnis der Gemälde,* Vienna 1991, 36–37
H. Leisner, *Pieter Bruegels d. Ä. Turmbauten zu Babel,* in: Exhibition Catalogue *Der Turmbau zu Babel,* Bamberg 1991, 43–53
H. Verougstraete – A. R. Van Schoute, *The Triumph of Death by Pieter Bruegel the Elder and Pieter Brueghel the Younger,* in: *The Triumph of Death by Pieter Brueghel the Younger,* compiled by J. I. W. Corcoran, Antwerp 1993, 35–53
M. Sullivan, *Bruegel's Peasants. Art and Audience in the northern Renaissance,* Cambridge University Press 1994
A. Wied, *Bruegel. Der Kampf zwischen Fasching und Fasten,* Milan – Vienna 1996
Miedema 1996: see sources, van Mander
J. Müller, *"Pieter der Drollige" oder der Mythos vom Bauern-Bruegel,* in: Exhibition Catalogue *Pieter Brueghel der Jüngere – Jan Brueghel der Ältere. Flämische Malerei um 1600. Tradition und Fortschritt,* Essen – Vienna 1997, 42–53
J. Müller, *Das Paradox als Bildform. Studien zur Ikonologie Pieter Bruegels d. Ä.,* Munich 1997 (about to be published)

Exhibition catalogue:
Pieter Bruegel d. Ä. als Zeichner, Berlin (Staatliche Museen Preußischer Kulturbesitz, Kupferstichkabinett) 1975 (Berlin 1975)
Le siècle de Bruegel. La peinture en Belgique au XVIe siècle, Brussels (Musées Royaux des Beaux-Arts de Belgique) 1963
Bruegel. De schilder en zijn wereld, Brussels (Musées Royaux des Beaux-Arts de Belgique) 1969
Bruegel. Une dynastie des peintres, Brussels 1980
L'Epoque de Lucas van Leyde et Pierre Bruegel. Dessins des anciens Pays-Bas. Collection Frits Lugt, Exhibition Catalogue K. G. Boon, Florence (Istituto Universitario Olandese di Storia dell'Arte) – Paris (Institut Néerlandais) 1980/81
The Age of Bruegel. Netherlandish Drawings in the Sixteenth Century (J. O. Hand, J. R. Judson, W. W. Robinson, M. Wolff), Washington (National Gallery of Art) 1987, with bibliography
Die Kunst der Graphik IV. Zwischen Renaissance und Barock. Das Zeitalter von Bruegel und Bellange, Vienna (Albertina Graphics Collection) 1967